Faith and Foreign Policy

FAITH AND FOREIGN POLICY

The Views and Influence of U.S. Christians and Christian Organizations

by
Stephen R. Rock

continuum

The Continuum International Publishing Group
80 Maiden Lane, New York, NY 10038
The Tower Building, 11 York Road, London SE1 7NX

www.continuumbooks.com

Library of Congress Cataloging-in-Publication Data
Rock, Stephen R.
Faith and foreign policy: the views and influence of U.S. Christians and Christian organizations/Stephen R. Rock.
   p. cm.
Includes bibliographical references and index.
ISBN-13: 978-0-8264-2030-5 (hardcover : alk. paper)
ISBN-10: 0-8264-2030-3 (hardcover : alk. paper)
ISBN-13: 978-0-8264-2320-7 (pbk. : alk. paper)
ISBN-10: 0-8264-2320-5 (pbk. : alk. paper) 1. United States–Foreign relations–1989–Decision making. 2. Christians–Political activity–United States. 3. Lobbying–United States. 4. Pressure groups–United States. I. Title.

JZ1480.R63 2011
327.73–dc22

2010035953

ISBN: 978-0-8264-2030-5 (HB)
       978-0-8264-2320-7 (PB)

Typeset by Newgen Imaging Systems Pvt Ltd, Chennai, India
Printed and bound in the United States of America

For Andy and Julia

Contents

List of Illustrations

Tables

Figure

List of Abbreviations

ABM	Anti-Ballistic Missile
AIPAC	American Israel Public Affairs Committee
AOG	Assemblies of God
ARDA	Association of Religion Data Archives
ARIS	American Religious Identification Survey
CAIP	Catholic Association for International Peace
CBD	Convention on Biological Diversity
CBF	Cooperative Baptist Fellowship
CFCs	chlorofluorocarbons
CFIC	Christian Friends of Israeli Communities
CITES	Convention on International Trade in Endangered Species of Wild Fauna and Flora
CJDP	Commission to Study the Bases of a Just and Durable Peace
CPA	Comprehensive Peace Agreement
CRCNA	Christian Reformed Church in North America
CUFI	Christians United for Israel
CWA	Concerned Women for America
DDT	dichloro-diphenyl-trichloroethane
DOP	Declaration of Principles on Interim Self-Government Arrangements
ECI	Evangelical Climate Initiative
EEN	Evangelical Environmental Network
EFCA	Evangelical Free Church of America
EHR	Evangelicals for Human Rights
ELCA	Evangelical Lutheran Church in America
ESA	Endangered Species Act
EUB	Evangelical United Brethren
FCC	Federal Council of Churches
FMCNA	Foreign Missions Conference of North America
GATT	General Agreement on Tariffs and Trade
GCCUIC	General Commission on Christian Unity and Interreligious Concerns
HIRR	Hartford Institute for Religion Research
IAST	Initiative Against Sexual Trafficking
ICC	International Criminal Court
ICEL	International Committee for English in the Liturgy
IDF	Israeli Defense Forces
IMF	International Monetary Fund
INF	Intermediate-Range Nuclear Forces
INS	Immigration and Naturalization Service

IPCC	Intergovernmental Panel on Climate Change
IRFA	International Religious Freedom Act
ISA	Interfaith Stewardship Alliance
ISR	Institute for Studies of Religion, Baylor University
LCMS	Lutheran Church—Missouri Synod
MECC	Middle East Council of Churches
MRS	Migration and Refugee Services, United States Conference of Catholic Bishops
NAACP	National Association for the Advancement of Colored People
NAE	National Association of Evangelicals
NAFTA	North American Free Trade Agreement
NCC	National Council of Churches (formally, the National Council of Churches of Christ in the United States of America)
NCCB	National Conference of Catholic Bishops
NCWC	National Catholic Welfare Conference
NGO	Nongovernmental Organization
NILI	National Interreligious Leadership Initiative for Peace in the Middle East
NRPE	National Religious Partnership for the Environment
PCID	Pontifical Council for Interreligious Dialogue
PCUSA	Presbyterian Church (USA)
PLO	Palestine Liberation Organization
PNA	Palestinian National Authority
PVO	Private Voluntary Organization
RCMS	Religious Congregations & Membership Study
RCRC	Religious Coalition for Reproductive Choice
RNEP	Robust Nuclear Earth Penetrator
SALT II	Second Strategic Arms Limitation Treaty
SBC	Southern Baptist Convention
SDI	Strategic Defense Initiative
TIP	Trafficking in Persons
TVPA	Trafficking Victims Protection Act
UCC	United Church of Christ
UMC	United Methodist Church
UNCCD	United Nations Convention to Combat Desertification
UNCIO	United Nations Conference on International Organization
UNFCCC	United Nations Framework Convention on Climate Change
UNGIFT	United Nations Global Initiative to Fight Trafficking
UNPF	United Nations Population Fund
USAID	United States Agency for International Development
USCC	United States Catholic Conference
USCCB	United States Conference of Catholic Bishops
WCC	World Council of Churches
WTO	World Trade Organization

Preface

This book lies at the intersection of important personal and intellectual interests. I am a life-long Christian, raised in the Lutheran Church of America and for many years now a United Methodist. Since my days in catechism classes, I have been intrigued by differences in the histories, cultures, and doctrines of various Christian denominations, as well as those of other religions. I am also a professional student of U.S. foreign policy, having taught courses in that area my entire career. While my earlier published work falls more properly within the field of international politics, a good portion of it relies on case studies drawn from the history of U.S. foreign relations.

This project was inspired by intense disagreement among members of the U.S. Christian community over the U.S. invasion of Iraq in March 2003. Within the congregation to which I belong, there existed deep differences of opinion regarding the moral permissibility and wisdom of attacking Iraq and overthrowing the regime of Saddam Hussein. The United Methodist Church, like most Mainline Protestant denominations and the Roman Catholic Church, was outspokenly opposed to the war, but Evangelical Protestant leaders and Evangelical Protestant denominations such as the Southern Baptist Convention generally supported it. What, I wondered, accounted for the sharp divergence of views? What other differences on foreign policy issues existed and what explained them? Did the religious beliefs and policy preferences of Christian groups within the United States influence the conduct and substance of U.S. foreign policy? If so, how and when? This book represents my attempt to answer these and other questions.

As a life-long member of Mainline Protestant churches, my religious convictions and my foreign policy preferences are, not surprisingly, more typical of Mainline Protestants as a group than they are of either Evangelical Protestants or Roman Catholics. I have tried hard to be self-conscious regarding my prejudices and fair to those with whom I might disagree on matters both theological and political. I hope that I have succeeded.

No one can complete a project of this magnitude without the help and support of others. For reading the manuscript and offering many helpful suggestions, I am grateful to my father, William R. Rock, professional historian and amateur theologian; the Reverend Robert Thompson-Gee, pastor of Poughkeepsie United Methodist Church; Peter S. Henne, my former research assistant and now a Ph.D. student at Georgetown University; and Professor James L. Guth of Furman University, who generously shared with me some of his own research. A series of student assistants aided me in various ways. In addition to Peter Henne, I owe particular thanks to Michael Frenkel and Nikola Trkulja. Sabbaticals provided by my employer, Vassar College, allowed me to finish the study more rapidly than would otherwise have been possible. My editor at Continuum, Marie-Claire Antoine, read draft chapters promptly, made many constructive comments, and was a consistent source of encouragement. Molly Morrison and her colleague Vidya Priya copyedited the manuscript with a light hand and a keen eye. P. Muralidharan, of Newgen Publishing and Data Services, who handled the typesetting, was patient in answering my questions and meticulous in making corrections from the proofs.

Being able to share the publication of this book with my family is a tremendous pleasure. To my parents, who provided the foundation for everything I have accomplished personally and professionally: Thank you, from the bottom of my heart. To my wife, Jenny Arden, who read the manuscript and with whom I celebrated 27 years of marriage in 2010: You have my profound gratitude and my undying love. To our children, Andy and Julia, who, during the course of this project were somehow transformed from children into young adults: I hope that someday you will truly understand the joy and pride that your mother and I have felt, and continue to feel, at watching you grow and seeing what you become. This book is for you.

CHAPTER 1

Faith and Foreign Policy: An Introduction

I base a lot of my foreign policy decisions on some things that I think are true. One, I believe there's an Almighty. And, secondly, I believe one of the great gifts of the Almighty is the desire in everybody's soul, regardless of what you look like or where you live, to be free.

George W. Bush[1]

Religion shapes the nation's character, helps form Americans' ideas about the world, and influences the ways Americans respond to events beyond their borders. Religion explains both Americans' sense of themselves as a chosen people and their belief that they have a duty to spread their values throughout the world. Of course, not all Americans believe such things—and those who do often bitterly disagree over exactly what they mean. But enough believe them that the ideas exercise profound influence over the country's behavior abroad.

Walter Russell Mead[2]

U.S. Christians and the War in Iraq

On March 20, 2003, military forces of the United States and other members of a multinational coalition invaded Iraq. The outbreak of war came as no surprise. For months, the U.S. government had sought to obtain a United Nations Security Council Resolution authorizing the use of force against the government of Saddam Hussein. When that effort failed, the Bush administration had declared its intention to proceed without U.N. authorization.

Christian leaders and institutions in the United States reacted in divergent ways to the threat of war in Iraq, and to the war itself. Mainline Protestant denominations vigorously and almost unanimously opposed the opening of hostilities.[3] The World Council of Churches (WCC), to which many Protestant denominations and the National Council of Churches (NCC) belong, asked in October 2002 that the U.S. government "desist from any military threats against Iraq" and that other members of the international community "resist pressures to join in preemptive military strikes against a sovereign state under the pretext of the 'war on terrorism.'"[4] The head of the General Board of Church and Society of the United Methodist Church

(UMC) condemned the anticipated attack as "reckless," and the president of the UMC's Council of Bishops stated that "a preemptive war by the United States against a nation like Iraq goes against the very grain of our understanding of the Gospel, our church's teachings, and our conscience."[5] Leaders of the United Church of Christ wrote, "We firmly oppose this advance to war."[6] The bishops of the Episcopal Church told Congress that "we do not believe war with Iraq can be justified at this time."[7] And a statement from leaders of Friends (Quaker) organizations in the United States expressed "profound grief and sorrow over our government's decision to go to war against Iraq," calling the Bush administration's policy "unnecessary, immoral, and unwise."[8]

Organs of the Roman Catholic Church in the United States also articulated serious reservations about the use of force in Iraq. In November 2002, the United States Conference of Catholic Bishops wrote, "We harbor no illusions about the behavior or intentions of the Iraqi government" and noted that they did not offer "definitive conclusions" regarding the moral status of the approaching conflict. Nevertheless, the bishops stated, "We fear that resort to war, under present circumstances and in light of current public information, would not meet the strict conditions in Catholic teaching for overriding the strong presumption against the use of military force" and they urged that "our nation and the world continue to pursue actively alternatives to war in the Middle East."[9]

By contrast, Evangelical Protestant denominations and leaders were much more favorably disposed toward the Bush administration's policy. A fall 2002 survey of 350 top evangelical leaders found 59 percent approved the use of military force against Iraq, while only 19 percent opposed it.[10] As Charles Marsh, Professor of Religion at the University of Virginia, later noted, "Many of the most respected voices in American evangelical circles blessed the president's war plans."[11] Televangelists Franklin Graham, Pat Robertson, and Jerry Falwell all supported the invasion of Iraq. Robertson is reported to have declared to his 700 Club viewers that the war was "a righteous cause out of the Bible."[12] Charles Stanley, pastor of the First Baptist Church in Atlanta and a former president of the Southern Baptist Convention, told his listeners that "we should offer to serve the war effort in any way possible."[13] The year after the war began, Falwell wrote an essay entitled, "God is Pro-War," in which he stated that "President Bush declared war in Iraq to defend innocent people. This is a worthy pursuit."[14] According to one observer, "In the fall [of 2002], when a preemptive military strike against Iraq turned into a serious possibility, it appeared that a major religious debate over the morality of war was heating up, pitting evangelicals against mainline Protestants, Catholics and Orthodox Christians."[15]

This debate never fully materialized. Although, unlike the mainline denominations and the Catholic hierarchy, their leaders and members tended to support the war, many evangelical institutions did not articulate a public position. The Assemblies of God declined to issue a statement supporting or condemning the war, noting that local pastors and congregations, as well as individual members, were free to speak for themselves.[16] A representative of the Lutheran Church—Missouri Synod (LCMS), in response to a question from a member of the denomination, answered: "Regarding the impending war in Iraq, it is apparent that members of the LCMS equally committed to Scriptural teaching may have differing views regarding justification for such a war. And they may present equally cogent arguments to support their views."[17] Richard Cizik, vice president for governmental affairs at the National Association of Evangelicals (NAE), was a strong proponent of war, arguing that an invasion of Iraq would not be "preemption but another step in responding to the continuum of terrorism, of evildoers."[18] However, when Cizik drafted a statement endorsing the forcible overthrow of Saddam Hussein, the NAE failed to approve it.[19]

The Southern Baptist Convention (SBC), the single largest Protestant denomination in the United States, openly supported the war. Richard Land, head of the SBC's Ethics and Religious Liberty Commission, termed those who opposed the use of force against Iraq "naïve" and advocated "whatever military means are necessary—unilateral or otherwise—to overthrow the Iraqi regime."[20] In June 2003, the SBC passed a resolution, "On the Liberation of Iraq," to "affirm President George W. Bush, the United States Congress, and our armed forces for their leadership in the successful execution of Operation Iraqi Freedom."[21]

The positions of individual Christians on the Iraq War did not always reflect those of the religious organizations to which they belonged. President Bush and Vice President Dick Cheney were members of the United Methodist Church, one of the most stridently antiwar denominations. Within every denomination, there were many members whose personal positions differed from the views articulated by the national leadership. A Pew Forum survey conducted in the week before the war began found that 62 percent of Catholics and Mainline Protestants favored the war, despite the formal opposition expressed by the official bodies of their churches. The same survey found that nearly a quarter of Evangelical Protestants did not support attacking Iraq, although most evangelical leaders and the SBC did. Nevertheless, as the poll results show, the pattern of support and opposition to the Iraq War among church leaders and organizations was mirrored to some degree in the pattern among individual believers. While more than three-quarters of Evangelical Protestants favored war in Iraq, fewer than two-thirds of Catholics and Mainline Protestants did so.[22]

Clearly, different religious groups in the United States held strong and diverse views concerning the Iraq War. Did the opinions and activities of these groups influence the policy of the United States government? It would be easy—and almost certainly wrong—to conclude that they did not. Obviously, opposition to the war by Mainline Protestant and Roman Catholic organizations failed to convince the Bush administration to refrain from initiating the conflict. This was in part because the antiwar sentiments expressed by church leaders were not shared by even a majority of the members of their denominations. But it was also because the Mainline Protestant and Catholic opposition to the war was offset, and perhaps outweighed, by the sometimes silent, sometimes vocal support of the war on the part of Evangelical Protestants—denominations, leaders, and individuals—who represented an important constituency of the Bush administration and the Republican Party. Had Evangelical Protestants strongly opposed the war, the administration would likely have been reluctant to proceed. As Michael Cromartie, an expert on evangelicalism at the Ethics and Public Policy Center, remarked the week before the opening of hostilities: "Just cold political calculus tells you if you had 50 million evangelicals rallying in downtown Washington against the war, it would cause great disturbance, but they're not there, and they won't be."[23] In that sense, it can be argued that attitudes of Evangelical Protestants exercised a considerable, possibly even decisive, impact on U.S. policy.

Classifying Christians

This book is about the relationship between religion and foreign policy in the United States. It has two main purposes. The first is to explain how, and under what circumstances, religion—religious beliefs, believers, and institutions—influences America's behavior abroad. The second is to identify and, more importantly, to explain, differences (and similarities) in foreign policy preferences and positions among various groups of U.S. Christians. Understanding these differences is essential to understanding the nature of contemporary U.S. foreign policy and, perhaps, to predicting its future course.

Why focus on Christianity and Christians? The reason is simple: The United States is an overwhelmingly Christian nation. The U.S. Religious Landscape Survey, conducted in 2007 by the Pew Forum on Religion & Public Life, found that 78.4 percent of adult Americans identified themselves as Christian. By comparison, Jews made up 1.7 percent of the population, with Buddhists, Muslims, Hindus, and adherents to other faiths constituting less than 1 percent each. According to the survey, after Christians, the second largest (16.1 percent) "religious group" in the United States was composed of those people who were not affiliated with any particular religion.[24] The dominance of Christianity was even greater in earlier periods of the nation's history. As recently as 1990, in fact, self-declared Christians made up 86.2 percent of the country's population.[25]

Identifying and explaining differences (and similarities) among various groups of U.S. Christians requires, of course, that such groups be defined. This is a more difficult task than it might initially appear. Most Christians in the United States today belong to one of three longstanding traditions: Roman Catholic, Protestant, or Orthodox. But these categories obscure an enormous amount of diversity. Although there are no official denominational sub-groupings among Catholics, and relatively few among Orthodox Christians, there exist somewhere between 150 and 200 different Protestant denominations. Beyond this, there also exist hundreds of nondenominational Protestant congregations, which, as traditional denominational loyalties fade, account for an increasingly large percentage of Protestant believers. Certain "mega-churches," such as Willow Creek Community Church, outside of

Chicago, are probably the best-known examples of this phenomenon, but most nondenominational churches are much smaller.[26]

Categorizing this vast diversity of religious organizations, and the individuals who populate them, is not an easy task. It is, however, essential to identifying and understanding meaningful differences on foreign policy issues. As Ted Jelen writes, "If a religious variable of any type is to have a significant net effect on any important aspect of American politics, that variable must describe a large number of people."[27]

This book devotes its attention to three groups of U.S. Christians: Roman Catholics, Mainline Protestants, and Evangelical Protestants. These categories are not exhaustive. That is, they do not include all Christians in the United States, omitting, for example, Christian Scientists and Orthodox organizations and believers as well as the Church of Jesus Christ of Latter Day Saints (Mormon). But they do include the overwhelming majority. According to the Pew Religious Landscape survey, Roman Catholics, the single largest denomination, account for roughly 24 percent of the adult population in the United States, and about 30 percent of all U.S. Christians. Evangelical Protestants constitute approximately 26 percent of the U.S. population and just over a third of U.S. Christians. Mainline Protestants represent 18 percent of the U.S. population and a little less than one-quarter of Christians in the United States. The three groups, taken together, account for more than two-thirds of the U.S. population and about 86 percent of all U.S. Christians.[28] Other surveys give comparable results. In 2006, a study conducted by the Baylor Institute for Studies of Religion found that Roman Catholics (21 percent), Evangelical Protestants (34 percent), and Mainline Protestants (22 percent) accounted for 77 percent of the total U.S. population and nearly 90 percent of all U.S. Christians.[29]

Roman Catholics, Evangelical Protestants, and Mainline Protestants are typically defined according to their denominational affiliation. That is, Roman Catholics are those who belong to or attend a Roman Catholic house of worship, while Evangelical and Mainline Protestants attend or belong to evangelical and mainline churches, respectively. Happily, there is widespread agreement among students of religion and other analysts as to which Protestant churches belong in which category. Major evangelical denominations include the Assemblies of God (AOG), the Southern Baptist Convention (SBC), the Church of the Nazarene, and the Lutheran Church—Missouri Synod (LCMS).[30] Among the major mainline denominations are the American Baptist Churches USA (sometimes referred to as Northern Baptist), Congregationalists, the Disciples of Christ, the Episcopal Church, the Evangelical Lutheran Church in America (ELCA), the Presbyterian Church (USA), the Reformed Church in America, the United Church of Christ (UCC) and the United Methodist Church (UMC).[31]

Many Evangelical and Mainline Protestant denominations belong to larger umbrella organizations formed for purposes of interdenominational cooperation, including cooperation in the realm of political advocacy. Most mainline denominations (as well as most Orthodox ones) are members of the National Council of Churches (NCC).[32] Established in 1950 as the successor to the Federal Council of Churches (1908), the NCC is headquartered in New York.

Many evangelical denominations—though not, it should be noted, the Southern Baptist Convention—belong to the National Association of Evangelicals (NAE).[33] The NAE's stated mission "is to extend the kingdom of God through a fellowship of member denominations, churches, organizations, and individuals, demonstrating the unity of the body of Christ by standing for biblical truth, speaking with a representative voice, and serving the evangelical community through united action, cooperative ministry, and strategic planning."[34] Unlike the NCC, which limits membership to churches, the NAE also counts among its members a variety of other kinds of organizations, including seminaries, colleges, and universities, as well as individual Christians. Indeed, no description of the evangelical community in this country would be complete without recognition of the importance of non-denominational organizations. Many of the nondenominational churches in the United States, including most of the mega-churches, are evangelical.[35] So, too, are a number of "para-church" religious organizations such as James Dobson's Focus on the Family, the Promise Keepers, Campus Crusade for Christ, and televangelist Pat Robertson's 700 Club. Major Protestant organizations in the United States today are shown in Table 1.1.

Table 1.1: Major Protestant Organizations in the United States

	Mainline	Evangelical
Umbrella Organization	National Council of Churches (NCC)	National Association of Evangelicals (NAE)
Major Denominations	American Baptist Churches USA (Northern Baptist) Congregationalist Disciples of Christ Episcopal Church Evangelical Lutheran Church in America Presbyterian Church (USA) Reformed Church in America United Church of Christ United Methodist Church	Assemblies of God Christian Reformed Church in North America Churches of Christ Church of the Nazarene Lutheran Church—Missouri Synod Southern Baptist Convention

*Omitted from this table are non-Christian organizations such as the Unitarian Universalist Association of Congregations and the Jehovah's Witnesses. Also omitted are nontraditional denominations such as the Church of Jesus Christ of Latter-Day Saints (Mormon); Church of Christ, Scientist; and the Seventh-day Adventist Church; as well as historically Black Protestant denominations.

Sources: American Religion Data Archive, Baylor Religion Survey.

Evangelical Protestants

Mainline and Evangelical Protestant denominations—and Mainline and Evangelical Protestants—are distinguished from one another chiefly on the basis of their religious doctrines. Evangelical Protestants typically regard the Bible as being the word of God and thus without error. Most have had a "born again" or conversion experience, which some consider essential to being a true Christian. Evangelicals, more than other Christians, believe that salvation can only come through faith in Jesus Christ, and they place great emphasis on evangelizing, or spreading the Gospel.[36] The presence of the word "evangelical" in the name of a particular church, it must be noted, does not necessarily signify an evangelical denomination subscribing to these views. During the Reformation, the term, *evangelisch*, meaning "of the Gospel," was used in Germany to highlight differences between Protestant (especially Lutheran) and Roman Catholic theology and practice. Over time, in certain parts of the world, "evangelical" became synonymous with "Protestant." Today, in the United States, as elsewhere, an "Evangelical Church" may or may not be an evangelical church. The Evangelical Lutheran Church in American (ELCA), the country's third largest Protestant denomination, is a mainline church.[37] So, too, was the Evangelical United Brethren (EUB) Church, which in 1968 merged with the Methodist Church to form the United Methodist Church, the country's second largest Protestant denomination.[38]

Evangelical Protestants include those Christians who are often labeled fundamentalists. As Steve Waldman, editor-in-chief of *Beliefnet*, writes, "Fundamentalists are a subset" of evangelicals.[39] While almost all evangelicals regard the Bible as being inerrant, fundamentalists believe it is literally true.[40] Historically, fundamentalists have been hostile toward other Christians, especially Catholics, and they have attempted to maintain the purity of their faith by isolating themselves from the evils of modern society. According to Walter Russell Mead, fundamentalists are defined by "a high view of biblical authority and inspiration; a strong determination to defend the historical Protestant faith against Roman Catholic, and modernist, secular, and non-Christian influence; and the conviction that believers should separate themselves from the non-Christian world."[41] This group has been the driving force in efforts to mandate the teaching of "creation science" and "intelligent design" as alternatives to Darwinian evolution and the theory of natural selection in public schools. Fundamentalists are "very strict" and "tend towards intolerance" of beliefs and practices (religious and nonreligious) different from their own.[42] The late Reverend Jerry Falwell, founder of the Moral Majority and of Liberty University, was a well-known fundamentalist. His controversial remarks, as a guest of Pat Robertson on the 700 Club the day after the terrorist attacks of September 11, 2001, which blamed the American Civil Liberties Union, People for the American Way, pagans, gays, lesbians, and feminists for prompting God to allow the attacks to occur, reflected his fundamentalist views.[43]

Some scholars argue for separating evangelicals and fundamentalists into two distinct groups. But this flies in the face of contemporary usage—among journalists and other observers, as well as among polling organizations and think thanks, such as the Pew Forum—and ignores, at least to some extent, what they have in common. As Mead notes, the "core beliefs" of evangelicals and fundamentalists share "common roots." Both fundamentalists and evangelicals "attach a great deal of importance to the doctrinal tenets of Christianity, not just to its ethical teachings." They believe that the emphasis of liberal Christians on ethics and consequently on "good works" departs from the central Christian precept that human salvation can come about only through the redeeming blood of Jesus Christ. Evangelicals, like fundamentalists, "believe that human beings who die without accepting Christ are doomed to everlasting separation from God" and that people who have not been "saved" are incapable of doing good. Many evangelicals hold fundamentalist views regarding the so-called end times. They believe that the prophecies contained in the book of Daniel and the book of Revelation predict events that will actually occur (or have occurred) and that can be recognized by those who interpret the Bible properly. The main difference between fundamentalists and evangelicals, writes Mead, is that the latter have a rosier worldview than the former. In particular, they are more optimistic about the possibility of saving souls and about the development of human society in a more moral direction. Consequently, evangelicals are less separatist than fundamentalists and more involved in the world.[44]

In addition to the fundamentalists, Evangelical Protestants also include pentecostals. Pentecostals are a group of Christians who hold theological beliefs very much like those of other evangelicals, but who place more emphasis on religious practice and using what they consider to be the "gifts of the Holy Spirit." These gifts, which according to the Bible (Acts 2) were bestowed by God on the day of Pentecost, include speaking in tongues (glossolalia), the interpretation of tongues, healing, and the working of miracles. A well-publicized but very small minority of pentecostal Christians handle poisonous snakes because they believe that the ability to handle snakes without harm is one of the marks of true believers set forth in Mk 16.17–18: "And these signs shall follow them that believe; In my name shall they cast out devils; they shall speak with new tongues; they shall take up serpents; and if they drink any deadly thing, it shall not hurt them; they shall lay hands on the sick, and they shall recover." Pentecostal worship is typically emotional—"exuberant and even ecstatic"—assuming the quality of revivals and tent-meetings. Worldwide, pentecostalism is the fastest growing segment of Christianity. Major pentecostal denominations in the United States include the Assemblies of God and the Church of God in Christ.[45]

Students of religion sometimes lump charismatics together with pentecostals and include them as part of the evangelical camp.[46] Charismatic Christians practice a style of worship that is very similar to that of pentecostals, but they do not belong to so-called pentecostal denominations. There are Roman Catholic and Mainline Protestant charismatics, as well as Non-Pentecostal Evangelical Protestant ones. Since Christians are often classified at least in part on the basis of their denominational affiliation, charismatics are frequently considered to be distinct from pentecostals. While some are Evangelical Protestants, others are not.[47]

It is important to recognize that public opinion surveys and scholarly works typically do not include "black evangelicals" among Evangelical Protestants, but assign them a category of their own (sometimes labeled "Black Protestants"). Journalistic and other more casual accounts of the contemporary religious scene in the United States frequently ignore this group altogether. Belonging mostly to historically African-American denominations, black evangelicals share many of the beliefs of their white evangelical counterparts. A Pew survey, for example, found that identical percentages (65 and 65) of black and white evangelicals believed that God had created human beings in their present form, accepting the creation account in the book of Genesis and rejecting Darwinian evolution.[48] The two groups have fairly similar views on certain "moral issues" such as same-sex marriage and abortion.[49] For cultural and historical reasons, however, black evangelicals tend to differ quite significantly from white evangelicals on political, social, and economic issues, and not surprisingly, political orientation. In a 2004 survey, 71 percent of black evangelicals identified as Democrats, while only 10 percent identified as Republicans. By contrast, 56 percent of white evangelicals considered themselves Republicans, and 27 percent considered themselves Democrats.[50] The number of black evangelicals in the United States is relatively small; less than 7 percent of the population belongs to historically black churches.[51] For these reasons, most references to Evangelical Protestants in both the social-scientific literature and in popular discourse are references to *white* Evangelical Protestants. That convention will be observed throughout this book.

Mainline Protestants

Mainline Protestants typically subscribe to views somewhat different from those of Evangelical Protestants on certain matters of doctrine. Although they usually regard the Bible as being "the word of God," instead of reading it as a factual account of historical events, they tend to read it figuratively. Old Testament stories such as Adam and Eve in the Garden of Eden are considered to reveal important truths about the nature of human beings, the nature of God, and the relationship between humans and God, but few Mainline Protestants (11.2 percent in one study) believe them to be literally true.[52] For this reason, most Mainline Protestants, like most Roman Catholics, do not see the need to choose between faith and science. The biblical account of creation and Darwinian evolutionary theory are not, in their minds, incompatible. One survey found that more than half of Mainline Protestants agreed with the proposition that "evolution is the best explanation for the origins of human life on earth." By contrast, nearly three-quarters of Evangelical Protestants disagreed.[53]

Some Mainline Protestants, like most evangelicals, regard the Bible as inerrant. Others, believe that, having been written by humans, in some cases centuries after the events that are recorded, it may contain mistakes. In the Baylor Religion Survey, nearly a quarter (22 percent) of Mainline Protestants regarded the Bible as an "ancient book of history and legends," while the Pew Forum found that 28 percent believe it "is a book written by men and is not the word of God."[54] Many Mainline Protestants see biblical writers as having been influenced by the political, social, and cultural contexts in which they wrote, and they argue that recognizing this is essential to understanding the meaning of the scriptures for contemporary Christians. While a number of Mainline Protestants have—like Paul on the road to Damascus—had sudden conversion experiences, this is not regarded as being the only way, or even the usual way, in which one can be "born again." They consider the example of the Disciple (and later Apostle) Peter, who came to faith in Jesus slowly and over time, to be equally valid. Mainline Protestants (83 percent) are more likely than Evangelical Protestants (57 percent) to accept the notion that persons of other faiths can receive God's grace and attain salvation.[55] And, perhaps as a result, although Mainline Protestants often believe in proselytizing, they tend to be less aggressive in seeking converts than their evangelical brothers and sisters.[56] Even among friends, many Mainline Protestants do not talk much about religion. The Pew Religious Landscape Survey found that 57 percent seldom or never shared their faith with others, as opposed to only 29 percent of Evangelical Protestants.[57]

Roman Catholics

Because the Roman Catholic Church is a single denomination, labeling Catholic institutions and believers is much less complicated than classifying different brands of Protestantism. Still, it is worth reviewing some of the doctrines and practices that distinguish Catholic organizations and believers from their Protestant counterparts.

The division between Roman Catholics and Protestants dates, of course, to the Protestant Reformation, which began in the sixteenth century. Some of the beliefs and practices that prompted reformers such as Martin Luther and John Calvin to break with Rome—the selling of indulgences and the notion that only clergy should have access to the scriptures, for example—are no longer relevant. But there remain core differences on a variety of issues. The Roman Catholic Church subscribes to the doctrine of "Petrine succession": that the Apostle Peter was anointed by Jesus to found the Christian Church and that popes, as successors to Peter, are the supreme leaders of this church. It is in part from this belief that the doctrine of papal infallibility—the notion that the pope, though an imperfect human being, is incapable of making mistakes on matters of church doctrine—derives. It is also in part on the basis of this doctrine that the Roman Catholic Church continues to maintain that it is the one "true church" and that all other Christian denominations are "deficient," a position that has, predictably, been an irritant in ecumenical relations.

Other doctrines that separate the Roman Catholic Church from Protestant churches include the notion of the "immaculate conception": the idea that Mary, the mother of Jesus, was conceived without sin. Indeed, the veneration of Mary, as practiced in many Catholic parishes, is quite foreign to most Protestants. The Catholic Church also subscribes to the idea of "transubstantiation," which holds that the bread and wine of the communion meal (the "Eucharist" or "Holy Eucharist" in Roman Catholic and some Protestant parlance), when consumed, actually becomes the body and blood of Jesus Christ. Most Protestant denominations maintain that Jesus' body and blood are symbolically, but not physically, present. Roman Catholic theology, unlike Protestant theology, includes the concept of "purgatory," a kind of halfway house between heaven and hell, in which souls that are ultimately destined for heaven, but which are not sufficiently pure to enter it immediately, are purged of their sins. As is well known, the Roman Catholic Church has a process by which members of the faith can, following their deaths, be beatified and become saints, and the veneration of such saints is another characteristic of Catholic faith and practice. As is also well known, the Roman Catholic Church admits only men to the ordained ministry, or priesthood, and, except in some cases in which already married Episcopal priests convert to Catholicism, it requires that they remain single and celibate.

On most other theological and doctrinal matters, positions of the Roman Catholic Church and Roman Catholics are not particularly different from those of Protestants. It is probably fair to say—and this will become clearer throughout later chapters— that Roman Catholic positions on many issues are closer to those of Mainline Protestants than to those of Evangelical Protestants. The Roman Catholic Church, for example, does not read the Bible literally, and neither do most Catholics. Percentages of Roman Catholics almost identical to those of Mainline Protestants say that they regard the scriptures as having been written by men and not the word of God.[58] Although the Catholic Church, like major Protestant denominations, maintains that faith in Jesus is the only means of attaining salvation, in public opinion surveys, Catholics, in numbers very similar to those of Mainline Protestants, express the belief that religions other than Christianity can lead to eternal life.[59] One major issue on which the Roman Catholic Church differs from most Mainline Protestant denominations and is similar to most Evangelical Protestant ones concerns the question of the point at which human life begins. Roman Catholics and Evangelical Protestants tend to believe that life begins at conception, while Mainline Protestants are more likely to be uncertain or to contend that it begins at birth. This has obvious implications for the positions of both churches and believers on the matter of abortion, and, consequently, as discussed in Chapter 4, on certain aspects of U.S. human rights policy.

Alternative Typologies of U.S. Protestants

Before proceeding to the next chapter, it is important to address three issues. First, although this book divides contemporary U.S. Protestants into evangelical and mainline categories, other taxonomic schemes exist and are sometimes employed. It was once fairly common practice for students of religion in the United States to locate individual Christians and Christian organizations along a conservative-liberal, or fundamentalist-liberal continuum. One noteworthy study, conducted in 1979, asked 25 experts on religion to rank major Protestant denominations from "most conservative" to "most liberal."[60] Other studies took the conservative-liberal continuum and segmented it into discrete categories: conservative/fundamentalist, moderate, and liberal.[61] These labels are still used, and some authors have performed a kind of "mix and match," borrowing elements from more than one typology. Walter Russell Mead, for example, in his essay, "God's Country?" contrasts evangelical with liberal (and fundamentalist) Protestants.[62]

The mainline-evangelical distinction is used in this book for two reasons. One is that it has become the convention, the dominant practice, among observers of the contemporary religious scene. This is particularly true of the media and the press, but it is also true of many think tanks and other organizations devoted to the study of religion and politics, and of scholars working in this area. A second and perhaps related reason is that in certain respects the evangelical-mainline typology is superior to the alternative conservative/fundamentalist-moderate-liberal typology. In particular, classifying Protestants as either mainline or evangelical better captures the similarities and differences in history and tradition among various denominations, acknowledges the growing importance of nondenominational churches and other institutions, helps to prevent confusion over whether terms such as "liberal" and "conservative" refer to theological orientations or positions on political, social, and economic issues, and avoids conceptualizing religion as an "ordinal variable," with liberal Protestantism being considered merely "a diluted form of orthodoxy."[63] Nevertheless, because the mainline-evangelical typology is not the only one employed by students of religion and politics in the United States, it is important to understand how these categories correspond to labels such as "conservative," "moderate," and "liberal."

Most Evangelical Protestants—including virtually all fundamentalists—would be considered conservative Christians. Mainline Protestants would be more likely to fall into the liberal category, while the moderate category would contain believers and organizations from both the evangelical and mainline camps. The terms "conservative," "moderate," and "liberal," in this context, refer to the theological and doctrinal beliefs held by individuals and/or articulated by their denominations. They are not meant to describe their views on political, social, or economic issues, although they frequently do. Conservative Christians hew strongly to traditional Christian beliefs: the virgin birth, the Trinitarian nature of God (three persons—Father, Son, and Holy Spirit—in one being), the factual accuracy of biblical accounts of events such as the stories of Adam and Eve and of Noah's flood, and salvation only through the saving grace of Jesus Christ. Liberal Christians, by contrast, are much less strongly committed to these beliefs. At the extreme liberal end of the spectrum, groups that are sometimes considered liberal Christian may not warrant the label "Christian." The Unitarian-Universalist Church, in addition to rejecting the Trinitarian conception of God, regards Jesus not as a supernatural being, the literal son of God and the provider of eternal life, but as merely "a sublime moral teacher."[64] It is for these reasons that Unitarian-Universalism was treated in the 2000 Religious Congregations and Membership Study (RCMS) not as "Mainline Protestant" but as

"Other Denomination," a category that also included Bahai, Buddhism, Hinduism, and Judaism.[65]

Differences in Numbers

A second issue that deserves attention is the fact that, as any reader who is familiar with the U.S. religious landscape knows, there are significant discrepancies in the numbers and percentages of various types of Christians—especially Evangelical Protestants—reported by different authors and organizations. Differences in methodology account for most of these.

The figures for percentages of Roman Catholics, Evangelical Protestants, and Mainline Protestants given earlier in this chapter are from surveys classifying individuals on the basis of their denominational affiliation. This is the method most commonly used, but it is not the only one. Surveys that do not employ denominational affiliation to categorize believers, or that use it in combination with other measures, often report quite different figures for certain groups. The 2001 American Religious Identification Survey (ARIS) conducted by researchers at the City University of New York asked respondents to place themselves into one of 35 different categories. In addition to a large number of denominations, choices also included labels such as "evangelical," "born again," and "fundamentalist." Remarkably—though predictably, given the way the survey instrument was constructed—the ARIS study found that "evangelicals" made up only a tiny portion of the U.S. population, that is, 0.5 percent.[66]

As a general rule, in surveys, the more groups into which religious believers may be placed (or into which they may place themselves), the smaller the number who will fall into a particular category. In a CNN/Time poll conducted in June 2002, only 15 percent of the respondents identified themselves as evangelical, while another 18 percent identified themselves as fundamentalist, and 34 percent as "born again."[67] As the authors of the Baylor Religion study noted, "'born again' is the favored religious label for those with ties to Black Protestant and Evangelical Protestant religious groups." This presumably accounted for the survey's otherwise surprising finding that "more people in Mainline Protestant denominations describe themselves best as 'Evangelical' than do persons affiliated with Evangelical Protestant denominations."[68]

Sometimes, surveys ask respondents not about their denominational affiliation, but about their religious beliefs and practices, and analysts use this data to assign them to particular groups. Differences in numbers can arise from the lack of agreement on what beliefs and practices characterize certain types of Christians. Some studies, for example, define evangelicals as individuals meeting only two criteria: a belief in the inerrancy of the Bible, and the experience of a sudden conversion or of being "born again." Others, however, require that different and/ or additional conditions be fulfilled. Gallup polls from the 1980s classified respondents as evangelicals if they described themselves as "born again" or as having had a "born again" experience, interpreted the Bible literally, and had encouraged others to become Christians.[69] According to the Barna Group, evangelical Christians must

> be born again; say their faith is very important in their life today; believe they have a personal responsibility to share their religious beliefs about Christ with non-Christians; believe that Satan exists; believe that the eternal salvation is possible only through grace, not works; believe that Jesus Christ lived a sinless life on earth; and describe God as the all-knowing, all-powerful, perfect deity who created the universe and still rules it today.[70]

Not surprisingly, the Barna Group finds that evangelicals make up only 8 percent of the U.S. population.[71]

Diversity within Religious Groups

Finally, it is essential to acknowledge the lack of uniformity of religious beliefs and foreign policy preferences among Christians of various stripes. It may seem that Roman Catholics, Evangelical Protestants, and Mainline Protestants are very different animals. But at the rank-and-file level, especially, the lines between the members of these groups are often not very distinct. There are "more conservative" and "more liberal" individuals within each tradition, and the differences between a more liberal evangelical and a more conservative mainliner, for example, may be quite small. The 2004 National Survey of Religion and Politics categorized respondents as Mainline or Evangelical Protestants on the basis of their denominational affiliation, then further classified the members of each group as "traditional," "centrist," or "moderate." The survey found, on certain issues, more variation among the subtypes within each category than between Evangelical and Mainline Protestants overall.[72] This and other analyses suggest that differences of opinion on foreign policy issues are "more strongly connected to religious beliefs than to simple ethnoreligious affiliation."[73] For this reason, public opinion surveys that classify believers purely on the basis of their denominational affiliation fail to capture fully, and may obscure altogether, the impact of doctrine and practice on foreign policy attitudes and preferences.

Of course, there does exist some correlation between religious beliefs and religious affiliation. But this correlation is imperfect. Within Mainline Protestant denominations, there are many members who hold "evangelical" beliefs. As noted above, the Baylor Religion Survey found that a small but hardly trivial minority (11.2 percent) of Mainline Protestants read the Bible literally.[74] Likewise, many members of Evangelical Protestant churches and denominations hold beliefs more typically associated with mainline churches. According to the Pew Religious Landscape Survey, over 40 percent of Evangelical Protestants do not subscribe to a literal interpretation of the Bible, including 7 percent who regard it as being written by men and not the word of God.[75]

Some analysts of religion and politics have identified a group of evangelicals that they term "freestyle evangelicals."[76] Freestyle evangelicals may make up as much as 40 percent of the white evangelical population. Members of this group hold largely conservative views on theological issues and moral issues—abortion and gay marriage, for example—but are more moderate in other ways. They are "deeply concerned about their children and communities, and as a consequence, concerned with education, health care, and the environment." According to analysts, freestyle evangelicals attend church less often than other evangelicals and are more receptive to contemporary forms of worship. Many of them live in suburban areas and belong to nondenominational congregations. Freestyle evangelicals are less conservative in their voting patterns than other evangelicals; Bill Clinton won a majority of their votes in the 1996 presidential election. Some freestyle evangelicals are, in fact, quite liberal in their stances on political, economic and social issues. Jim Wallis and the Sojourners organization that he heads frequently advocate positions that are very similar to, if not indistinguishable from, positions advocated by Mainline Protestant denominations and the Roman Catholic hierarchy, as well as by secular liberals. Former U.S. president Jimmy Carter, whose foreign policy is discussed in the next chapter, is often regarded as being a freestyle evangelical.

The differences among Evangelical Protestants, Mainline Protestants, and Roman Catholics are greatest at the institutional level and smallest among the laity. Even at the denominational level, however, the dichotomous characterization of U.S. Protestants as either evangelical or mainline obscures differences within each group. Some evangelical denominations articulate positions more characteristic of those held by mainline churches, and vice versa. To cite just one example: The Lutheran Church–Missouri Synod, which is almost always classified as an evangelical denomination, explicitly rejects the notion, held by a number of evangelicals and other evangelical denominations, that Christians can predict when the Second Coming of Jesus will occur by placing historical and contemporary events in the context of biblical prophecies.[77] On this particular theological issue, the LCMS adheres to a position espoused by most mainline denominations.

Because there is considerable variation within the Evangelical and Mainline Protestant camps—and among Roman Catholics, too—it is rarely (perhaps never) correct to say that "Evangelical Protestants believe this" or "Roman Catholics and Mainline Protestants believe that." Clear differences do exist among the groups, but they are differences of tendency and proportion rather than absolutes. Qualifiers such as "some," "most," or "many" are almost always necessary and, as the reader may have noticed already, are employed frequently throughout this volume.

Looking Ahead

Walter Russell Mead, one of the foremost students of foreign policy in the United States, has written that religion and religious ideas "exercise profound influence over the country's behavior abroad."[78] This book shares that assessment. Religion is far from being the sole, or even the main, determinant of U.S. foreign policy, but it does matter. Religious beliefs, believers, and institutions affect the foreign policy process in the United States and, in some cases, significantly influence America's international behavior. Chapter 2 identifies some of the ways in which they do so: through an underlying impact on cultural attributes, particularly American exceptionalism; via education, communication, mobilization, voting, lobbying, and other political activities; and through the religious beliefs and related foreign policy attitudes of policymakers themselves. The chapter also discusses a number of episodes in which U.S. foreign policy was shaped by one or more of these factors, ranging from Ronald Reagan's Central American policy to the human rights policies of the Jimmy Carter and George W. Bush administrations.

Chapters 3 through 7 focus on the attitudes of U.S. Christians with respect to certain foreign policy issues—the use of military force, human rights, the Middle East, international law and organizations, and international environmental protection—explaining them in terms of individuals' religious beliefs, church doctrine and culture, and other factors. They examine cases in which religious leaders, denominational institutions, and other church and para-church organizations have attempted to influence U.S. policy on these issues, sometimes successfully and sometimes not. Chapter 8 summarizes the main conclusions of the book and considers the extent to which, in light of current trends, religion might influence U.S. foreign policy in the future.

Notes

1. Bush, speech to the Orange County Business Council, Irvine, California, April 24, 2006, http://georgewbush-whitehouse.archives.gov/news/releases/2006/04/20060424–2.html.
2. Walter Russell Mead, "God's Country?" *Foreign Affairs*, 85, no. 5 (September–October 2006): 24, www.jstor.org/stable/20032068.
3. Bill Broadway, "Religious Leaders' Voices Rise on Iraq," *Washington Post*, September 28, 2002, www.proquest.com.
4. World Council of Churches Central Committee, "Statement on the Threats of Military Action against Iraq," www2.wcc-coe.org/ccdocuments.nsf/index/pub-5-en.html#iraq.
5. Jim Winkler, statement of August 30, 2002, http://home.earthlink.net/~coalition4peace/United%20Methodist%20Statement.htm. Sharon A. Brown Christopher, "Act with Restraint in Dealing with Iraqi President Saddam Hussein - A Pastoral Letter," October 4, 2002, www.gbgm-umc.org/leoniaumc/pastoral%20letter%20from%20the%20president%20of%20united%20methodist%20bishops.htm.
6. UCC, "Statement of United Church of Christ Leaders Opposing U.S. War Against Iraq," www.ucc.org/justice.iraq1.htm.
7. Episcopal Church, "Letter from the Bishops of the Episcopal Church, USA, Meeting in Cleveland, Ohio, Sending Prayers and Support as Members of Congress Make Decision of Whether to Authorize the Use of Force Against Iraq," October 1, 2002, www.episcopalchurch.org/3654_13324_ENG_HTM.htm.
8. "A Statement from Leaders of Friends Organizations in the U.S. Regarding the War in Iraq," March 20, 2003, www.quaker.org/iraqwar.html.

9. United States Conference of Catholic Bishops (hereinafter USCCB), "Statement on Iraq," November 13, 2002, www.usccb.org/bishops/iraq.shtml.
10. "Evangelical Views of Islam," *Beliefnet*, www.beliefnet.com/story/124/story_12447_1. html.
11. Charles Marsh, "Wayward Christian Soldiers," *New York Times*, January 20, 2006, www. nytimes.com/2006/01/20/opinion/20marsh.html?ex=1295413200&en=9611bfdb755d0d 6d&ei=5090&partner=rssuserland&emc=rss.
12. I have been unable to find a completely reliable source for this comment, which appears on blogs and many other websites.
13. Marsh, "Wayward Christian Soldiers."
14. Jerry Falwell, "God is Pro-War," *World Net Daily*, January 31, 2004, http://worldnetdaily. com/news/article.asp?ARTICLE_ID=36859.
15. Bill Broadway, "Evangelicals' Voices Speak Softly about Iraq," *Washington Post*, January 25, 2003, www.washingtonpost.com/ac2/wp-dyn/A40893-2003Jan24?
16. Jim Brown and Bill Fancher, "Assemblies of God Will Let Churches Speak for Themselves on Issue of War," *AgapePress*, February 25, 2003, http://headlines.agapepress.org/ archive/2/252003c.asp.
17. Lutheran Church—Missouri Synod (hereinafter LCMS), "War," www.lcms.org/pages/ internal.asp?NavID=2109.
18. Broadway, "Religious Leaders' Voices Rise on Iraq."
19. Broadway, "Evangelicals' Voices Speak Softly about Iraq."
20. Broadway, "Religious Leaders' Voices Rise on Iraq."
21. Southern Baptist Convention (hereinafter SBC), "On the Liberation of Iraq," www.sbc. net/resolutions/amResolution.asp?ID=1126.
22. Pew Forum on Religion & Public Life (hereinafter Pew Forum), "Different Faiths, Different Messages: Americans Hearing about Iraq from the Pulpit, but Religious Faith Not Defining Options," March 19, 2003, www.pewforum.org/publications/surveys/iraq-war.pdf.
23. National Public Radio (hereinafter NPR), "Profile: Silent Evangelical Support of Bush's Proposed War against Iraq," *Morning Edition*, February 26, 2003, www.npr.org/ programs/morning/transcripts/2003/feb/030226.hagerty.html.
24. Pew Forum, "U.S. Religious Landscape Survey. Religious Affiliation: Diverse and Dynamic," February 2008 (hereinafter "U.S. Religious Landscape Survey," Report 1), 10; available for download at http://religions.pewforum.org/reports.
25. CUNY Graduate Center, "American Religious Identification Survey (2001)," www. gc.cuny.edu/faculty/research_briefs/aris/key_findings.htm.
26. Mega-churches are usually defined as Protestant churches that average 2000 or more congregants per week at services. The Hartford Institute for Religion Research (HIRR) maintains a database of mega-churches in the United States. See HIRR, "Megachurch Definition," http://hirr.hartsem.edu/megachurch/database.html. While it is commonly thought that most mega-churches are nondenominational, this is true of only about one-third of them. Of the nearly two-thirds having a denominational affiliation, the largest number are Southern Baptist.
27. Ted G. Jelen, "Research in Religion and Mass Political Behavior in the United States: Looking Both Ways After Two Decades of Scholarship," *American Politics Quarterly*, 26, no. 1 (January 1998): 127. *Expanded Academic ASAP*. Web.
28. Pew Forum, "U.S. Religious Landscape Survey," Report 1, 11.

29. Baylor Institute for Studies of Religion, "American Piety in the 21st Century: New Insights to the Depth and Complexity of Religion in the US," Selected Findings from the Baylor Religion Survey, September 2006, www.baylor.edu/content/services/document. php/33304.pdf. The Baylor Religion Survey differed from the Pew Religious Landscape Survey in that the former asked respondents not only for their denominational affiliation, but also the name and location of their place of worship. This technique allowed researchers to categorize as Roman Catholic, Evangelical Protestant, or Mainline Protestant many Christians who belonged to or attended nondenominational churches or who were uncertain as to their denominational affiliation. The study's authors noted that this lowered the number of Americans classified as nonreligious and increased the number classified as Evangelical Protestants as compared to other similar surveys.

30. Association of Religion Data Archives, "Evangelical Protestant Denominations," www. thearda.com/mapsReports/reports/evangelical.asp.

31. Association of Religion Data Archives, "Mainline Protestant Denominations," www. thearda.com/mapsReports/reports/mainline.asp.

32. A list of NCC member organizations can be found at www.ncccusa.org/members/index. html.

33. For a complete list of denominations, other organizations, and educational institutions that belong to the NAE, see www.nae.net/membership/current-members.

34. NAE, "Mission Statement," www.nae.net/about-us/mission-statement.

35. According to the Hartford Institute for Religion Research, 56 percent of the megachurches in the United States are Evangelical. If one includes Pentecostal (8 percent), Charismatic (8 percent), and Fundamentalist (2 percent) in the Evangelical category, the figure rises to 74 percent. See HIRR, "Megachurch Definition."

36. Lyman A. Kellstedt, "The Meaning and Measurement of Evangelicalism," in *Religion and Political Behavior in the United States*, ed. Thomas G. Jelen (New York: Praeger, 1989), 3–21. See also John Green, "Evangelicals v. Mainline Protestants," *Frontline*, April 29, 2004, www.pbs.org/wgbh/pages/frontline/shows/jesus/evangelicals/evmain.html. Note that if Christians are classified only on the basis of these doctrinal beliefs, without regard to denominational affiliation, some Roman Catholics could, in principle, be considered evangelicals. However, their numbers are so small as to be almost negligible. Kellstedt's analysis of data from the 1984 National Election Study show that "Catholic Evangelicals" constituted less than 4 percent of the Catholics surveyed. Kellstedt, "Meaning and Measure of Evangelicalism," 7.

37. The ELCA was formed in 1988 by the merger of the Lutheran Church in America, the American Lutheran Church, and the Association of Evangelical Lutheran Churches.

38. The EUB Church was itself a product of a 1946 merger between the Evangelical Church and the Church of the Brethren in Christ.

39. Waldman and Green, "Evangelicals v. Fundamentalists," *Frontline*, April 29, 2004, www. pbs.org/wgbh/pages/frontline/shows/jesus/evangelicals/vs.html. See also, Kellstedt, "Meaning and Measurement of Evangelicalism," 6.

40. A Pew Forum Survey found that 89 percent of Evangelical Protestants believed the Bible was the word of God, and 59 percent read it literally. See Pew Forum on Religion & Public Life, "U.S. Religious Landscape Survey: Religious Beliefs and Practices: Diverse and Politically Relevant," June 2008 (hereinafter "U.S. Religious Landscape Survey," Report 2), 31; available for download at http://religions.pewforum.org/reports.

41. Mead, "God's Country?"

42. Waldman and Green, "Evangelicals v. Fundamentalists."
43. These remarks were widely reported in the press. For an editorial criticizing them, see the *Pittsburgh Post-Gazette*, September 17, 2001, www.post-gazette.com/forum/20010917edfal17p3.asp.
44. Mead, "God's Country?"
45. "Pentecostalism vs. Fundamentalism," *Beliefnet*, www.beliefnet.com/News/Politics/2001/01/Pentecostal-vs-Fundamental.aspx.
46. Kellstedt, "Meaning and Measurement of Evangelicalism," 6.
47. "Pentecostalism vs. Fundamentalism."
48. Scott Keeter and David Masci, "Science in America: Religious Belief and Public Attitudes," Pew Research Center, December 18, 2007, http://pewresearch.org/pubs/667/science-in-america-religious-belief-and-public-attitudes.
49. John C. Green, "The American Religious Landscape and Political Attitudes: A Baseline for 2004." Pew Forum for Religion & Public Life, September 9, 2004, 42, 45, http://pewforum.org/docs/index.php?DocID=55.
50. Green, "American Religious Landscape and Political Attitudes," 9.
51. Pew Forum, "U.S. Religious Landscape Survey," Report 1, 10.
52. By contrast, nearly half of Evangelical Protestants read the Bible literally. See Baylor ISR, "American Piety in the 21st Century," 14.
53. Pew Forum, "U.S. Religious Landscape Survey," Report 2, 95.
54. See Baylor ISR, "American Piety in the 21st Century," 1; and Pew Forum, "U.S. Religious Landscape Survey," Report 2, 31.
55. Pew Forum, "U.S. Religious Landscape Survey," Report 2, 58.
56. Green, "Evangelicals v. Mainline Protestants."
57. Pew Forum, "U.S. Religious Landscape Survey," Report 2, 51.
58. Pew Forum, "U.S. Religious Landscape Survey," Report 2, 31.
59. Pew Forum, "U.S. Religious Landscape Survey," Report 2, 58.
60. See Dean R. Hoge, "A Test of Theories of Denominational Growth and Decline," in *Understanding Church Growth and Decline, 1950–1978*, ed. Dean R. Hoge and David A. Roozen (New York: Pilgrim Press, 1979), 185. Their list, based on 21 responses, was as follows: Assemblies of God, Seventh-Day Adventist, Church of Jesus Christ of Latter-Day Saints (Mormon), Lutheran Church—Missouri Synod, Church of the Nazarene, Southern Baptist Convention, Churches of Christ, Reformed Church in America, American Lutheran Church, Presbyterian Church, American Baptist Churches, Lutheran Church in America, Christian Church (Disciples of Christ), United Presbyterian Church, United Methodist Church, Episcopal Church, and United Church of Christ.
61. See, for example, Tom W. Smith, "Classifying Protestant Denominations," *Review of Religious Research*, 31, no. 3 (March 1990): 225–45, www.jstor.org/stable/3511614.
62. Mead, "God's Country?"
63. See Brian Steensland, Jerry Z. Park, Mark D. Regnerus, Lynn D. Robinson, W. Bradford Wilcox and Robert D. Woodbury, "The Measure of American Religion: Improving the State of the Art," *Social Forces*, 79, no. 1 (September 2000): 291–318, www.jstor.org/stable/2675572.
64. Mead, "God's Country?"
65. Association of Religion Data Archives, "Other Denominations," www.thearda.com/mapsReports/reports/other.asp.
66. CUNY Graduate Center, "American Religious Identification Survey (2001)."

67. CNN/Time poll conducted by Harris Interactive, June 19–20, 2002, www.pollingreport. com/religion2.htm.
68. Baylor ISR, "American Piety in the 21st Century," 15. In addition to Born Again, Fundamentalist, and Evangelical, other categories into which respondents could place themselves were Bible-Believing, Mainline Christian, Theologically Conservative, Theologically Liberal, Moral Majority, Seeker, Religious Right, Charismatic, Pentecostal, and None of these.
69. Kellstedt, "The Meaning and Measurement of Evangelicalism."
70. Barna Group, "Survey Explores Who Qualifies as an Evangelical," January 18, 2007, www.barna.org/barna-update/article/13-culture/111-survey-explores-who-qualifies-as-an-evangelical.
71. Barna Group, "Survey Explores Who Qualifies as an Evangelical."
72. Green, "American Religious Landscape and Political Attitudes."
73. James L. Guth, "Militant and Cooperative Internationalism Among American Religious Publics, 2008." Prepared for the Annual Meeting of the International Studies Association, February 16–20, 2010, 12.
74. The Pew Religious Landscape Survey placed this figure much higher, at 22 percent. Pew Forum, "U.S. Religious Landscape Survey," Report 2, 31.
75. Pew Forum, "U.S. Religious Landscape Survey," Report 2, 31. Surprisingly, the Baylor Survey actually found that a majority of Evangelical Protestants (52.2 percent) did not subscribe to a literal interpretation of the Bible. Baylor ISR, "American Piety in the 21st Century," 14.
76. Steven Waldman and John Green, "Freestyle Evangelicals: The Surprise Swing Vote," *Beliefnet*, www.beliefnet.com/story/129/story_12995_1.html.
77. LCMS, *Concerning the Coming of our Lord Jesus Christ and our Being Gathered to Him . . . A Lutheran Response to the "Left Behind" Series*. A Report of the Commission on Theology and Church Relations of the Lutheran Church—Missouri Synod, April 2004 (St. Louis, MO: Lutheran Church—Missouri Synod, 2004). www.lcms.org/graphics/assets/media/CTCR/LeftBehind.pdf.
78. See note 2, above.

CHAPTER 2

The Influence of Religion on U.S. Foreign Policy

Religion and Foreign Policy

That religion affects the foreign policy of the United States may seem uncontroversial. The rise, beginning in the 1980s, of the so-called Religious Right, with its connections to the administrations of Ronald Reagan and George W. Bush, as well as to the Republican Party more generally, led many observers to conclude that U.S. foreign policy was dominated by a conservative Christian agenda.

Nevertheless, until the mid-1990s, few scholars took seriously the notion that religion plays a significant role in shaping America's international behavior.[1] Indeed, the idea that religion exercises a marked impact on U.S. foreign policy runs counter to much of international relations theory. For more than half a century, realism has been the leading perspective on the interactions among states. Emphasizing the anarchic nature of the international system—that is, the fact that there is no global authority to maintain order and protect states from one another—realists have prescribed a foreign policy that places the highest priority on national security and the maintenance of a favorable balance of power. "Realists," writes Elliott Abrams, "have long argued that the international system, and our own foreign policy, must be based on hard calculations of power and interest."[2]

In addition to prescribing foreign policy, realism also seeks to explain it. So-called classical realists such as Hans Morgenthau and E. H. Carr sought to account for the international behavior of states partly in terms of their internal attributes: ideology, form of government, and type of economic system, among others.[3] But the dominant strain of realism since the publication of Kenneth Waltz's *Theory of International Politics* in 1979—commonly referred to as "structural realism" or "neorealism"— sees no role for any domestic factors.[4] John Mearsheimer, author of *The Tragedy of Great Power Politics*, is quite explicit on this point: "the structure of the international system, not the particular characteristics of individual great powers," causes them to behave in certain ways. States, he argues, cannot be classified as "more or less aggressive on the basis of their economic or political systems."[5]

A proponent of a brand of structural realism termed "offensive realism," Mearsheimer contends that states seek to ensure their security by maximizing their power, attempting to achieve a position of hegemony.[6] By contrast, "defensive realists" such as Kenneth Waltz argue that states seek to maintain a balance of power, not to attain a preponderance of it.[7] Both variants of structural realism, it is crucial to note, locate the sources of state behavior in the structure of the international system—typically defined according to the number of poles (great powers) and the distribution of power among them—and each state's position within that system. Thus, for example, the isolationism of the United States (at least in regard to Europe) throughout most of the nineteenth century can be explained as a function of two factors: (1) a relatively stable balance of power in multipolar Europe, which prevented any European country from gaining a sufficient advantage over its rivals to threaten the United States, and (2) the relatively inferior (as compared to European) military, especially naval, capabilities of the United States, which meant that it could not effectively project its power across the Atlantic Ocean. By 1917, however, the balance of power in Europe had become precarious, and the United States had a blue-water navy, the second largest in the world. Hence, intervention in World War I was both necessary and possible; the same was the case in World War II. After World War II, according to Mearsheimer, the United States was forced to maintain a large military force in Europe in order to prevent a Soviet domination of the continent.[8]

Liberalism, the principal alternative to realism in international relations theory during most of the past half century, also sees little or no role for religion in U.S. foreign policy.[9] There exist three main strands of liberal thinking. One, economic or commercial liberalism, dates back to the free trade doctrines of Adam Smith and David Ricardo. Articulated in the mid-nineteenth century by Richard Cobden and reflected in the so-called Manchester School of English thought, commercial liberalism argues that economic interdependence among states—especially among those with market capitalist economic systems—inclines them toward peace because the costs of disrupting mutually beneficial trading and financial ties are simply too great.[10] More contemporary explications of commercial liberalism can be found in the works of Paul Copeland and Richard Rosecrance, among others.[11]

A second strain of liberal international theory, often called institutionalism, or neoliberal institutionalism, focuses on the allegedly pacifying effects of international institutions. International organizations, suggest proponents of this approach, help maintain peace among states by a variety of mechanisms, including collective security (the purpose of the League of Nations and the primary function of the United Nations, as originally intended), mediating conflict, reducing uncertainty, creating habits of cooperation, and generating a sense of common identity.[12]

The third branch of liberal international theory is ideological or political liberalism. Adherents of this perspective contend that the ideologies and political structures of states profoundly influence their foreign policies and their relations with one another. At the heart of ideological liberalism is democratic (or liberal) peace theory.[13] Some democratic peace theorists argue that democratic (or liberal) states in general have less aggressive foreign policies than their nondemocratic counterparts.[14] The more common claim, however, is that democratic (or liberal) states are pacific in their relations with one another, although they may act in quite bellicose fashion toward their nondemocratic neighbors. Why do democracies not fight one another? Some scholars emphasize the structures and processes of democratic political systems, including elections, checks and balances, and the role of public opinion. These, they maintain, serve to constrain leaders from pursuing overly aggressive foreign policies. Other theorists focus more on the philosophical and normative underpinnings of such systems, arguing that shared values—for example, tolerance of difference, respect for popular sovereignty, commitment to nonviolent conflict resolution— keep liberal states at peace.[15] The most sophisticated analyses suggest that democratic politics and liberal norms, in combination with one another, are responsible for the so-called democratic peace.[16]

Some students of U.S. foreign policy have concluded that it is driven largely if not entirely by liberal international theory. Tony Smith, for example, has described American grand strategy as being one of "national security liberalism," aimed at promoting liberal democracy, open markets, and international institutions. The United States pursued these objectives not simply because they were intrinsically good or economically profitable but because they contributed (or were believed to contribute) to the safety and security of the nation.[17] Similarly, John Ikenberry argues that U.S. foreign policy since the end of World War II has reflected a sustained, systematic effort to spread democracy, expand free trade and economic openness, and establish and support international organizations.[18] Indeed, he contends, this foreign policy agenda is so deeply engrained and enjoys such widespread support among American political elites that it cannot be abandoned. Writes Ikenberry, "The United States is doomed to pursue a liberal grand strategy."[19]

Since the close of the Cold War, which marked, if not (in Francis Fukuyama's famous phrase) "the end of history," at least a significant decline in the ideological competition between liberalism and socialism, international relations scholars have been devoting more attention to cultural influences, including religion.[20] In 1993, Samuel Huntington predicted that in the emerging post-Cold War era "the great divisions among humankind and the dominating source of conflict will be cultural. Nation states will remain the most powerful actors in world affairs, but the principal conflicts of global politics will occur between nations and groups of different civilizations. The clash of civilizations will dominate global politics." According to Huntington, religion was the "most important" cultural feature distinguishing one civilization from another, and he assigned religious labels to more than half of his civilizational groupings: Islamic, Confucian, Hindu, and Slavic-Orthodox.[21]

Building on Huntington's work, Richard Payne sought to analyze the impact of American culture on U.S. foreign policy. In *Clash with Distant Cultures*, Payne identified a number of American cultural attributes—exceptionalism, race-consciousness, and violence, among others—and traced their effects on U.S. policy toward Iraq in the years before and during the 1991 Persian Gulf War, U.S. policy in the Middle East, and U.S. policy in Bosnia during the 1990s. Although Payne did not devote a significant amount of attention to the influence of religion, he noted that the United States is an uncommonly religious and mainly Christian country and that "during the Reagan administration, the religious component of America's foreign and domestic policies was pronounced, partly because of the power of fundamentalist Christians."[22]

The September 2001 terrorist attacks on the World Trade Center and the Pentagon by Islamist militants backed by a conservative Islamic regime in Afghanistan sparked still greater interest in the role of religion in international affairs. The last decade has witnessed the appearance of a number of works addressing aspects of religion and American behavior abroad. In 2008, former conservative evangelical turned skeptic Lee Marsden authored *For God's Sake: The Christian Right and US Foreign Policy*, and in 2009 Robert Wuthnow published *Boundless Faith: The Global Outreach of American Churches*. Perhaps most importantly, a group of scholars, headed by James Guth, John Green, Lyman Kellstedt, and Corwin Smidt, has been conducting empirical studies of the affect of religious beliefs on public opinion concerning foreign policy issues.[23]

In his contribution to *The Influence of Faith: Religious Groups and U.S. Foreign Policy*, political scientist Mark Amstutz notes that "religion remains salient" in U.S. society but asks, "Does it influence foreign policy? More specifically, do churches and faith-based nongovernmental organizations (NGOs) affect the conduct of U.S. foreign relations?" His answer is that "they play only a modest, indirect role."[24] Andrew Kohut and Bruce Stokes believe that, except for Middle East policy, "religion has little bearing on how [Americans] think about international affairs."[25]

As noted in the opening chapter, this book argues that the influence of religion on U.S. foreign policy is far more pervasive than these authors—and the general thrust of international relations theory—suggests. Religion influences U.S. foreign policy in a variety of ways. Some religious beliefs have become so embedded in American culture that their religious origins are not always appreciated by inhabitants of the United States. Religious institutions attempt to instill their values in American citizens, and many of them lobby policymakers in an effort to make their voices heard. To the extent that religious beliefs affect voting, they influence whom the American people choose to lead them and, indirectly, the foreign policies the leaders will pursue. Finally, of course, the religious views of policymakers, including the president of the United States, may influence the country's behavior abroad.

Religion, U.S. Culture, and American Exceptionalism

One of the most pervasive, yet often unappreciated, effects of religion on U.S. foreign policy is the role it plays in what is often referred to as "American exceptionalism." Exceptionalism is the belief that the United States is different from, and superior to, other states. As Davis and Lynn-Jones write, "American exceptionalism not only celebrates the uniqueness and special virtues of the United States, but also elevates America to a higher moral plane than other countries."[26] That the United States may not in fact be morally superior to other states, as some have argued, is largely beside the point.[27] It is the belief, not the reality, that matters.[28] Exceptionalist statements by policymakers are not hard to find. In 1899, during the Spanish-American War, Secretary of War Elihu Root proclaimed that "the American solider is different from all other soldiers of all other countries since the world began. He is the advance guard of liberty and justice, of law and order, of peace and happiness."[29] President Ronald Reagan, in 1983, told the Convention of Religious Broadcasters,

> I have always believed that this blessed land was set apart in a special way, that some divine plan placed this great continent between the two oceans to be found by people from every corner of the earth—people who had a special love for freedom and the courage to uproot themselves, leave their home land and friends to come to a strange land.[30]

The notion that the United States is uniquely benign, indeed beneficent, in its international behavior was articulated clearly by then-presidential candidate George W. Bush in 2000: "America has never been an empire. We may be the only great power in history that had the chance, and refused—preferring greatness to power, and justice to glory."[31]

The belief that the United States is exceptional permeates American society. Although Daniel Bell suggested in 1975 that the Vietnam War and Watergate had brought exceptionalist beliefs to an end,[32] little more than a decade later, Davis and Lynn-Jones noted a marked resurgence in such sentiments.[33] One 1983 poll found that 81 percent of Americans believed that the United States had a "special role" to play in the world, while only 14 percent regarded it as being no different from other countries.[34] In a recent poll, 71 percent of Americans said they were "very proud" to live in the United States. By contrast, only 38 percent of French citizens and 21 percent of German and Japanese citizens claimed pride in their countries of residence.[35] Although exceptionalist views are somewhat more characteristic of those on the right of the American political spectrum than of those on the left, according to Richard Payne, "Exceptionalism is embraced by conservatives and liberals alike."[36]

American exceptionalism has a number of origins, but its roots lie in a particular version of Christian Protestantism. Early European arrivals in North America found biblical meaning in the establishment of their settlements. Believing that the Roman Catholic Church and, later, the leaders of the Church of England had "perverted" the Christian faith, the Puritans regarded New England as the place in which God's promise to the Israelites, recorded in the book of Isaiah, to create in the last days "a new heaven and a new earth," might be fulfilled.[37] Some Puritan leaders regarded their settlements as the "New Jerusalem" prophesied in the book of Revelation:

> And I saw a new heaven and a new earth: for the first heaven and the first earth are passed away; and the sea is no more. And I saw the holy city, new Jerusalem, coming down out of heaven of God, made ready as a bride adorned for her husband. And I heard a great voice out of the throne saying, "Behold, the tabernacle of God is with men, and he shall dwell with them, and they shall be his peoples, and God himself shall be with them, and be their God: and he shall wipe away every tear from their eyes; and death shall be no more; neither shall there be mourning, nor crying, nor pain, any more: the first things are passed away."[38]

The founders of the Massachusetts Bay Colony declared that "this is the place where the Lord will create a new Heaven, and a new earth in new Churches, and a new Commonwealth together."[39] John Winthrop, elected governor of the colony in 1629, told passengers bound for New England the following year that God had established it to serve as a perfect model for other societies to emulate: "We shall be as a city upon a hill. The eyes of all people are upon us."[40]

As Davis and Lynn-Jones have suggested, this "religious vision fused with the faith in reason, progress, and man's perfectibility characteristic of the Enlightenment." Jefferson and other founders of the United States "took Lockean liberalism as their starting point instead of Calvinist theology. But they all concluded that America was a 'separated' nation where mankind could make a new beginning."[41] Alexis de Tocqueville observed in the middle of the nineteenth century that "for Americans the ideas of Christianity and liberty are so completely mingled that it is almost impossible to get them to conceive of one with out the other."[42] Lockean liberalism and the Puritans' notion of the "city on a hill" combined to create what some analysts have called America's "civil religion," whose chief article of faith is the superiority, and the universality, of American ideals and values. This civil religion is so deeply embedded in U.S. culture that its religious origins have become obscured, and contemporary adherents include many Americans who are not Puritans, Protestants, or even necessarily Christians.[43]

American exceptionalism has had myriad implications for U.S. foreign policy. At certain points in the history of the United States it has encouraged the country to withdraw from international affairs, isolating itself in such a way as to protect its purity by avoiding contact with the decadent Old World.[44] This tendency is embodied in what Mead has termed the "Jeffersonian" approach to U.S. foreign policy, which emphasizes the dangers to uniquely American values of excessive involvement abroad.[45] John Quincy Adams warned in 1821 that the United States, "by once enlisting under other banners than her own . . . would involve herself, beyond the power of extrication, in all the wars of interest and intrigue, of individual avarice, envy, and ambition, which assume the colors and usurp the standard of freedom." Concluded Adams, "She might become the dictatress of the world: she would no longer be the ruler of her own spirit."[46] Such sentiments were echoed by Idaho Senator William Borah and others nearly a century later as they prevented the United States from joining the League of Nations.[47]

At other points in the history of the United States, and particularly in more recent years, exceptionalism has helped to create a messianic tendency in U.S. foreign policy. Woodrow Wilson proclaimed after World War I that "America had the infinite privilege of fulfilling her destiny and saving the world."[48] Wilson's plan to involve the United States in the League of Nations was thwarted, but under Franklin Roosevelt's leadership, America played the central role in the founding of the United Nations roughly three decades later. Ronald Reagan's efforts to spread democracy by supporting anticommunist guerrilla movements during the 1980s reflected a belief in the saving mission of the United States. The same was true of the neoconservative-led push to promote democracy in the Middle East and Persian Gulf on the part of the administration of President George W. Bush. Bush's use of the military to overthrow dictators such as Saddam Hussein and to impose democracy at the point of a gun represented in some ways the most extreme, aggressive form of American messianism, combining traditional Wilsonian ideals and the violent methods associated by Mead with the "Jacksonian" school of U.S. foreign policy.[49]

Exceptionalist beliefs have had other implications for U.S. behavior abroad. The reluctance by various administrations to negotiate, or even to hold conversations, with foreign governments regarded as evil is one example. Ronald Reagan, discussing relations with the Soviet Union, asked rhetorically, "How do you compromise between good and evil? . . . How do you compromise with men who say . . . there is no God?"[50] Reagan eventually did compromise with the nuclear-armed Soviet Union on the Intermediate-Range Nuclear Forces (INF) arms control agreement. But some analysts have suggested that exceptionalism and the attendant moralistic quality of U.S. foreign policy leads Americans to prefer war to diplomacy with less powerful enemies. John Spanier has noted:

> If the United States is by definition moral, it obviously cannot compromise, for a nation endowed with a moral mission can hardly violate its own principles. If it did, national interest would be undermined and the national honor stained. Moreover, to compromise with the immoral enemy is to be contaminated by evil. To reach a settlement with the enemy instead of wiping it out is to acknowledge American weakness. This attitude toward diplomacy, viewed as an instrument of compromise, reinforces the American predilection for vio-lence as a means of settling international problems. War allows the nation to destroy its evil opponent, while permitting it to pursue its moral mission uncompromised.[51]

This attitude has almost certainly contributed to what many observers have called the militarization of U.S. foreign policy, including the Bush administration's preference for military solutions in U.S. relations with members of what the president famously termed the "Axis of Evil": Iraq, North Korea, and Iran.

Another effect of exceptionalism has been the willingness of the United States to act in defiance of international law and international organizations. During the 1980s, as part of the so-called Contra War against the Sandinista government of Nicaragua, the Reagan administration mined Nicaraguan harbors. The Nicaraguan regime brought a case before the International Court of Justice, arguing that the mining, as well as other U.S. actions, violated Nicaraguan sovereignty and various elements of international law. The Court found against the United States, but the U.S. government, which had previously declared that it did not recognize the Court's jurisdiction, simply ignored the decision. In 2003, having failed to convince the United Nations Security Council to authorize an invasion of Saddam Hussein's Iraq based on allegations of Iraqi possession of weapons of mass destruction, the administration of George W. Bush proceeded to attack anyway, convinced of the rectitude of the administration's position. Two weeks prior to the invasion, Bush had told reporters that he was not troubled at the prospect of launching military action in the absence of U.N. support, stating that "if we need to act, we will act. And we really don't need United Nations approval to do so."[52] According to the Israeli newspaper, *Haaretz*, Bush later told the Palestinian prime minister, Mahmoud Abbas, "God told me to strike at al Qaida and I struck them, and then he instructed me to strike at Saddam, which I did."[53] While American administrations have typically proclaimed their respect for international law and the organizations that exist to interpret and implement it, it is evident that many have felt that they answer to a higher law, one which it is the exclusive province of the United States to interpret and, if necessary, enforce.

Religious Institutions

There exist in the United States today literally thousands of faith-based organizations. These fall into three main categories. The first are those whose primary function is religious. Such institutions include local churches and, in many cases, the larger denominational organizations to which they belong. The Roman Catholic Church, the United Methodist Church, and the Southern Baptist Convention are such denominations, while the National Council of Churches (NCC) and the National Association of Evangelicals (NAE) are larger umbrella organizations. The second group consists of nonprofit organizations that, although religiously based, are concerned less with theological and ecclesiastical matters than with social and political issues, such as abortion, gay marriage, and social welfare policy. The Christian Coalition of America and James Dobson's Focus on the Family are good examples of this sort of organization. The third category is interest groups or lobbying organizations that are at least ostensibly secular in nature, but which draw much of their support from people of faith. The outstanding example is the

American Israel Public Affairs Committee (AIPAC), which is comprised mainly of American Jews.

Religious institutions can influence foreign policy in a number of ways. Perhaps the most important of these is education. Most of this education—to which Mark Amstutz refers as "preaching and teaching"—is conducted in local churches and parishes, and in religious education classes at church-run schools. Much of it is, of course, fundamentally theological in nature and concerns the doctrines and beliefs of the individual organizations. As I shall show in later chapters of this book, these doctrines and beliefs can themselves have important implications for the views of believers on questions of foreign policy. But much of the education also involves the transmission of broader values and ideas—charity, forgiveness, intolerance of evil— that have implications for public policy in general and foreign policy in particular. Roman Catholic and Mainline Protestant churches have, for many decades, empha- sized the importance of Christian responsibility to society and the welfare of other people. In churches of all types, it is not uncommon to hear sermons on the practical applications of doctrinal principles or the ways in which biblical precepts serve as a guide to living and acting in today's world.

Sometimes, of course, the preaching is overtly political. A March 2003 Pew Survey found that 57 percent of those Americans who regularly attended religious services had heard from their clergy about the possibility of war with Iraq. Fourteen percent reported that their priests or pastors had expressed opposition to such a war, while 7 percent reported that their ministers had spoken in support. Although members of Evangelical Protestant denominations were much more likely to hear pro-war sermons than their Mainline Protestant and Roman Catholic counterparts, the per- centages of clergy speaking on the war were roughly the same across denominations. The survey also found that 33 percent of the American public were influenced "some" or "a great deal" by religious leaders in forming their opinions on the Iraq war. Among major religious groups, the percentage was highest among black Protestants (58 percent) and Evangelical Protestants (46 percent) and lowest among Roman Catholics (29 percent) and Mainline Protestants (18 percent).[54]

Denominational organizations frequently engage in efforts to educate both their own members and the public at large. The primary mechanism by which they do this is the issuing of policy statements and teaching documents.[55] The Roman Catholic Church, through the U.S. Conference of Catholic Bishops, and Mainline Protestant denominations publish a large number of documents on foreign policy issues. It difficult to assess the degree to which these documents influence the attitudes of U.S. citizens or the policymaking process. Mainline Protestant statements on issues such as nuclear weapons, anti-personnel land mines, the Middle East, and the Persian Gulf, for example, seem to have had little or no impact on the substance of U.S. policy.[56] Sometimes, of course, this may simply be because other religious organizations are articulating opposing positions. As noted in the opening chapter, while the Roman Catholic Church and most Mainline Protestant denominations opposed the opening of the war in Iraq, Evangelical denominations were more supportive; the single largest Protestant denomination, the Southern Baptist Convention, issued a statement explicitly backing Bush administration policy. The fact that the positions articulated by some churches are not manifested in U.S. policy is not necessarily evidence of the unimportance of these positions as much as a reflection of the articulation of opposing—and offsetting—views.

When Christian denominations speak with a single voice, their views are much more likely to influence foreign policy. As noted in Chapter 7, during the first decade of the twenty-first century, Evangelical Protestant leaders and institutions began to advocate positions on the protection of the global environment similar to those advocated previously by Roman Catholic and Mainline Protestant organizations. At least in part as a result, the U.S. government, under the leadership of George W. Bush, began to take environmental issues more seriously, finally recognizing, for example, what it had long denied: that there is overwhelming scientific evidence for human-induced climate changes. In 2005, the president acknowledged, for the first time, "that pollution generated by humans is contributing to global warming,"[57] and in his 2007 State of the Union Address, Bush cited the need to become "better stewards of the environment" and to "confront the serious challenge of global climate change."[58] While the rhetoric was not matched by meaningful action on the part of the U.S. government, the fact that the Bush administration shifted its official position suggests the possibility of further movement in the direction of international cooperation on environmental issues, particularly under a Democratic administration.

One denominational document that observers generally recognize as having influenced U.S. foreign policy is the 1983 pastoral letter, *The Challenge of Peace: God's Promise and Our Response*, produced by the National Conference of Catholic Bishops (NCCB) and the United States Catholic Conference (USCC). Written in the early years of the Reagan administration, which was pursuing a significant military build-up in an atmosphere of heightened tensions between the United States and the Soviet Union, the Catholic bishops addressed head-on the question of whether or not nuclear deterrence was a morally acceptable policy. In a careful and closely reasoned argument, drawing on papal statements and other documents setting forth Catholic principles regarding the use of force in international politics, the bishops concluded that nuclear deterrence enjoyed only conditional morality. That is, it could be considered morally acceptable (1) only as a temporary measure to prevent the outbreak of nuclear (or other) war, and (2) only if the U.S. government were actively pursuing other mechanisms to replace it as the guarantor of peace and national security. Thus, the bishops urged that the United States should diligently pursue arms control and disarmament, and should work toward developing nonviolent means of resolving conflicts.[59]

Employing biblical principles and theological arguments in the service of articulating a foreign policy position, the bishops' letter served as something of a model for future documents produced by the NCCB, the USCC, and their successor organization, the United States Conference of Catholic Bishops (USCCB), as well as by Mainline Protestant denominations. In the short term, *The Challenge of Peace* had a "measurable impact" on the attitudes of Roman Catholics.[60] It played a significant role in foreign and defense policy discourse during the 1980s and contributed to the so-called nuclear freeze movement, the objective of which was to halt the construction of any additional nuclear weapons. While it is impossible to find a direct causal connection, the letter may have contributed to the emphasis placed by then-president Ronald Reagan on the Strategic Defense Initiative (SDI), which, he argued, would render nuclear weapons (and thus nuclear deterrence) "impotent and obsolete."[61] And it may have contributed to Reagan's decision to offer, at a meeting with Soviet president Mikhail Gorbachev in Reykjavik, Iceland, to negotiate an agreement by which both the United States and the Soviet Union would eliminate their entire nuclear arsenals. Ironically, this potential pact foundered on Reagan's refusal to abandon SDI, but the failure was followed, in 1987, by the Intermediate-Range Nuclear Forces (INF) agreement, which did remove the most dangerous nuclear missiles from the continent of Europe.[62]

Religious institutions also attempt to influence U.S. foreign policy by lobbying. As Allen Hertzke notes, "National religious leaders operate much as other lobbyists do. They propose bills and amendments, testify before congressional committees, track legislation, provide information on the effects of public policies, and bring pressure to bear by mobilizing their constituencies in congressional districts and states."[63] The National Council of Churches, to which most Mainline Protestant (as well as Orthodox and a few evangelical) denominations belong, consists of 36-member organizations representing more than 45 million Christians. Headquartered in New York City, the NCC's Justice and Advocacy Commission coordinates the efforts of the Public Policy Office in Washington, DC, as well as the office on International Affairs and Peace. Employing a variety of methods, the NCC seeks to make "the views of the ecumenical community known to government."[64]

The National Association of Evangelicals (NAE) represents 60 Christian denominations, in addition to a multiplicity of nonchurch organizations, such as Campus Crusade for Christ, and academic institutions ranging from seminaries to universities. Together, these groups account for approximately 30 million U.S. Christians. The Office of Government Affairs is the NAE's lobbying arm. Employing many of the same methods as the NCC, the Office of Government Affairs, according to the NAE, "represent[s] evangelical concerns to the government and . . . mobilize[s] evangelicals to engage in the public sphere."[65] In recent years, the NAE has increasingly turned its attention to international affairs, as has the evangelical segment of American Christianity more generally.

Christian organizations and their lobbying efforts have, according to experts on religion and politics in the United States, at certain points played a prominent role in U.S. foreign policy. Hertzke notes that during the 1980s, U.S. policy in Central America was "an issue of passionate concern for the mainline Protestants, the peace protestants, the major Catholic organizations, and even some evangelical groups."

In 1986, when President Reagan proposed to give another $100 million in aid to the Contras fighting the Sandinista government of Nicaragua, "religious organizations . . . organized demonstrations in Washington against Contra aid, initiated letter-writing campaigns, and sponsored visits to Congress by clerical leaders returning from the region with fresh reports of Contra atrocities." On March 20, 1986, the House of Representatives voted against Reagan's request, "a notable demonstration of lobby effectiveness in light of the president's personal appeals to many wavering congressmen."[66] While Reagan eventually convinced Congress to appropriate the money, support for his Central American policy continued to erode. The president was forced to rely on subterfuge—secretly and illegally selling arms to Iran—in order to finance the war against the Nicaraguan government, and Reagan's successor, George H. W. Bush, abandoned efforts to persuade Congress to continue providing aid to the Contras.

More recently, Hertzke has observed, the rise of a faith-based movement, driven primarily but not exclusively by Evangelical Protestants, has had profound implications for U.S. human rights policy. This movement, he writes, "has successfully pressed a series of landmark legislative initiatives, each of which faced fierce opposition." These initiatives, some of which are discussed in Chapter 4, included the International Religious Freedom Act of 1998, the Trafficking Victims Protection Act of 2000, the Sudan Peace Act of 2002, and the North Korean Human Rights Act. Hertke argues that the movement has placed on the U.S. human rights agenda "issues previously slighted—or insufficiently pressed—by secular groups, the prestige press, and the foreign policy establishment."[67] Other analysts agree. In 2003, *New York Times* reporter Elizabeth Bumiller wrote that

> Administration officials and members of Congress say the religious coalition has had an unusual influence on one of the most religious White Houses in American history. The groups have driven aspects of foreign policy and won major appointments, and they were instrumental in making sure that the president [Bush] included extensive remarks on sex trafficking in his speech to the United Nations General Assembly in September [2003].[68]

As in domestic politics, Evangelical Protestants have pushed U.S. foreign policy in ways that seek to preserve what they regard as the right to life of unborn children. According to William Martin, "In large part because of opposition from the Religious Right, the United States did not contribute to the UN Population Fund in 1998, jeopardizing a program that provides contraceptives to nearly 1.4 million women in 150 countries."[69]

Evangelical Protestants and their organizations have exercised perhaps their most significant influence on U.S. Middle East policy. In *The Israel Lobby and U.S. Foreign Policy,* John Mearsheimer and Stephen Walt posit the existence of a "loose coalition of individuals and organizations that actively work to shape U.S. foreign policy in a pro-Israel direction."[70] At the core of the lobby is the American Israel Public

Affairs Committee (AIPAC), which the *New York Times* has called "the most important organization affecting America's relationship with Israel."[71] Conservative evangelicals serve as a valuable "junior partner" to the predominately Jewish AIPAC. Important Christian Zionists include Gary Bauer, the late Jerry Falwell, and Pat Robertson, as well as Dick Armey and Tom DeLay, former majority leaders in the House of Representatives. Among the organizations founded by conservative Christians to promote a pro-Israel foreign policy are Christians United for Israel (CUFI), Christian Friends of Israeli Communities (CFIC), and the National Christian Leadership Conference for Israel.[72] According to Mearsheimer and Walt, the Israel lobby, which pressures members of Congress and the executive branch, and shapes public discourse in ways favorable to Israel, is responsible for the United States government pursuing a one-sided Middle East policy that benefits Israel not only at the expense of Palestinians and other Arabs, but at the expense of American national interests.[73] AIPAC, like many organizations, probably exaggerates its own accomplishments, but its website claims a large number of important achievements, ranging from securing essential foreign aid for Israel to obtaining passage of legislation designating Hezbollah's television station as a terrorist entity.[74] Although some analysts have contended that Mearshimer and Walt significantly overstate the influence of the Israel lobby, there is no question of its importance, and many observers have noted the increasingly powerful role played in it by evangelical Christians.[75]

Electoral Politics

Ultimately, of course, the effectiveness of religious lobbying, like other lobbying, depends largely on the ability—or at least the perceived ability—of religious and religiously oriented institutions to mobilize segments of the American electorate. In recent years, Evangelical Protestants have voted much more as a bloc than have their Mainline Protestant and Roman Catholic counterparts. In the 2000 presidential election, for example, Mainline Protestants favored George W. Bush over Al Gore by 53 to 43 percent, while Catholics favored Gore over Bush by a 50 to 47 percent margin. By contrast, white Evangelical Protestants voted overwhelmingly for Bush, 68 to 30 percent. This pattern was, if anything, more marked 4 years later. In the 2004 presidential election, Catholics favored Bush over Democratic nominee John Kerry, 52 to 47 percent; Mainline Protestants favored Bush, 55 to 45 percent; and Evangelical Protestants favored Bush, 78 to 21 percent.[76]

Similar patterns can be observed in Congressional elections. In 2004, white Evangelical Protestants favored Republican candidates for House and Senate positions by a wide margin, 75 to 24 percent. Two years later, in an election in which the Republican Party lost control of both houses of Congress, Evangelical Protestants favored Republican candidates by a nearly identical 72 to 27 percent. Mainline Protestant voters, on the other hand, preferred Republican candidates by much narrower margins: 54 to 44 percent in 2004, and 51 to 47 percent in 2006. Roman

Catholic voters were also fairly evenly split, going Republican, 50 to 49 percent in 2004, and Democratic, 55 to 44 percent in 2006.[77]

Evangelical Protestants vote more monolithically than other U.S. Christians in part because they have focused more exclusively on a small set of largely domestic "values" issues of which abortion and gay marriage are perhaps the most important. Their votes are also more heavily influenced by their religious convictions than the votes of Roman Catholics or Mainline Protestants. In a 2003 Pew Forum survey, 48 percent of Evangelical Protestants said that religion "frequently" guides their voting, while another 20 percent stated that it "occasionally" does. Figures for Mainline Protestants were 10 and 14 percent, respectively, and for Roman Catholics, 12 and 20 percent.[78] Evangelical Protestants are well organized, too. Quoting Robert Putnam, Hertzke has written that "American evangelicals have built the 'largest, best-organized grassroots' social networks of the last quarter century."[79] The Christian Coalition, for example, has sponsored "Citizenship Sundays" in local congregations across the country, encouraging people to register to vote and providing them with education on various social and political issues. The organization provides news to its members regarding its legislative agenda, and "action alerts" on items of particularly pressing importance. Before the November 2007 national election, the Christian Coalition distributed 70 million "voter guides" in all 50 states, with the stated purpose of informing voters of the positions of candidates for various offices.[80] The National Association of Evangelicals offers member congregations a bulletin insert of "Washington Insight," its monthly publication designed to "keep the local church current on the important policy issues facing the evangelical community." Focus on the Family also provides bulletin inserts.

Given their large numbers—most surveys put them at between one-quarter and one-third of the U.S. electorate—and their tendency to vote more monolithically than either Roman Catholics or Mainline Protestants, Evangelical Protestants are in a position to significantly influence the outcome of national elections. Had Evangelical Protestants split their votes in the same proportions as Catholics or Mainline Protestants in 2000 and 2004, George W. Bush would have lost both races by substantial margins. In the 1980s, Ronald Reagan and Republican candidates for Congress also benefited from high levels of evangelical support.

The influence, through voting, of religious beliefs on foreign policy may be quite indirect. Foreign policy issues are frequently not decisive in determining a person's vote. Moreover, polls have suggested that religion typically does not influence Americans' perspectives on foreign policy issues to the same extent as it does certain domestic ones. In a Pew Forum survey of March 2003, only 10 percent of respondents stated that their personal religious beliefs were the most important factor in their views regarding war with Iraq. By contrast, 23 percent reported that religious beliefs were the most important influence on their views regarding the death penalty; corresponding figures for abortion and gay marriage were 28 percent and 40 percent, respectively.[81] It is possible that religiously influenced views on domestic policy issues are more important determinants of a person's vote than are foreign policy preferences. At the same time, however, "for many religious voters preferences on social, economic *and* foreign policies tend to push them in consistent directions."[82]

In any event, elections clearly matter. Who is elected president and which party controls Congress have profound implications for U.S. foreign policy. Counterfactual arguments—those that speculate how history would have been different had certain things happened that did not happen, or had not happened that did—cannot by their very nature be proved. But it seems evident, for example, that, as president, Al Gore would have pursued a foreign policy agenda quite different from that of George W. Bush. Certainly, Gore would have pursued international cooperation on the environment in a way that Bush did not. His human rights agenda would have emphasized issues of social and economic justice, rather than religious freedom. One suspects that he would have initiated an invasion of Afghanistan after the terrorist attacks of September 11, 2001, but it is doubtful that under his leadership U.S. military forces would have attacked Iraq, overthrown Saddam Hussein, and attempted to establish a democratic regime in that country. His Middle East policy would almost certainly have been more balanced: less pro-Israel and more pro-Palestinian. Of course, Gore might have been constrained, until 2006, by a Republican Congress, but this only suggests the degree to which control of the legislative branch of government matters, too.

Policymakers' Beliefs

The most direct manner in which religion affects U.S. foreign policy lies in the beliefs and attitudes of policymakers themselves. These views cannot be inferred on the basis of a person's religious affiliation. Richard Nixon, for example, was a Quaker, but he was certainly not a pacifist, escalating as he did the Vietnam War by bombing Cambodia and Laos in the spring of 1970. As noted previously, the chief architects of the U.S. war against Iraq, President Bush and Vice President Cheney, were United Methodists and thus members of one of the Protestant denominations most vigorously opposed to the war.

But the religious beliefs and attitudes of policymakers do matter. James Guth has demonstrated that voting on social, economic, and foreign policy issues in the U.S. House of Representatives is influenced by members' "religious affiliations, as well as theological perspectives and religious involvement." For those in Congress who are Evangelical Protestants, Mainline Protestants, and white Roman Catholics, "theological orientation" is the "facet of religion that shapes member choices."[83] One might plausibly expect a similar religious influence on the behavior of U.S. presidents.

Among recent occupants of the White House, few have had the connection between their faith and their foreign policies scrutinized to the same extent as George W. Bush. Perhaps this was because of Bush's strong political base among Evangelical Protestants and his courting of their support. Perhaps it was because of his appointment of vocal evangelicals to a variety of high-ranking positions. Perhaps it was due to his public declarations of faith. Perhaps it was because certain of his policies were so strongly opposed by those who disagreed with them.

In any event, Bush, as was widely reported during his presidency, lived a somewhat dissolute existence as a younger man. In his 40s, he apparently had a sudden conversion experience. According to Bush himself, this occurred in 1985, following a series of meetings with the Reverend Billy Graham, although other observers have questioned this account, suggesting that Bush had come to God the previous year, in 1984, in a prayer meeting with the aptly named evangelist Arthur Blessitt.[84] Regardless, Bush on numerous occasions credited finding God with saving his life and especially for enabling him to overcome an addiction to alcohol. His colleagues and even most of his critics believed that his professions of faith were genuine, rather than being manufactured for political purposes.

Bush was somewhat reticent about disclosing his religious views in detail. He never, for example, stated whether or not he believed the Bible is inerrant and must be read literally, although he did, in 2000, call for creationism to be taught in public schools. In 1994, on beginning his first campaign for governor of the state of Texas, Bush told the *Houston Post* that only those who had accepted Jesus Christ as their personal Lord and Savior could go to heaven.[85] This is in principle a universal Christian belief, but one that is less frequently articulated (and less widely believed) by Mainline Protestants than by evangelicals. During his 2000 presidential campaign he backtracked, denying that he had ever claimed that Christians alone possessed the means of salvation.[86] Although the president did not employ either the term "evangelical" or the term "born again" to describe himself, most scholars—and many other contemporary observers—concluded that he "fits in naturally with evangelicals, in style as well as substance."[87]

On the surface, much of Bush's foreign policy appeared to be driven by his religious beliefs. The president himself told the Orange County Business Council in April of 2006 that "I base a lot of my foreign policy decisions on some things that I think are true. One, I believe there's an Almighty. And, secondly, I believe that one of the great gifts of the Almighty is the desire in everybody's soul, regardless of what you look like or where you live, to be free."[88] If the desire for freedom is a gift from God, and a universal human aspiration, then surely those whom the United States sought to liberate would be grateful for its efforts. Without this belief, it is difficult to understand the unshakable (and mistaken) conviction, despite a myriad of warnings to the contrary, on the part of Bush and his advisers that U.S. forces in Iraq would be welcomed as heroes and liberators.

According to some observers, Bush regarded his policy in Iraq and in the war on terror more generally as the fulfillment of a divine plan. As noted above, he allegedly told the Palestinian prime minister that God himself had told him to go after Saddam Hussein. Seymour Hersh wrote in 2005,

> Bush's closest advisers have long been aware of the religious nature of his policy commitments. In recent interviews, one former senior official, who served in

Bush's first term, spoke extensively about the connection between the President's religious faith and his view of the war in Iraq. After the September 11, 2001, terrorist attacks, the former official said, he was told that Bush felt that "God put me here" to deal with the war on terror. The President's belief was fortified by the Republican sweep in the 2002 congressional elections; Bush saw the victory as a purposeful message from God that "he's the man," the former official said. Publicly, Bush depicted his reelection as a referendum on the war; privately he spoke of it as another manifestation of divine purpose.[89]

As discussed in the following chapter, Evangelical Protestants more than Mainline Protestants or Roman Catholics tend to see the world in terms of black and white. They frequently regard governments as having been established by God to promote good and combat evil. For these and other reasons, they often support the use of force in international politics, particularly against enemies of the United States. Bush's language in discussing the war on terror and the Iraq War was suggestive of such beliefs. His repeated references to "evil-doers" and his statements "that those who are not with us are against us" called to mind the predicted Battle of Armageddon, in which the forces of God and the forces of Satan will engage in a final showdown. There is no direct evidence that Bush himself held such apocalyptic views. At the same time, much of his rhetoric was consistent with them and with an essentially fundamentalist evangelical worldview.[90] His unpremeditated and apparently reflexive labeling of the war on terror as a "crusade" in the aftermath of September 11, 2001, is just one other example.[91]

It is possible—and has often been alleged—that other aspects of Bush's foreign policy were influenced by his religious views. As noted in later chapters, views of conservative evangelicals often include, among other things, the belief that the "end times" and the Second Coming of Jesus Christ are near, that the central work of Christians is to bring non-Christians to Jesus, and that the earth and its resources were given to human beings by God for their benefit. Bush's reluctance to admit, until late in his second term, that global warming was a problem and that human activities were at least in part responsible for it is consistent with the view of the environment as something to be exploited rather than preserved. His steadfast support for Israel may have been related to the view that Israel plays a critical role in the fulfillment of biblical prophecies contained in the books of Daniel and Revelation. His emphasis on religious freedom around the world as a human rights issue and his relative lack of interest in social and economic conditions may also have been a consequence, at least in part, of his religious convictions. Lee Marsden has written that "Bush's foreign policy, when stripped of the realist pragmatism necessary to protect its economic, political and strategic interests, [was] an extension of his religious faith."[92]

Members of the Bush administration, on the other hand, reject many of the alleged connections between Bush's foreign policy and his religious views. Bush's foreign policy adviser and chief speechwriter, Michael Gerson, writes that "the direct political influence of the president's religious beliefs [was] considerable—but not in the way the critics often imagine." Gerson acknowledges that what he terms Bush's "mild and conventional evangelical spirituality" was responsible for his "deep belief in the power and appeal of liberty," but he denies that Bush's religious convictions made him "sectarian, intolerant, and triumphalistic about American purposes in the world." As to the claim that "the president's Middle East policies were driven by a Christian eschatology," Gerson writes, "I never once heard President Bush mention these matters."[93] In the end, it seems clear that Bush's foreign policy was significantly influenced by his religious beliefs, but the precise nature of the effects is difficult to ascertain.

A second president whose foreign policies were, it is often argued, driven by his religious convictions was Jimmy Carter. Formally, Carter's upbringing was Southern Baptist, but in adulthood he read the works of a number of important Protestant theologians, primarily Reinhold Niebuhr, and also Tillich, Barth, Bonhoffer, and Kierkegaard.[94] John F. Kennedy had, of course, been forced to talk about his religious beliefs during the 1960 presidential campaign in an effort to convince some American voters that he would not allow his Catholicism (and presumably his loyalty to the pope) to skew his policies in ways that might not be in the interest of the United States. But Carter was the first presidential candidate in modern U.S. history to make his religiosity a centerpiece of his campaign. Unlike Bush, he openly referred to himself as "born again," a label that caused some concern among analysts and pundits during the 1976 presidential campaign about the degree to which he might allow his religious views to affect the policies of his administration.[95]

Although Carter was, by affiliation, a member of a largely evangelical denomination, it is important to remember that in his formative years, as well as during the years of his presidency, the Southern Baptist Convention was considerably less conservative than it is today. It was not until the 1990s that a fundamentalist movement, begun in the 1970s by Paige Patterson and Paul Pressler, managed to take control of the SBC's seminaries and drive moderate Baptists from leadership positions in the seminaries and the Convention itself.[96] Dismayed by these events, Jimmy Carter dissociated himself from the SBC in 2000.[97] In 2001, addressing the moderate Cooperative Baptist Fellowship (CBF), an organization formed in response to the fundamentalist takeover of the SBC, he urged other disaffected Baptists to "forget" the SBC and to form new partnerships in an effort to advance more "traditional" Baptist views.[98]

Whether a function of his upbringing, his reading of Protestant theologians, or some other factors, Carter's religious beliefs were "mainstream."[99] During his presidency, these beliefs found expression in two main areas of foreign policy. According to his speechwriter, Hendrick Herzberg, "Carter believed in peace—in preventing war—and in human rights. These two values were the lodestars by which he guided his conduct of foreign affairs. And . . . these values were expressions of his sense of religious and moral duty."[100]

Nowhere was Carter's pursuit of peace more in evidence than in his Middle East policy. In 1978, he brokered the so-called Camp David Accords between Egypt and Israel.[101] By convincing Egyptian president Anwar Sadat to extend diplomatic recognition to Israel in exchange for Israel's return of the Sinai Peninsula to Egypt, he helped to stabilize the Middle East and dramatically improve Israel's security. The two countries, which had fought wars in 1948, 1956, 1967, and 1973, have not fought since, and although Israel has remained under almost continual assault from Palestinian terrorists, its existence as a state is no longer in jeopardy.

Carter was determined to minimize the dangers of nuclear war by limiting offensive nuclear weapons. Unlike previous presidents, he sought a "radical reduction of ICBMs," and he told the Joint Chiefs of Staff, shortly before his inauguration, that he thought 200 missiles on each side might be sufficient for mutual deterrence.[102] After taking office, he "ordered that the United States prepare a proposal for deep cuts and far more sweeping controls and limitations than anything introduced before."[103] Carter's ambitions were thwarted in part by Soviet objections and in part by congressional opposition. Members of his own party, including such hawks as Paul Nitze and Eugene Rostow, testified before the Senate in an effort to prevent Paul Warnke, Carter's choice as chief arms control negotiator, from being confirmed. Warnke was confirmed, but it had become obvious that Carter could not successfully pursue an arms reduction agenda that his opponents feared would leave the United States weakened in the struggle against worldwide communism.[104] Even the relatively modest limits on weapons contained in the second Strategic Arms Limitation Treaty (SALT II) proved to be too much for Congress to swallow, and after ratification hearings conducted by a divided Senate Foreign Relations Committee, Carter withdrew the pact from consideration.[105]

In addition to his quest for peace in the Middle East and his efforts at arms control, during his presidency Carter moved to improve relations with China, recognizing the government in Beijing and withdrawing diplomatic recognition from the government on the island of Taiwan. Under his leadership, the United States returned the Panama Canal to Panama, and the U.S. government sought to normalize relations with the Castro regime in Cuba.

Carter's most dramatic initiatives occurred in the area of human rights. Critical of the Nixon and Ford administrations for subordinating human rights concerns to national security and economic interests, Carter sought to make human rights the centerpiece of his foreign policy agenda.[106] In October 1977, he signed, on behalf of the United States, the International Covenant on Civil and Political Rights and the International Covenant on Economic, Social, and Cultural Rights, each of which had been open for signature for more than a decade. The Carter administration voted to deny multilateral aid to countries deemed particularly egregious violators of human rights, suspended or eliminated bilateral aid to others, and, in several cases, imposed trade sanctions. Administration officials made "innumerable speeches and other public statements" emphasizing the importance of their human rights agenda.[107] Under Carter's leadership, the Department of State first began issuing "country reports" on the status of human rights in a wide variety of countries. Initially controversial, both within the U.S. government and in some of the countries being reported upon, these reports continue to be produced annually and are a source of detailed and generally accurate information regarding human rights practices around the world.[108]

Carter's human rights policy was widely criticized for its inconsistency and its strategic shortsightedness. The president was, for example, accused of soft-pedaling criticism of U.S. enemies such as the Soviet Union and China, while badgering and alienating right-wing authoritarian regimes that were important Cold War allies. Some of these criticisms were legitimate, and Carter's human rights initiatives, for a host of political, bureaucratic, and other reasons, certainly accomplished less than he had hoped. But the important thing, from the perspective of this study, is that these initiatives were motivated, if not entirely, then to a considerable degree, by his religious views. Zbigniew Brzezinski, Carter's national security adviser and the member of his administration perhaps least enthusiastic about the president's human rights policies, nonetheless acknowledged that "the commitment to human rights reflected Carter's own religious beliefs, as well as his political acumen. He deeply believed in human rights and that commitment remained constant during his Administration."[109]

Summary

The purpose of this chapter has been to demonstrate that religion, religious beliefs, and religious institutions have played, and are likely to continue to play, a substantial role in the foreign policy of the United States. Religious beliefs become part of the culture of society, affecting its values and the ways in which its citizens view their country and the world. Religious institutions educate, mobilize adherents, and lobby in support of their policy preferences. Believers vote, helping to elect leaders who pursue particular policies. And policymakers themselves are sometimes influenced in their foreign policy agendas, by their own religious beliefs and values. The various mechanisms by which religion influences U.S. foreign policy are shown in Figure 2.1.

It would be foolish to suggest that religious factors trump strategic, economic, and political considerations. The failures of Jimmy Carter's arms control and human rights policies are evidence to the contrary. At the same time, it is clear that religious factors do sometimes exercise an important, perhaps even decisive role in U.S. foreign policy. What are the conditions under which religion is likely to be most important? This question will be answered in the concluding chapter.

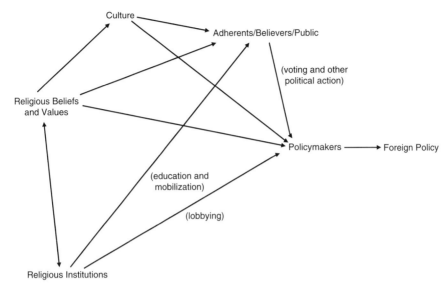

Figure 2.1: How Religion Influences U.S. Foreign Policy

Notes

1. James L. Guth, John C. Green, Lyman A. Kellstedt, and Corwin E. Smidt, "Faith and Foreign Policy: A View from the Pews," *Review of Faith and International Affairs* (Fall 2005): 3.
2. Elliott Abrams, "Introduction," in *The Influence of Faith: Religious Groups and U.S. Foreign Policy*, ed. Abrams (Lanham, MD: Rowman & Littlefield, with the Ethics and Public Policy Center, 2001), vii.
3. Hans J. Morgenthau, *Politics among Nations: The Struggle for Power and Peace*, 4th ed. (New York: Alfred A. Knopf, 1967); E. H. Carr, *The Twenty Years' Crisis, 1919–1939: An Introduction to the Study of International Relations* (London: Macmillan & Co., 1941).
4. Kenneth N. Waltz, *Theory of International Politics* (Reading, MA: Addison-Wesley Publishing Co., 1979). To be fair, it must be noted that most structural realists, including Waltz, acknowledge that domestic factors influence foreign policy; they simply exclude them from their theories.
5. John J. Mearsheimer, *Tragedy of Great Power Politics* (New York: W. W. Norton & Co., 2001), 53, 54. Some structural realists maintain that structural realism is intended solely to explain international outcomes—wars, for example—and cannot be used to account for the external behaviors of individual states. Randall Schweller writes that structural realism "is a theory of international politics and not one of foreign policy." Waltz declares that structural realism "does not explain the particular policies of states" and that scholars who criticize it for failing to do so "mistake a theory

of international politics for a theory of foreign policy." Yet he subsequently claims that his neorealist balance-of-power theory "leads us to expect states to behave in ways that result in balances forming" and that, "from the theory, one predicts that states will engage in balancing behavior." Indeed, as Colin Elman has observed, neorealism can be used to generate testable hypotheses about how states behave, and structural realists have, despite their disclaimers, employed their theories both to explain and to predict such behavior. See Randall L. Schweller, "Fantasy Theory," *Review of International Studies*, 25, no. 1 (January 1999): 149, www.jstor.org/stable/20097582; Waltz, *Theory of International Politics*, 121, 125, 128; and Colin Elman, "Horses for Courses: Why *Not* Neorealist Theories of Foreign Policy?" *Security Studies*, 6, no. 1 (Autumn 1996): 7–53.

6. Mearsheimer, *Tragedy of Great Power Politics*, 4–14, 17–22.

7. Waltz, *Theory of International Politics*.

8. Mearsheimer, *Tragedy of Great Power Politics*, 252–57.

9. The best single elaboration of liberal international theory is Bruce Russett and Jon R. Oneal, *Triangulating Peace: Democracy, Interdependence, and International Organizations* (New York: W. W. Norton & Co., 2001).

10. An early elaboration is Norman Angell, *The Great Illusion: A Study of the Relation of Military Power in Nations to Their Economic and Social Advantage* (New York: Putnam, 1910).

11. Dale C. Copeland, "Economic Interdependence and War: A Theory of Trade Expectations," *International Security*, 20, no. 3 (Winter 1995–1996): 5–41, www.jstor.org/stable/i323313; Richard Rosecrance, *The Rise of the Trading State: Commerce and Conquest in the Modern World* (New York: Basic Books, 1986).

12. The literature on this topic is vast. See, among others, David Mitrany, *A Working Peace System* (Pittsburgh, PA: Quadrangle Books, 1966); Robert Axelrod and Robert O. Keohane, "Achieving Cooperation under Anarchy: Strategies and Institutions," *World Politics*, 38, no. 1 (October 1985): 226–54, www.jstor.org/stable/2010357; Robert O. Keohane, "International Institutions: Two Approaches," *International Studies Quarterly*, 32, no. 4 (December 1988): 379–96, www.jstor.org/stable/2600589; Robert O. Keohane, *International Institutions and State Power: Essays in International Relations Theory* (Boulder, CO: Westview Press, 1989); Lisa L. Martin, "Institutions and Cooperation: Sanctions During the Falkland Islands Conflict," *International Security*, 16, no. 4 (Spring 1992): 143–78, www.jstor.org/stable/i323297; and Inis L. Claude, Jr., *Swords into Plowshares: The Problems and Progress of International Organization*, 4th ed. (New York: Random House, 1984). For a critical analysis of institutions, see John J. Mearsheimer, "The False Promise of International Institutions," *International Security*, 19, no. 3 (Winter 1994–95): 5–49, www.jstor.org/stable/2539078.

13. Michael Doyle's explication is the earliest and still one of the best. See Doyle, "Kant, Liberal Legacies, and Foreign Affairs," Part I, *Philosophy & Public Affairs*, 12, no. 3 (Spring 1983): 205–35, www.jstor.org/stable/2265298; and Doyle, "Liberalism and World Politics," *American Political Science Review*, 80, no. 4 (December 1986): 1151–61, www.jstor.org/stable/1960861. See also Bruce Russett, *Grasping the Democratic Peace: Principles for a Post-Cold War World* (Princeton, NJ: Princeton University Press, 1993).

14. See, for example, Rudolph J. Rummel, "Democracies *Are* Less Warlike than Other Regimes," *European Journal of International Relations*, 1, no. 4 (December 1995): 457–79, available for download at http://ejt.sagepub.com/content/vol1/issue4/.

15. A good survey of the literature can be found in James Lee Ray, *Democracy and International Conflict: An Evaluation of the Democratic Peace Proposition* (Columbia: University of

South Carolina Press, 1995). Many of the major contributions are contained in Michael E. Brown, Sean M. Lynn-Jones, and Steven E. Miller (eds.), *Debating the Democratic Peace*, an *International Security* Reader (Cambridge, MA: MIT Press, 1996).

16. See John M. Owen, "How Liberalism Produces Democratic Peace," *International Security*, 19, no. 2 (Autumn 1994): 87–125, www.jstor.org/stable/2539197.

17. Tony Smith, "National Security Liberalism and American Foreign Policy," in *American Foreign Policy: Theoretical Essays*, 4th ed., ed. G. John Ikenberry (New York: Longman/Addison-Wesley, 2002), 258–74.

18. G. John Ikenberry, "America's Liberal Grand Strategy: Democracy and National Security in the Post-War Era," in *American Foreign Policy: Theoretical Essays*, 4th ed., ed. Ikenberry (New York: Longman/Addison-Wesley, 2002), 274–96.

19. Ikenberry, "America's Liberal Grand Strategy," 293.

20. Francis Fukuyama, *The End of History and the Last Man* (New York: Free Press, 1992). See also Fukuyama, "The End of History," *National Interest* (Summer 1989), www.unc.edu/home/rlstev/Text/Fukuyama%20End%20of%20History.pdf.

21. Samuel P. Huntington, "Clash of Civilizations?" *Foreign Affairs*, 72, no. 2 (Spring 1993): 22, 25, www.jstor.org/stable/20045621. See also Huntington, *The Clash of Civilizations and the Remaking of World Order* (New York: Simon & Schuster, 1996). Other works on the importance of culture in international politics include Peter J. Katzenstein (ed.), *The Culture of National Security: Norms and Identity in World Politics* (New York: Columbia University Press, 1996); Akira Iriye, *Cultural Internationalism and World Order* (Baltimore, MD: Johns Hopkins University Press, 1997); and Valerie M. Hudson (ed.), *Culture and Foreign Policy* (Boulder, CO: Lynne Rienner & Co., 1997).

22. Richard J. Payne, *The Clash with Distant Cultures: Values, Interests, and Force in American Foreign Policy* (Albany, NY: State University of New York Press, 1995), 29.

23. Many of these studies are cited in subsequent chapters and are listed in the Selected Bibliography.

24. Mark R. Amstutz, "Faith-Based NGOs and U.S. Foreign Policy," in *The Influence of Faith: Religious Groups and U.S. Foreign Policy*, ed. Elliott Abrams (Lanham, MD: Rowman & Littlefield, with the Ethics and Public Policy Center, 2001), 175.

25. Andrew Kohut and Bruce Stokes, *America against the World: How We are Different and Why We are Disliked* (New York: Henry Holt, 2006), 94.

26. Tami R. Davis and Sean M. Lynn-Jones, "Citty upon a Hill," *Foreign Policy*, no. 66 (Spring 1987): 20–38, www.jstor.org/stable/1148662.

27. See, for example, Howard Zinn, "The Power and the Glory: Myths of American Exceptionalism," *Boston Review* (Summer 2005), http://bostonreview.net/BR30.3/zinn.html.

28. There is another version of exceptionalism that holds that the United States really is different from other states, though not necessarily superior to them. This view rests on a number of factors, including the geographic isolation of the United States, the absence in this country of any significant socialist movement, the pervasiveness of Lockean liberalism, Americans' lack of experience living under nondemocratic political systems (e.g., monarchy, fascism), the country's unusual level of success in foreign wars, and other factors. See Davis and Lynn-Jones, "Citty upon a Hill," 22–23; and James Q. Wilson, "American Exceptionalism," *The American Spectator*, September 2006, http://spectator.org/archives/2006/10/02/american-exceptionalism. See also Louis Hartz, *The Liberal Tradition in America* (New York: Harcourt, Brace, 1955).

29. Quoted in Zinn, "American Exceptionalism."
30. Quoted in Payne, *Clash with Distant Cultures*, 22–23.
31. Speech of November 19, 1999, at the Ronald Reagan Presidential Library, Simi Valley, California, www.mtholyoke.edu/acad/intrel/bush/wspeech.htm.
32. Daniel Bell, "The End of American Exceptionalism," *The Public Interest* 41 (1975): 193–224. Available for download at http://pao.chadwyck.com/journals/displayItemFromId. do?QueryType=journals&ItemID=g035#listItem81.
33. Davis and Lynn-Jones, "Citty upon a Hill."
34. Cited in Davis and Lynn-Jones, "Citty upon a Hill," 29–30.
35. Cited in Wilson, "American Exceptionalism," 36.
36. Payne, *Clash with Distant Cultures*, 25.
37. Isa. 65.17.
38. Rev. 21.1–4.
39. Davis and Lynn-Jones, "Citty upon a Hill," 22; as quoted in Richard Barnet, *Roots of War* (New York: Penguin, 1972), 251.
40. John Winthrop, "A Model of Christian Charity," http://religiousfreedom.lib.virginia. edu/sacred/charity.html.
41. Davis and Lynn-Jones, "Citty upon a Hill," 22.
42. Alexis de Tocqueville, *Democracy in America*, Vol. 1 (New York: Doubleday & Co., 1969), 293.
43. Payne, *Clash with Distant Cultures*, 28–29. See also Cynthia Toolin, "American Civil Religion from 1789 to 1981: A Content Analysis of Presidential Inaugural Addresses," *Review of Religious Research*, 25, no. 1 (September 1983): 39–49, www.jstor.org/ stable/3511310; and Robert N. Bellah, "Civil Religion in America," *Daedalus*, 96, no. 1 (Winter 1967): 1–21, www.jstor.org/stable/20027022.
44. Davis and Lynn-Jones, "Citty upon a Hill," 21.
45. Walter Russell Mead, *Special Providence: American Foreign Policy and How it Changed the World* (New York: Routledge, 2002), 183–86.
46. Quoted in Mead, *Special Providence*, 185.
47. Mead, *Special Providence*, 185–86.
48. Quoted in Davis and Lynn-Jones, "Citty upon a Hill," 25.
49. Mead, *Special Providence*, chapters 5 and 7.
50. Quoted in Davis and Lynn-Jones, "Citty upon a Hill," 28; from *New York Times*, August 19, 1980, 1.
51. John Spanier, *Games Nations Play*, 7th ed. (Washington, DC: Congressional Quarterly Press, 1990), 185.
52. Press conference of March 6, 2003, www.cnn.com/2003/US/03/06/bush.speech. transcript/index.html.
53. Arnon Regular, "'Road Map is a Life Saver for Us,' PM Abbas Tells Hamas," www. haaretz.com/hasen/pages/ShArt.jhtml?itemNo=310788&contrassID=2&subContrass ID=1&sbSubContrassID=0&listSrc=Y.
54. Pew Forum, "Different Faiths, Different Messages."
55. Amstutz, "Faith-Based NGOs and U.S. Foreign Policy," 178.
56. Many of these statements are discussed or cited in subsequent chapters.
57. National Resources Defense Council (NRDC), "The Bush Record," www.nrdc.org/ bushrecord/airenergy_warming.asp.
58. Bush, State of the Union Address, 2007, http://georgewbush-whitehouse.archives.gov/ news/releases/2007/01/20070123-2.html.

59. National Conference of Catholic Bishops, *The Challenge of Peace: God's Promise and Our Response* (Washington, DC: United States Catholic Conference, 1983), www.usccb.org/sdwp/international/TheChallengeofPeace.pdf.

60. Kenneth D. Wald, "Religious Elites and Public Opinion: The Impact of the Bishops' Peace Pastoral," *Review of Politics*, 54, no. 1 (Winter 1992): 143, www.jstor.org/stable/1407929.

61. Ronald Reagan, speech to the nation, March 23, 1983, www.fas.org/spp/starwars/offdocs/rrspch.htm.

62. On the Reykjavik summit meeting, see Svetlana Savranskaya and Thomas Blanton (eds.), "The Reykjavik File: Previously Secret Documents from U.S. and Soviet Archives on the 1986 Reagan-Gorbachev Summit." From the collections of The National Security Archive, George Washington University, Washington DC. National Security Archive Electronic Briefing Book No. 203, www.gwu.edu/~nsarchiv/NSAEBB/NSAEBB203/index.htm.

63. Allen D. Hertzke, *Representing God in Washington: The Role of Religious Lobbies in the American Polity* (Knoxville, TN: University of Tennessee Press, 1988), 44.

64. National Council of Churches, "Public Witness Resources from the NCC," www.ncccusa.org/publicwitness/index.html.

65. NAE, "Our Mission & Work," www.nae.net/about-us/mission-statement.

66. Hertzke, *Representing God in Washington*, 129, 130.

67. Allen D. Hertzke, "The Role of Evangelicals in the New Human Rights Movement," Speech given at the USC Annenberg School for Communication Conference on "Religion, Politics, and Public Policy," September 22, 2004, 2, 7, http://faculty-staff.ou.edu/H/Allen.D.Hertzke-1/speeches.html.

68. Elizabeth Bumiller, "Evangelicals Sway White House on Human Rights Issues Abroad," *New York Times*, October 26, 2003, section 1, p. 1, www.nytimes.com/2003/10/26/world/evangelicals-sway-white-house-on-human-rights-issues-abroad.html?pagewanted=1.

69. William Martin, "The Christian Right and American Foreign Policy," *Foreign Policy*, 114 (Spring 1999): 68, www.jstor.org/stable/1149591.

70. John J. Mearsheimer and Stephen M. Walt, *The Israel Lobby and U.S. Foreign Policy* (New York: Farrar, Straus and Giroux, 2007), 112. The book followed the authors' highly controversial essay, "The Israel Lobby," *London Review of Books*, March 23, 2006, www.lrb.co.uk/v28/n06/print/mear01_.html; and "The Israel Lobby and U.S. Foreign Policy," a working paper for the John F. Kennedy School of Government, Harvard University, available at http://ksgnotes1.harvard.edu/Research/wpaper.nsf/rwp/RWP06-011.

71. Quoted on AIPAC's homepage, www.aipac.org/.

72. Mearsheimer and Walt, *Israel Lobby and U.S. Foreign Policy*, 132–34.

73. Obviously, this argument is inconsistent with Mearsheimer's structural realist orientation, elaborated earlier in the opening chapter.

74. See "AIPAC Achievements," www.aipac.org/about_AIPAC/default.asp.

75. Stephen Zunes, "Is the Israel Lobby Really that Powerful?" *Tikkun*, 21, no. 4 (July/August 2006): 49, www.tikkun.org/article.php/Zunes-IstheIsraelLobbyThatPowerful. For more on evangelical Christians and their connections to Israel, see Chapter 4.

76. Pew Research Center for the People & the Press, "Religion and the Presidential Vote: Bush's Gains Broad-Based," December 6, 2004, http://people-press.org/commentary/?analysisid=103.

77. Scott Keeter, "Election '06: Big Changes in Some Key Groups," Pew Research Center for the People & the Press, November 16, 2006, http://pewresearch.org/pubs/93/election-06-big-changes-in-some-key-groups.
78. Pew Forum, "Religion and Politics: Contention and Consensus (Part II)," July 24, 2003, http://pewforum.org/docs/?DocID=28#1.
79. Hertzke, "The Role of Evangelicals in the New Human Rights Movement," 6.
80. For information, see the Christian Coalition's website, www.cc.org.
81. Pew Forum, "Different Faiths, Different Messages."
82. James L. Guth, personal correspondence with author. See Guth, "Bush and Religious Politics," in *Ambition and Division: Legacies of the George W. Bush Presidency*, ed. Steven E. Schier (Pittsburgh, PA: University of Pittsburgh Press, 2009), 103.
83. James L. Guth, "Religion and Roll Calls: Religious Influences on the U.S. House of Representatives, 1997–2002." Presented at the annual meeting of the American Political Science Association, August 30–September 2, 2007, abstract, 21.
84. See Craig Unger, "How George Bush Really Found Jesus," *Salon.com*, November 8, 2007, www.salon.com/books/feature/2007/11/08/house_of_bush/print.html. Unger's account is based on a documentary, "With God on Our Side: George W. Bush and the Rise of the Religious Right," which included interviews with Donald Poage, a Texas oilman and member of Bush's Bible-study group, who was apparently present during Bush's meeting with Blessitt.
85. Alan Cooperman, "Openly Religious, to a Point," *Washington Post*, September 1, 2004, A01, www.washingtonpost.com/wp-dyn/articles/A24634-2004Sep15.html.
86. Interview with *Beliefnet* (Fall 2000), www.beliefnet.com/story/47/story_4703.html.
87. Cooperman, "Openly Religious, to a Point."
88. See Chapter 1, note 1. See also Bill Brubaker, "Bush Admits Mistakes in Iraq, Defends Tactics," *Washington Post*, April 24, 2006, www.washingtonpost.com/wp-dyn/content/article/2006/04/24/AR2006042400850.html.
89. Seymour M. Hersh, "Annals of National Security: Up in the Air. Where is the Iraq War Headed Next?" *New Yorker*, December 5, 2005, www.newyorker.com/archive/2005/12/05/051205fa_fact.
90. See David Domke, *God Willing? Political Fundamentalism in the White House, the "War on Terror," and the Echoing Press* (London: Pluto Press, 2004).
91. James Carroll, "The Bush Crusade," *The Nation*, September 20, 2004, www.commondreams.org/views04/0902-06.htm.
92. Lee Marsden, *For God's Sake: The Christian Right and US Foreign Policy* (London and New York: Zed Books, 2009), 107.
93. Michael J. Gerson, *Heroic Conservatism: Why Republicans Need to Embrace America's Ideals (And Why They Deserve to Fail If They Don't)* (New York: HarperOne, 2007), 99.
94. Bruce Mazlish and Edwin Diamond, *Jimmy Carter: A Character Portrait* (New York: Simon and Schuster, 1979), chapter 11.
95. Carter does not seem to have had a sudden conversion experience, but to have been "born again" in the way that is more typical of Mainline Protestants: "growing his faith through a series of experiences." See Betty Glad, *Jimmy Carter: In Search of the Great White House* (New York: W. W. Norton & Co., 1980), 118.
96. The definitive account is Robison B. James, Barbara Jackson, Robert E. Shepherd, Jr., and Cornelia Showalter, *The Fundamentalist Takeover in the Southern Baptist Convention: A Brief History*, 4th ed. (Macon, GA: Cooperative Baptist Fellowship of Georgia, 2006), www.sbctakeover.com/TakeoverBook.pdf.

97. Greg Warner, "Jimmy Carter Says He Can 'No Longer Be Associated' with the SBC," *Baptist Standard*, October 23, 2000, www.baptiststandard.com/2000/10_23/pages/carter.html.

98. Bob Allen, "Carter Calls on 'Traditional' Baptists to Move On," *Baptist Standard*, July 9, 2001, www.baptiststandard.com/2001/7_9/pages/carter.html.

99. Betty Glad, *An Outsider in the White House: Jimmy Carter, His Advisors, and the Making of American Foreign Policy* (Ithaca, NY and London: Cornell University Press, 2009), 19.

100. Hendrick Hertzberg, "Jimmy Carter," from an essay written for *Character Above All*, www.pbs.org/newshour/character/essays/carter.html.

101. Glad, *Outsider in the White House*, 142–63.

102. Glad, *Outsider in the White House*, 48.

103. Gaddis Smith, *Morality, Reason, and Power: American Diplomacy in the Carter Years* (New York: Hill and Wang, 1986), 74.

104. Smith, *Morality, Reason, and Power*, 74–76.

105. Glad, *Outsider in the White House*, 107–16.

106. Although written by a conservative who was decidedly unsympathetic to the Carter administration, the best study of Carter's human rights policies is Joshua Muravchik, *The Uncertain Crusade: Jimmy Carter and the Dilemmas of Human Rights Policy* (Lanham, MD: Hamilton Press, 1986).

107. Smith, *Morality, Reason, and Power*, 53–54.

108. Muravchik, *Uncertain Crusade*, 230–32.

109. Quoted in Muravchik, *Uncertain Crusade*, 6; from Zbigniew Brzezinski, *Power and Principle* (New York: Farrar, Straus, Giroux, 1983), 49.

CHAPTER 3

The Use of Military Force

Religion has played an important role in U.S. foreign policy—and particularly policies regarding the use of military force—at least since the beginning of the Cold War. When the Soviet Union began to challenge U.S. national interests in the late 1940s and early 1950s, the difference between "Christian" America and "godless" communism helped heighten Americans' fears of the USSR and their determination to resist its advances.

As Stephen Bates has noted, "To describe communism as practiced in the Soviet Union, one might talk of the totalitarianism and terror, the dictatorship of the proletariat, the centralized economy, or the denials of civil liberties; but what Americans knew above all else . . . was that communism was 'against religion.'"[1] Religious leaders had been preaching this message for years. Most Protestant churches in the United States during the 1920s and 1930s inveighed against the evils of communism, although "none did so as vehemently as the evangelical fundamentalists," led by renowned evangelists Billy Sunday and, later, Billy Graham.[2] Opposition to communism on the part of the Roman Catholic Church, which dated back to the late nineteenth century, was, if anything, more vociferous.[3]

The distaste for atheistic communism that existed in American society was deliberately encouraged by successive U.S. administrations in the interest of uniting the American population in favor of the strategy of containment and related policies, including the Truman Doctrine, the buildup of nuclear weapons and reliance on nuclear deterrence, and the prosecution of wars in Korea and Vietnam. Dianne Kirby writes that "President Harry Truman made religion an integral part of his Cold War campaign to persuade the American people to abandon isolationism, embrace globalism and world leadership, and roll-back communism."[4] During the Eisenhower presidency, "In God We Trust" became the official motto of the United States and the phrase, "under God," was added to the Pledge of Allegiance.[5]

To be sure, the U.S. government's emphasis on the religious divide between the United States (and the West more generally) and the atheistic communist world was not intended solely for domestic American consumption. It was also aimed at those in other countries who might be seduced by the promises of communism. Kirby states, "Marxist atheism was seen as a potential focus for undermining the popular appeal of communist doctrine. This was particularly important in relation to the masses of poor, for whom communism naturally held a significant attraction, as these were equally the people for whom religion was a comfort and a consolation."[6]

Religion, then, as William Inboden has written, served both "as a cause and as an instrument" of the Cold War.[7] This is not to suggest that the Cold War was exclusively, or even primarily, a religious conflict. Changes in the relative power positions of the United States and the Soviet Union, the power vacuum created in Eastern and Central Europe by the defeat of Germany in World War II, and the widely divergent political and economic systems of the two sides were probably more central. But the Cold War did have a prominent religious component. H. W. Brands has noted,

> Officially, of course, the United States could not wage war, even Cold War, in the name of religion. . . . Unofficially, however, the contest against communism was commonly construed religiously, as a struggle against "Godless communism." Americans who knew nothing else of communism knew that it was atheistic, and therefore a threat to every God-fearing nation and person on the planet. . . . The ideological struggle with the Communists became almost theological: a naïve observer of Cold War America could have been forgiven for thinking that the fate not merely of the world, but of heaven and earth, hung on the outcome of the contest with the Kremlin.[8]

"Without this theological context," Inboden contends, "the Cold War cannot be understood."[9]

The source of Americans' aversion to communism was not simply that Soviet and communist ideology was anti-*Christian*, but that it was explicitly anti-*religious*. Public opinion surveys from the first decade of the twenty-first century show that U.S. Christians are more favorably disposed toward people of other faiths, including Muslims, than they are toward nonbelievers. In a Pew Forum poll taken less than 2 years after the September 11, 2001 attacks on the Pentagon and World Trade Center, 31 percent of Americans stated that they would have reason to vote against a Muslim presidential candidate, while 41 percent said that they would have reason to vote against an atheist candidate.[10] In the middle of the twentieth century, the bias against nonbelievers was, if anything, more pronounced. In 1954, The *Christian Century* wrote that "it had become 'un-American to be unreligious.'"[11] According to Bates, President Eisenhower's famous remark that "our government makes no sense unless it is founded on a deeply held religious belief—and I don't care what it is," reflects the United States "all-but-unique religiosity" and "the apparent national conviction that any religion is better than none."[12]

During the early years of the Cold War, there existed relatively minor differences of opinion regarding the Communist threat among the major branches of Christianity in the United States. As noted above, Evangelical Protestant leaders and the Roman Catholic Church were stridently anti-Commmunist. Mainline Protestant denominations were initially somewhat less so; indeed, during the latter stages of World War II, they had pressed the U.S. government to pursue international cooperation in order to usher in an era of peace following the defeat of the Axis Powers. Nevertheless, within a few years they had come to see the totalitarian threat from communism as being equal to, or perhaps greater than, the danger of nuclear war. To combat it, they believed, the United States must maintain a nuclear arsenal and, if necessary, use it. A commission of the Federal Council of Churches (FCC) reported in 1950:

> For the United States to abandon its atomic weapons, or to give the impression that they would not be used, would leave the non-Communist world with totally inadequate defense. . . . We believe that American military strength, which must include atomic weapons as long as any other nation may possess them, is an essential factor in the possibility of preventing both world war and tyranny. If atomic weapons or other weapons of parallel destructiveness are used against us or our friends in Europe or Asia, we believe that it could be justifiable for our government to use them in retaliation with all possible restraint.[13]

Later that year, a group of leaders of the National Council of Churches (the successor organization to the FCC) expressed support for the first use of nuclear weapons if the situation required it.[14]

As the Cold War progressed, the divisions within American Protestantism grew. The views of Evangelical Protestants remained relatively stable, although their numbers and their political influence increased. Within Mainline Protestant churches, however, liberal leaders and theologians became predominant, and the more conservative "Christian Realist" faction, represented by Reinhold Niebuhr, diminished in vitality. By the 1960s, serious differences of opinion existed within American Protestantism regarding the Vietnam War. More interesting and perhaps more important was the evolving position of the Roman Catholic Church concerning the fight against Communism. In 1945 or 1950, "significant Catholic opposition to a war against Communism" would have been "virtually inconceivable." Yet "from 1966 onward, the [U.S. Catholic] bishops grew steadily more critical of the Vietnam conflict, and in 1972 they endorsed amnesty for draft evaders."[15] Public opinion polls from this period revealed that Roman Catholics favored escalating the war in even lower numbers than Mainline Protestants. During the 1940s and early 1950s, American Protestants had been united in vigorous, even virulent, anti-Catholicism, but the increasing convergence of views between Catholics and Mainline Protestants concerning Vietnam markedly diminished anti-Catholicism among the latter group and within U.S. society more broadly. "Opposition to the Vietnam War," writes Leo Ribuffo, brought Roman Catholics "further into the American mainstream." When John F. Kennedy ran for president in 1960, many Americans fretted that his loyalty to the Roman Catholic Church and to the pope might surpass his loyalty to the United States. "When Eugene McCarthy ran for president in 1968, almost nobody worried about his religion even though he discerned a connection between his Catholic faith and his opposition to the war."[16]

Since the Vietnam War, the views of Evangelical Protestants, Mainline Protestants, and Roman Catholics regarding the use of military force have continued to evolve, although their broad outlines have not changed significantly. Generally speaking, Roman Catholics and Mainline Protestants tend to be skeptical of the utility and the morality of war, while Evangelical Protestants, and especially fundamentalists, tend to be more favorably disposed toward it. As a preliminary to examining these views in detail, it is useful to consider just how Christians have thought about armed conflict and the use of military force during the past two millennia.

Pacifism, Just War, and Crusade in the Christian Tradition

Historically, there have existed within Christianity three distinct views on war.[17] For the first several centuries after its founding, the church maintained a largely pacifist position. This may have been a reflection of the fact that Christians during this period, being a relatively small and frequently persecuted group, were rarely in a position to use organized violence effectively. Moreover, the words and actions of Jesus, related in the Bible, seemed to rule out the use of deadly force, even in self-defense. In the Sermon on the Mount, as recorded by Matthew, Jesus said, "Blessed are the peacemakers, for they shall be called the children of God." He also told the assembled crowd: "You have heard that it was said, 'An eye for an eye, and a tooth for a tooth.' But I tell you, do not resist an evil person. If someone strikes you on the right cheek, turn to him the other also."[18] Luke's account is similar: "But I tell you who hear me: Love your enemies, do good to those who hate you, bless those who curse you, pray for those who mistreat you. If someone strikes you on one cheek, turn to him the other also."[19] On the night before his crucifixion, when Jesus was seized by the authorities, one of his followers took a sword and cut off the ear of one of his captors. Jesus healed the man's ear and rebuked his follower, instructing him, "Put up your sword. All who live by the sword die by the sword."[20]

The pacifist tradition dominated Christianity until the fourth century. In 312, the Emperor Constantine converted and issued the Edict of Milan, declaring that henceforth Christianity would be tolerated. In 383, Christianity became the official religion of the Roman Empire. With these developments came the evolution of so-called just war theory. The just war tradition represented an effort to reconcile the biblical injunction against killing with the practical realities of a world in which the use of force was sometimes necessary. It acknowledged episodes in the Bible—particularly in the Old Testament—where wars appear to be ordained by God and passages in both the Old and New Testaments that seem to allow for the use of violence in the service of justice.[21] Although elements of just war thinking were present in the writings of early Christian leaders such as St. Ambrose, the bishop of Milan from 374 to 397, St. Augustine is usually credited as being "the father of modern Just War theory."[22] The work of Augustine was followed by that of Thomas Aquinas, Francisco de Vitoria, and other Roman Catholic theologians. Just war theory has, over the centuries, become secularized, and in some contemporary versions, its Christian underpinnings are virtually undetectable.[23] The foremost just war theorist of the late twentieth and early twenty-first centuries, Michael Walzer, for example, is a secular Jew who grounds his theory in notions of human rights, especially the rights to life and liberty. Such rights are sometimes seen as being divinely given—Jefferson, after all, wrote that men were endowed with them by their Creator—but this is not the norm in contemporary human rights theory, and it is not the approach taken by Walzer, who declines to speculate as to their origins.[24]

Just war theory consists of two parts: (1) *jus ad bellum* (the justice *of* war), which sets forth the conditions under which a government may legitimately resort to the use of force, and (2) *jus in bello* (justice *in* war), which establishes rules for fighting a war in a morally permissible manner. Some scholars have recently added a third component, *jus post bellum* (justice *following* war), which deals with the rights and responsibilities of the victors, and especially their occupational forces, after a conflict has ended.[25] Although just war theorists sometimes disagree on the precise meaning of particular criteria and whether or not they are fulfilled in specific contexts, there exists a broad consensus on what the rules are. To engage in war, a state must have a just cause. Most just war theorists limit just cause to self-defense, but some allow for the use of force to prevent or end genocide or other serious humanitarian crises. Moreover, the use of force must be authorized by a competent authority (in most cases, the national government), be undertaken only after all other means of resolving a dispute have been exhausted (the "last resort" condition), be motivated by right intention, have a reasonable prospect of success, be expected to produce a preponderance of good over evil, and have peace as its intended outcome.[26] To fight in a morally permissible manner, states must not deliberately kill civilians or noncombatants (the so-called principle of discrimination), and they must employ force in such a way that the harm done is not disproportionate to the good they seek to accomplish (the so-called principle of proportionality).

The third position on war in the Christian tradition is crusade. The Christian version of "holy war," crusade envisions using force aggressively to defeat evil and, in some cases, spread Christianity. The term itself, of course, derives from the series of crusades fought by European Christians, primarily, though not exclusively, against Muslims in the Middle East and Southern Europe from the eleventh to the thirteenth centuries. The first crusade was proclaimed by Pope Urban II in 1095, as a response to the Byzantine Emperor's request for support against Muslim incursions. Its purpose, ostensibly, was to liberate Jerusalem and reconquer other areas of the Holy Land that had fallen under Muslim control. As defined by Scotty McLennan, crusade has

> traditionally involved applying an absolutist good-versus-evil distinction not just to enemy military forces, but to whole peoples. Crusaders have repudiated not only evil deeds that the enemy does, but also the enemy as a whole. Matters of degree have been morally irrelevant from a crusader viewpoint. God has been seen to champion only one side and not lament the loss of enemy lives. The crusader's view is morally simplistic, seeing conflict as an either-or, a battle between pure good and unadulterated evil.[27]

Urban II's description of Muslims as a people "wicked, accursed, and alienated from God" is consistent with this definition.[28]

No major Christian denomination in the United States today subscribes to a crusade view regarding the use of military force. There are almost certainly individual believers who do. A few nondenominational Evangelical Protestant leaders such as Franklin Graham have, in the context of the recent wars in Afghanistan and Iraq, made statements that can be interpreted as containing elements of crusade-thinking. Some of these will be discussed later in this chapter. For the most part, however, contemporary U.S. Christians, and especially their religious institutions, subscribe to either pacifist or just war principles.

The Peace Churches

Within the United States today, the Christian pacifist tradition is most evident in the historical "peace churches." The best known of these denominations, all of which are Protestant, is the Society of Friends, commonly called Quakers. A statement of Quaker service agencies regarding the opening of the war in Iraq captures nicely the Quaker view:

> War is not the answer, not now and not ever. War does not bring about peace. War does not bring about security. War hurts innocent people and generates new resentment and new impetus for revenge in generations to come. Faith in violence as a means of solving political problems is both dangerous and contrary to our understanding of God's way. . . . We renounce the use of violence, and affirm the power of non-violence and love, to bring about the cause of peace and justice for all.[29]

The Church of the Brethren, in its 1970 "Statement of the Church of the Brethren on War," expressed similar sentiments. The document noted that since the founding of the church in 1708, it had "repeatedly declared its position against war." It called upon its members to "not participate in war, learn the art of war, or support war" and encouraged them to "divorce themselves as far as possible from direct association with defense industries in both employment and investment." Expressing "sorrow and deep concern" at the trend in U.S. foreign policy "toward a permanently militaristic outlook," the Church pledged to work toward the abolition of conscription and to support conscientious objectors. It declared its opposition to "the use of taxes by the government for war purposes and military expenditures," and promised to seek "government provision for an alternative use of such tax money for peaceful, non-military purposes."[30]

The Mennonite Church is the third of the major peace churches. Article 22 of its "Confession of Faith in a Mennonite Perspective," states:

> We believe that peace is the will of God. God created the world in peace, and God's peace is most fully revealed in Jesus Christ, who is our peace and the peace of the whole world. Led by the Holy Spirit, we follow Christ in the way of peace, doing justice, bringing reconciliation, and practicing nonresistance even in the face of violence and warfare. . . . As followers of Jesus, we participate in his

ministry of peace and justice. He has called us to find our blessing in making peace and seeking justice. We do so in a spirit of gentleness, willing to be persecuted for righteousness' sake. As disciples of Christ, we do not prepare for war, or participate in war or military service. The same Spirit that empowered Jesus also empowers us to love enemies, to forgive rather than to seek revenge, to practice right relationships, to rely on the community of faith to settle disputes, and to resist evil without violence.[31]

Interestingly, the peace churches straddle the mainline-evangelical divide among U.S. Protestants. While the Mennonites and the Church of the Brethren are evangelical denominations, the Friends are a mainline denomination.

Just War Churches

In addition to the historical peace churches, a few other Mainline Protestant denominations have adopted a pacifist or near-pacifist position. In 1985, the General Synod of the United Church of Christ declared the UCC a "Just Peace Church," placing it "in opposition to the institution of war." The Synod wrote that "since Just War criteria itself [sic] now rules out war under modern conditions, it is imperative to move beyond Just War thinking to the Theology of a Just Peace."[32] Since 1931, the Episcopal Church has held that "War is incompatible with the teaching of Our Lord Jesus Christ."[33] The majority of both Mainline and Evangelical Protestant institutions, as well as the Roman Catholic Church, however, subscribe to some version of just war theory.

The Roman Catholic Church explicitly adheres to a just war perspective. In their 1983 Pastoral Letter on War and Peace, *The Challenge of Peace: God's Promise and Our Response*, the National Conference of Catholic Bishops wrote that "Catholic teaching begins in every case with a presumption against war and for peaceful settlement of disputes. In exceptional cases, determined by the moral principles of the just-war tradition, some uses of force are permitted."[34]

Most Protestant denominations also have adopted a just war position. The Committee to Study War and Peace of the evangelical Christian Reformed Church in North America (CRCNA) acknowledged in 2006 that changes in the nature of warfare during the previous 100 years had made the application of just war principles more difficult, but noted, "We are agreed that just-war criteria must remain essential in assessing the just and unjust use of force."[35] These criteria, the committee wrote, offer guidance to political officials and military commanders concerning when and how to fight wars, as well as to citizens in deciding whether or not to support and participate in them. The mainline Evangelical Lutheran Church in America states, "We seek guidance from the principles of the 'just/unjust war' tradition," including the *jus ad bellum* principles of "right intention, justifiable cause, legitimate authority, last resort, declaration of war aims, proportionality, and reasonable chance of success," and the *jus in bello* principles of "noncombatant immunity and proportionality."[36] The United Methodist Church makes no reference to "just war" in its official documents. Still, the UMC's "Consequences of Conflict," adopted in

1992, states that the use of force must be evaluated "in accordance with historic church teaching limiting resort to war, including questions of proportionality, legal authority, discrimination between combatants and noncombatants, just cause, and probability of success."[37]

With the exception of the peace churches, then, Roman Catholics, Evangelical Protestants, and Mainline Protestants share, for the most part, a belief that war can sometimes be a legitimate instrument of national policy.

Differences Regarding the Use of Force

At the same time, it is clear that Roman Catholics and Mainline Protestants are considerably more averse to the use of force by the U.S. government than their Evangelical Protestant counterparts. Since the 1970s Mainline Protestants have been at the forefront of antiwar efforts in the United States. The National Council of Churches opposed the so-called Contra War waged by the administration of President Ronald Reagan against the Sandinista government of Nicaragua and called for an end to U.S. military assistance to the right-wing government of El Salvador. Mainline denominations supported a Sanctuary Movement in which local congregations sheltered Salvadoran refugees in an effort to prevent their deportation by federal authorities.[38] Mainline Protestant churches generally opposed U.S. action in the 1991 Gulf War, and they almost unanimously opposed the more recent war against Iraq, which began in the spring of 2003.[39]

The Roman Catholic Church in the United States, as noted above, believes that war is presumptively immoral and can be justified only in "exceptional" circumstances.[40] In *The Harvest of Justice is Sown in Peace* (1993), the National Conference of Catholic Bishops pointed to the tradition of nonviolence as a major component in Christian thinking, acknowledged that many Catholics believed their faith required a "full commitment to nonviolence," and stated that the nonviolent tradition, like the just war tradition, offered "significant moral insight." While maintaining that just war principles provide "an important moral framework for restraining and regulating the limited use of force by governments and international organizations," the bishops noted that "serious questions still remain about whether modern war in all its savagery can meet the hard tests set by the just-war tradition." Without directly mentioning the United States, they wrote that "some contemporary strategies and practices seem to raise serious questions when seen in the light of strict just-war analysis." Implicitly criticizing the so-called Powell Doctrine and other aspects of U.S. policy at the time, the bishops stated, "Strategies calling for use of overwhelming and decisive force can raise issues of proportionality and discrimination."[41]

The opposition of the Catholic bishops to the Iraq War, mentioned in the opening chapter, was simply the latest in a long line of policy pronouncements consistent with an aversion to armed conflict. In 1983, in their famous *The Challenge of Peace: God's Promise and Our Response*, the bishops concluded that the use of nuclear weapons would be immoral and that nuclear deterrence, which threatened the use of such weapons, was justified only as an interim strategy intended to prevent the use of such weapons by others. Reliance on nuclear deterrence, wrote the bishops, had to be "a step on the way toward a progressive disarmament."[42] The Catholic bishops have issued statements in support of the START I and START II Treaties, the Comprehensive Test Ban Treaty, and the Ottawa Treaty banning antipersonnel landmines. They have opposed various weapons modernization programs, including the Pentagon's plans to develop a nuclear "bunker-buster," the so-called Robust Nuclear Earth Penetrator (RNEP).[43] They have chastised the U.S. government for excessive military spending at the expense of human development, and they have criticized the United States for being the world's largest purveyor of weapons, arguing that America "bears great responsibility for curbing the [international] arms trade," a trade that the Second Vatican Council termed "one of the greatest curses on the human race."[44]

Mainline Protestant denominations have, in the past several decades, taken similar stances. In June 2002, activist authors Jonathan Schell and David Cortright, together with Randall Forsberg, head of the Institute for Defense and Disarmament Studies and founder of the Nuclear Freeze movement, issued an "Urgent Call to End the Nuclear Danger." Noting that "a decade after the end of the Cold War, the peril of nuclear destruction is mounting," the authors advocated the eventual abolition of nuclear weapons and called on the United States in the meantime to adopt a no first-use policy, cease the development, testing, and production of nuclear warheads, ratify the Comprehensive Test Ban Treaty, and work with Russia to cut the U.S. and Russian nuclear arsenals to 1000 warheads on each side.[45] The "Urgent Call" was endorsed by a number of mainline denominations, including the Disciples of Christ and the Reformed Church in America.[46] Among the tasks identified by the Evangelical Lutheran Church in America (ELCA) in its social statement, *For Peace in God's World*, were to "give high priority to arms control and reduction" and to "control and reduce the arms trade."[47] Like the United Methodist Church, the ELCA called for the elimination of landmines.[48] Between 1979 and 2003, the Episcopal Church adopted resolutions opposing the production of chemical weapons, calling for a nuclear freeze, advocating a no first-use policy, supporting a ban on landmines, promoting the abolition of nuclear weapons, supporting the Comprehensive Test Ban Treaty, and deploring the sale and export of conventional arms.[49]

Evangelical Protestant churches have taken positions on few, if any, issues concerning nuclear deterrence and strategy, defense policy, arms control, and specific weapons systems. Moreover, in contrast to their mainline counterparts, they have typically supported the use of military force by the United States. As noted in Chapter 1, the Southern Baptist Convention and the vast majority of evangelical leaders favored the invasion of Iraq. On October 3, 2002, Richard Land of the Southern Baptist Convention (SBC) authored a letter to President Bush. The "Land Letter," as it became known, also bore the signatures of Chuck Colson, chairman of the Prison Fellowship Ministries, William Bright, founder and chair of Campus Crusade for Christ, James Kennedy, president of Coral Ridge Ministries Media, Inc., and Carl Herbster, president of the American Association of Christian Schools. Land's missive explicitly referred to "the time-honored criteria of just war theory as

developed by Christian theologians in the late fourth and early fifth centuries, A.D."
Unlike the Roman Catholic bishops and Mainline Protestant leaders, however, Land
and his colleagues argued that a war against Iraq would satisfy all relevant just war
principles. Controversially, they posited a close connection between the Iraqi regime
of Saddam Hussein and members of Al Qaeda, the terrorist organization responsible
for the attacks on the Pentagon and World Trade Center, in claiming that a war with
Iraq would be defensive in nature.[50]

With respect to the use of military force and related issues, there clearly exist, at
the denominational and leadership levels, marked differences between Evangelical
Protestants on the one hand and Mainline Protestants and Roman Catholics on the
other. Studies reveal similar though less dramatic differences among laypersons. The
Pew Religious Landscape Survey found, for example, that 38 percent of Evangelical
Protestants believed that peace was best ensured through military strength, while
only 29 percent of Mainline Protestants and only 25 percent of Roman Catholic
respondents agreed.[51] Based on his analysis of data from the 2008 National Survey of
Religion and Politics, James Guth concluded that among U.S. Christians, "Evangelical
Protestants and other religious traditionalists were more likely [than other groups]
to favor policies consistent with [militant internationalism]," a viewpoint characterized by belief in "the necessity of a strong military, willingness to use force to protect
American interests, and a zero-sum interpretation of international conflict."[52]

Explaining the Differences

What accounts for these differences? Several factors seem to be important. One is
that Evangelical Protestants are more likely to see the world in terms of black and
white, while Mainline Protestants and Roman Catholics are more likely to see it in
shades of gray. More specifically, evangelicals are more likely to view international
conflicts in the context of a cosmic battle between the forces of good (God and the
United States) and evil. It is no accident that Ronald Reagan delivered his famous
"Evil Empire" speech before the National Association of Evangelicals. In words
hearkening back to the rhetoric of the early Cold War, discussed above, the president
declared that the Soviet Union was "the focus of evil in the modern world," and
he warned that those who viewed the arms race between the Soviet Union and the
United States as a "giant misunderstanding" were guilty of removing themselves
"from the struggle between right and wrong and good and evil."[53] Throughout the
Cold War, Evangelical Protestants regarded the officially atheist Soviet Union and
communism more generally with a mixture of hostility, suspicion, and fear. With the
end of the Cold War and the terrorist attacks of September 11, 2001, the new
enemy—the focus of evil—became Islam. As Richard Cizik of the NAE has stated,
"Evangelicals have substituted Islam for the Soviet Union. The Muslims have become
the modern-day equivalent of the Evil Empire."[54]

A second explanation has to do with the view of God held by different Christian
organizations and believers. One sometimes hears that Evangelical Protestants

subscribe to an "Old Testament" view of God, while Mainline Protestants subscribe to a "New Testament" view. This is an oversimplification. Nevertheless, the dominant metaphors for God do differ somewhat in the two traditions. In the mainline denominations, God is typically a God of love, and his love extends to all people, whether they are Christian or not. In evangelical churches, God tends to be regarded primarily as a lawgiver and judge, or as a warrior. This is not to say that evangelicals do not regard God as a loving God, or that mainline believers do not think they and others will be judged by God, only that the two groups give different emphases to God's attributes.[55]

Perceptions of God as fundamentally a loving, nurturing being or as an enforcer of the law may be related to beliefs regarding God's gender. Although almost all Christian denominations hold the official position that God is neither male nor female, some use purely masculine nouns and pronouns to refer to "him," while others use feminine language and imagery as well. Beginning in the 1980s, pressed by feminist theologians as well as members of the laity, more liberal Mainline Protestant denominations began to move toward gender-neutral language in their worship. This trend was especially notable in the liturgies of various churches where alongside traditional texts new forms appeared in which the term "Lord" was replaced by "Sovereign," and the word "Father" by "Creator."

In 2006, the General Assembly of the Presbyterian Church (USA) voted to "receive" "The Trinity: God's Love Overflowing," which had been brought before the body by the Congregational Ministries Division of the church. Stating that "Female imagery of the triune God has yet to be adequately explored," the document noted that "the overflowing love of God finds expression in the biblical depiction of God as compassionate mother, beloved child, and life-giving womb." It argued that traditional masculine references to God had been used "to support the idea that God is male and that men are superior to women," and said, "We repent" for such "distortions of trinitarian doctrine." The document suggested that in addition to referring to the Trinity as "Father, Son, and Holy Ghost," the triune God might also be described in other ways, including "Mother, Child, and Womb," "Lover, Beloved, Love," "Creator, Savior, Sanctifier," and "Rock, Redeemer, Friend." As of this writing, the report has not been formally approved, but Presbyterian congregations are free to use the new language, which reflects the increasing "feminization" of God that has been occurring in many Mainline Protestant denominations over the past several decades.[56]

Despite fears among conservative Catholics during the 1990s of a "feminist reconstruction of Roman Catholic worship," the Catholic Church in the United States has moved very slightly, if at all, in this direction.[57] In 1990, the U.S. Catholic bishops issued *Criteria for the Evaluation of Inclusive Language Translations of Scriptural Texts Proposed for Liturgical Use*.[58] The document called for replacing masculine nouns such as "men" with gender-neutral terms (e.g., people, humans) where appropriate and noted that it might be useful "to repeat the name of God, as used earlier in the text, rather than to use the masculine pronoun in every case." But nowhere did the bishops authorize feminine or gender-neutral language in referring to God. Indeed, they declared that "the traditional biblical usage for naming the Persons of the Trinity as 'Father,' 'Son,' and 'Holy Spirit' is to be retained," and they specifically stated that "the feminine pronoun is not to be used to refer to the Person of the Holy Spirit."

Were the U.S. bishops more inclined to permit more gender-neutral language, they would almost certainly be prohibited from doing so by the Vatican. In 1996, Cardinal Joseph Ratzinger (now Pope Benedict XVI), head of the Congregation for the Doctrine of the Faith, took the extraordinary step of ordering the National Conference of Catholic Bishops to withdraw its imprimatur from an already-published translation of the Psalms produced by the International Committee for English in the Liturgy (ICEL). It was evident that Rome would not tolerate any significant use of gender-neutral language, nor would it accept "dynamically equivalent" (as opposed to literal) translations from the Latin. Little has changed since that time. In February 2008, the Vatican issued a statement that Catholics who had been baptized "in the name of the Creator, and of the Redeemer, and of the Sanctifier," or "in the name of the Creator, and of the Liberator, and of the Sustainer," had not been validly baptized, and that persons who had been married following such a baptism were not married in the eyes of the Church.[59]

Evangelical Protestants are divided on the issue. The largest denominations, however, are adamantly opposed to language that envisions God as being female. The Lutheran Church—Missouri Synod, in a major document, "Biblical Revelation and Inclusive Language," noted that "feminine and maternal" attributes were sometimes ascribed to God, but stated that "the language of the Old and New Testaments simply does not allow the view that God is a mother in parallel and coordinate fashion with his being a father." Like the Roman Catholic Church, which sees the use of masculine references to God in the Bible as conveying critical truths about God's nature, the LCMS holds that "the masculine language and imagery which the Scriptures use for God is purposeful and therefore must not be neutralized." Specifically, "The first person of the Trinity is to be addressed as 'Father' rather than as 'Parent' or 'Mother.'"[60] When, in 2002, the International Bible Society and Zondervan Publishing House published a new, more gender-neutral translation of the Bible (Today's New International Version, or TNIV), the Southern Baptist Convention passed a resolution that expressed its "profound disappointment" at the "inaccurate translation" and asked that all organs of the SBC refrain from using it.[61] More recently, Albert Mohler, president of the Southern Baptist Theological Seminary, has blasted the movement toward the use of gender-neutral language in Mainline Protestant denominations, calling it "nonsense."[62] A 2008 editorial in *Christianity Today*, the leading evangelical journal, said that the reference to the Trinity as "Creator, Redeemer, and Sanctifier" was "somewhere between heresy and idolatry."[63]

What possible relationship could beliefs about God's gender have on the views on U.S. Christians regarding the use of military force? Since at least the 1980s, feminist students of international relations have argued that war is a masculine institution.[64] With rare exceptions, they do not claim that war is male institution, an activity in which only men participate. Female political leaders such as Golda Meir, Margaret

Thatcher, and Indira Gandhi have authorized the use of deadly force. Women have fought for decades, perhaps centuries, in armies and guerrilla organizations, and they have engaged in terrorist activities, including suicide bombings. Still, "masculine" characteristics—a desire to dominate, notions of heroic self-sacrifice, and so forth—are so-called because of their original association with men, while "feminine" characteristics—for example, a desire to cooperate rather than to compete, to nurture rather than to kill—are so-called because they were initially, and to some extent still are, associated with women. If the employment of military force is a masculine activity, and one regards God as being male, then presumably God has no objection to war and might in some cases favor it. By contrast, if one regards God as being at least in part female, and hence possessing more feminine qualities, one is presumably less likely to favor the use of force because it appears contrary to the nature and the will of God. Since evangelicals are more likely than Mainline Protestants (or Roman Catholics) to consider God exclusively male, they would be expected to favor the use of military force to a greater extent.

Views of God held by U.S. Christians do not differ solely on the issue of gender. The Baylor Religion Survey of September 2006 asked respondents about their concept of God along two dimensions: God's level of engagement (the extent to which individuals believe that God is directly involved in worldly and personal affairs) and God's level of anger (the extent to which individuals believe God is angered by human sins and tends toward punishing, severe, and wrathful characteristics). On this basis, the study's authors identified four basic conceptions of God: Authoritarian (high engagement, high anger), Benevolent (high engagement, low anger), Critical (low engagement, high anger), and Distant (low engagement, low anger). The survey found considerable differences in perceptions of God among Christian groups in the United States. Mainline Protestants tended to view God as either Distant (29.3 percent) or Benevolent (26.6 percent). Fewer than one-quarter (23.7 percent) believed in an Authoritarian God. Figures for Roman Catholics were similar: Distant God, 29.2 percent; Benevolent God, 28.2 percent; and Authoritarian God, 22.6 percent. On the other hand, a majority of Evangelical Protestants (52.3 percent) expressed belief in an Authoritarian God. Only 10.8 percent regarded God as being Distant.[65]

A third factor accounting for the difference between Mainline Protestants, Roman Catholics, and Evangelical Protestants on use of force issues may be their views regarding the nature of the relationship between God and the United States. Evangelical Protestants are particularly "strong believers in American exceptionalism," and they are more likely than either Roman Catholics or Mainline Protestants to regard the United States as a country uniquely blessed by God.[66] In a 2002 Pew Form survey, which asked respondents whether they believed the United States enjoyed special protection from God, 71 percent of Evangelical Protestants said yes, as compared to 40 percent of Mainline Protestants and 39 percent of Roman Catholics. Evangelical Protestants (83 percent) were also more likely than either Roman Catholics (58 percent) or Mainline Protestants (57 percent) to believe that America's strength as a country was based on the religious faith of its people.[67] Evangelical Protestants, more than Mainline Protestants and Catholics, regard the United States as having a special role in the world. Although, in the days following September 11, 2001, some evangelical leaders suggested that the terrorist attacks on the World Trade Center and the Pentagon were God's punishment for America's sinfulness, a more prominent theme was the belief expressed by President George W. Bush: that the United States (and he personally as its leader) had been divinely chosen to "rid the world of evil."[68]

A fourth factor accounting for the greater willingness of Evangelical Protestants than Mainline Protestants or Roman Catholics to countenance the use of force by the United States may have to do with their views regarding governmental authority. The Roman Catholic Church, the only religious organization in the world to control its own state (the Vatican), does not expect its members to demonstrate a high level of deference to the governments of other states. Mainline Protestant denominations also tend not to be particularly deferential to governmental authority, as the title of the Episcopal Church's statement, "The Cross Before the Flag," suggests.[69]

On the other hand, evangelical denominations and leaders tend to advocate a high level of deference to civil institutions, believing them to have been established by God. They also tend to see the use of force as essential to the purpose of government. This view is based largely on a passage in the book of Romans, in which Paul writes, "the one who is in authority . . . is the servant of God, an avenger who carries out God's wrath on the wrongdoer." Charles Stanley, pastor of the First Baptist Church in Atlanta, and founder of In Touch Ministries, said in a sermon to his 15,000-member congregation,

> The government is ordained by God with the right to promote good and restrain evil. This includes wickedness that exists within the nation, as well as any wicked persons or countries that threaten foreign nations. . . . [A] government has biblical grounds to go to war in the nation's defense or to liberate others in the world who are enslaved.[70]

In an interview with National Public Radio, Richard Land stated that "Romans 13 makes it very clear that 'God ordained the civil magistrate to punish those who do evil and to reward those [who] do that which is right.' So, clearly, the civil magistrate is ordained by God to use various means, up to and including lethal force, to punish evildoers."[71] According to the Lutheran Church—Missouri Synod, "God has instituted [earthly governments] to restrain the wicked, to thwart the designs of evildoers, and to preserve the civil order. To do this task war is sometimes necessary."[72]

It is likely that Evangelical Protestants—and perhaps Roman Catholics and Mainline Protestants, too—are even more deferential to governmental authority when the head of the government is seen as one of their own. In the run-up to the opening of the Iraq War, evangelical leaders and believers were inclined to support the administration's position partly because they trusted President Bush, who spoke their language and whom they regarded as one of them. Will Townsend, pastor of an evangelical church, told a reporter in 2003, "So, yeah, the idea that he is a Christian, that he is listening to the word of the Lord, that he's asking the Lord's wisdom, that he's saying, 'Guide me,' OK, yeah, I mean, I trust that."[73] In the same interview, Richard Cizik of the NAE confirmed that evangelicals "trust this president, George W. Bush, and his assessment of the nature of the threat."[74] Steven Waldman of *Beliefnet* argued in 2006 that "the key to evangelical support for Bush has never primarily been about his positions on issues (such as abortion or homosexuality) but his personal faith story. Simply put, they trust him because he's a Christian."[75] In the Baylor Religion Survey, nearly one-third of Evangelical Protestants reported that they trusted Bush "a lot," as compared to fewer than one-quarter of Roman Catholics, and between one-fifth and one-sixth of Mainline Protestants.[76]

Finally, there is the view of evil and of Satan. Evangelicals are more likely than either Mainline Protestants or Roman Catholics to regard Satan as real and to regard some human beings as the embodiment of evil and the devil's agents. As noted above, the Barna Group considers a belief in the reality of Satan to be one of the defining characteristics of an evangelical. The Assemblies of God explicitly state that Satan is a "real entity."[77] There is nothing in the official documents of the Southern Baptist Convention that articulates this position, but the SBC does believe in "a literal hell."[78] Leaders of the SBC commonly refer to Satan as though he is a real being, and when a Barna Group survey found that only 34 percent of Baptists (Southern and others, including members of mainline denominations) believed in the literal reality of Satan, they expressed dismay.[79]

Mainline Protestants are more likely to regard Satan as a metaphor for evil. They do not deny that evil exists, but often regard it as being a product of human society and human actions, rather than the result of a deliberate campaign by a supernatural being. Most mainline denominations do not take an official stance on this issue. The Evangelical Lutheran Church in America, for example, recognizes that some of its members regard Satan as a real entity, while others see Satan as symbolic.[80] Still, especially in more theologically liberal churches, the majority of believers do not subscribe to the literal reality of the devil. The Barna Group survey cited in the preceding paragraph found that 80 percent of Episcopalians did not regard Satan as real.[81]

It is easy to understand how these factors help to explain the differences regarding the use of force and related issues between Evangelical Protestants on the one hand and Roman Catholics and Mainline Protestants on the other. If one sees the world engaged in a struggle between good and evil, with one's enemies the agents of Satan and one's own country the special servant of God, and if one views God primarily as a masculine God of law and justice who metes out punishment for sins, then one is likely to approve the use of force against America's enemies. If, on the other hand, one is not sure that America's enemies are evil, one does not believe that their leaders are agents of the devil, one does not believe that the United States is God's hand in the world, and one views God as a partly feminine God of love and nurturance or a distant God who rarely, if ever, intervenes in human affairs, then the use of force is likely to be much less appealing.

Correlations between certain of these factors and Christians' views on war have been confirmed by public opinion survey research. In the Baylor Religion Survey, for example, 63 percent of those holding an Authoritarian view of God—a position much more characteristic of Evangelical Protestants than either Roman Catholics or Mainline Protestants—thought the U.S. invasion of Iraq was justified, as compared to 47 percent of those holding a Benevolent view and only 29 percent holding a Distant view. Of those who believed God favors the United States—again, a view more characteristic of Evangelical Protestants than of Mainline Protestants or Roman Catholics—79 percent felt that the Iraq War was justified, as opposed to 37 percent of those who did not believe that God favors the United States.[82] From his analysis of 1990–1991 National Election Survey data, Ted Jelen concluded that "Evangelical beliefs among Protestants [had] generally 'hawkish' effects" on foreign policy attitudes.[83]

The Iraq War

There are two further reasons, beyond those discussed already, that Evangelical Protestants, more than either Roman Catholics or Mainline Protestants, have supported the use of military force by the United States in certain specific cases, such as the Iraq War. The first is evangelism. As noted in the introductory chapter, one of the defining characteristics of evangelicals is their commitment to spreading the Gospel and winning new souls to Jesus Christ.

Many Evangelical Protestants saw the U.S. invasion of Iraq as an opportunity to convert Muslims to Christianity. In a *Beliefnet* survey conducted in the fall of 2002, 81 percent of the evangelical leaders polled considered evangelizing Muslims abroad to be "very important," while another 16 percent regarded it as being of some importance.[84] By the time the war began in March 2003, or shortly thereafter, major evangelical organizations were ready to act on this conviction.

The International Mission Board of the Southern Baptist Convention had plans to send hundreds of volunteers from the United States to Iraq. World Relief, the humanitarian organ of the National Association of Evangelicals, established a camp for Iraqi refugees in neighboring Jordan. Samaritan's Purse prepared 60,000 aid boxes for distribution to Iraqi civilians. According to Franklin Graham, the organization had ready "5000 hygiene kits, 5000 kits of pots and utensils, thousands of yards of plastic to make tents, and enough medicine to take care of 100,000 people for three months." By April 2004, roughly a year after the war began, about 30 evangelical missionaries were working in Baghdad on an ongoing basis, while another 150 had been there on shorter assignments. More than 900,000 Arabic-language Bibles had arrived from the United States, along with hundreds of tons of food and medical supplies.[85]

Much of the impetus for these efforts was, of course, humanitarian. Missionaries and other volunteers arrived in Iraq to provide food, clothing, shelter, and other necessities of life for members of the distressed Iraqi population. But, as the provision of Arabic-language Bibles suggests, seeking converts was also a powerful motivation. John Green noted at the time that "many evangelicals feel war in Iraq is part of a broader religious mission," that they "see 'opportunities' arising as a result of the war—as a way of 'taming' Islam and giving Christianity a greater platform in the Middle East."[86]

In a CNN interview, Albert Mohler, president of the Southern Baptist Theological Seminary, acknowledged the humanitarian needs of the Iraqi people, but he argued that their spiritual needs were even greater.[87] Nonreligious observers and many Mainline Protestant and Roman Catholic leaders called for caution and warned that aid efforts conducted by outspoken evangelicals such as Franklin Graham might backfire by alienating those for whom the assistance was intended. Charles Kimball, chair of the Department of Religion at Wake Forest University, who shared both the CNN interview and a Fox radio interview with Mohler, warned against prose-lytizing Muslims and expressed the belief that Christians did not have a monopoly on salvation, stating that "there are indeed many paths and we would do well to be the best Christians, the best Jews, the best Muslims."[88] "What we have here," observed Mohler correctly, "is a distinction between evangelicals and those who are not evangelicals. I believe, and other evangelicals believe, that eternity is hanging in the balance, that the only way to salvation is faith in the Lord Jesus Christ."[89]

Because they viewed the stakes as being so high, Mohler and other evangelicals rejected the idea that evangelizing should be scaled back because of fears that it might offend Muslim sensibilities and increase tensions between Christians and Muslims in Iraq. Said Mohler, "I agree with Dr. Kimball, that there are urgent humanitarian needs that really must be met and I agree with that wholeheartedly. I also agree with his call for sensitivity. But we cannot be so sensitive that we abandon the Gospel. And we must understand that these people have an even deeper need than food and clothing and shelter."[90] Richard Land stated that "it is every Christian's requirement to share Jesus Christ's gospel with everyone on the planet, including every Muslim. If that causes anger and violence, it only shows we must speak more loudly."[91] Todd Nettleton of the Voice of the Martyrs, an evangelical organization based in Oklahoma, expressed the view of many evangelicals bluntly and succinctly: "Yes, sharing Christ's love causes conflict. But the alternative is allowing people to go to hell."[92]

Evangelicals determined to proselytize in Iraq had ambitions extending well beyond that country. According to Kyle Fisk, executive administrator of the National Association of Evangelicals, "President Bush said democracy will spread from Iraq to nearby countries. A free Iraq also allows us to spread Jesus Christ's teachings even in nations where the laws keep us out." Indeed, said Fisk, "Iraq will become the center for spreading the gospel of Jesus Christ to Iran, Libya, throughout the Middle East."[93]

Evangelical support for the invasion of Iraq, which, at least implicitly, saw the use of force as a means of spreading Christianity and converting the heathen, contained aspects of a crusade view of war, as described above. Franklin Graham called Islam a "very evil and wicked religion," while Jerry Vines, a former president of the Southern

Baptist Convention, termed the prophet Muhammad, the founder of Islam, a "demon-possessed pedophile."[94] Robert Pyne, of the Dallas Theological Seminary, argued that evangelicals did see the Iraq War as a type of crusade, noting, "They identify the American cause with this war as the cause of Christ."[95] International Mission Board president Jerry Rankin told the Southern Baptist Convention in June 2003 that God himself, not the United States government, had given Southern Baptists the opportunity to evangelize Muslims in Iraq, and he implored members of the denomination to rally to the cause:

> God is breaking down the walls. It is God's time for the Gospel to penetrate those barriers in the Muslim world. It is not happening because of International Mission Board strategies or Western diplomacy or military might. It is the providence and power of God moving to fulfill His purpose, that He will be exalted among all the nations and peoples and tongues. The only question is whether or not we will respond to the challenge and opportunity. We must realize that God has blessed and prospered us as Southern Baptists, not to take pride in our programs and what we can do here, but to be a light to the nations, to carry his salvation to the ends of the earth. Will we be found faithful? . . . Will we pray that the walls will come tumbling down? Will we give that missionaries can go? Will we be willing to give of our lives to go and join in the effort?[96]

At this writing, the ambitions of Evangelical Protestant leaders and organizations in Iraq remain far from fully realized. As critics had predicted, efforts to convert Muslims met with considerable resistance. American missionaries were killed. Because the situation in Iraq was so unstable in the years following 2003, it was very difficult, if not impossible, for missionaries and volunteers to travel to certain parts of the country and to do the work they had planned to do. Ironically, Christian churches and believers in Iraq suffered from their perceived association with the United States and American Christian organizations. Nevertheless, evangelical leaders continue to hope that a stable, democratic Iraq will afford them a chance to win Muslim souls to Christ.

A second and related factor behind evangelicals' support for military action in Iraq had to do with their attitudes toward Islam. As noted above, Evangelical Protestants hold a generally dim view of that religion and its followers. The Christian Reformed Church, for example, states that "Islam is a thorn in the growth of the Kingdom. It holds a billion or more souls in its grip, puncturing any hope of eternal life with God unless led out of this thicket of spiritual brambles."[97] A 2002 survey of leaders of evangelical organizations sponsored by *Beliefnet* and the Ethics and Public Policy Center found that 89 percent believed it was "very important," in interacting with Muslims, to insist on the truth of the Gospel. Only 54 percent thought it was "very important" to engage in dialogue with Muslims.[98] Evangelical Protestant leaders have consistently rejected the notion that Christians and Muslims worship the same God, partly because Muslims, regarding Jesus as fully human and as a prophet but not a savior, do not subscribe to the Trinitarian notion of God that is at the core of Christian theology. When President Bush said in November 2003 that he believed that the God of Islam and the God of Christianity were one and the same, his remark "sent immediate shock waves through Christian Web sites and radio broadcasts."[99] Bush, according to Richard Land, was "simply mistaken." Said Land, "The Bible is clear on this: The one and true god is Jehovah, and his only begotten son is Jesus Christ."[100] Ted Haggard, president of the National Association of Evangelicals, agreed: "The Christian God encourages freedom, love, forgiveness, prosperity and health. The Muslim god appears to value the opposite. The personalities of each god are evident in the cultures, civilizations and dispositions of the peoples that serve them. Muhammad's central message was submission; Jesus' central message was love. They seem to be very different personalities."[101]

Mainline Protestants, by contrast, emphasize the historical and theological similarities between Christians and Muslims. They stress that the two religions are monotheistic, that "Allah" is the Arabic word for God, and that Abraham is the patriarch of both Christianity and Islam, as well as of Judaism.[102] They also place a high priority on interfaith dialogue. The Evangelical Lutheran Church in America, for example, has a Department of Ecumenical Affairs that promotes both ecumenical and interfaith relations. The ELCA's publication, "Honoring Our Neighbor's Faith," seeks to further Lutherans' understanding of other Christian denominations as well as Judaism, Hinduism, Buddhism, and Islam.[103] The United Methodist Church's General Commission on Christian Unity and Interreligious Concerns (GCCUIC) engages, along with other Christian groups, in dialogue with other faith traditions in order to build "understanding and trust."[104] The UMC's *Book of Resolutions* states that "we United Methodist Christians, not just individually, but corporately, are called to be neighbors with other faith communities (such as Buddhist, Jewish, Muslim, Hindu, and Native American), and to work with them to create a human community, a set of relationships between people at once interdependent and free, in which there is love, mutual respect, and justice."[105] In 1992, the GCCUIC proposed a statement, which was adopted by the UMC's General Conference, on "Our Muslim Neighbors," which noted that Christianity and Islam shared "common roots," identified a number of similarities between the Qur'an and the Bible, and argued that "the Christian faith itself impels us to love our neighbors of other faiths and to seek to live in contact and mutually beneficial relationship, in community with them."[106] In the days and weeks following the terrorist attacks of September 11, 2001, local congregations of Mainline Protestant denominations (as well as Orthodox denominations and the Roman Catholic Church) "began inviting Muslims to explain their faith at a flurry of interfaith events and dialogue sessions."[107]

The Roman Catholic Church, as noted previously, has sometimes angered not only persons of other faiths, but also other Christian denominations, with its insistence that Catholicism is the only "true" religion. Most recently, in 2007, Pope Benedict XVI approved a document prepared by the Church's theological watchdog, the Congregation for the Doctrine of the Faith, which declared that other Christian churches were not true churches, but only "ecclesial communities," because they did not have apostolic (Petrine) succession and their clergy were therefore not validly ordained. The document also asserted that Protestant denominations did not possess the "means of salvation."[108] Yet, the Catholic Church, like most Mainline Protestant denominations, pursues interfaith dialogue with considerable vigor and emphasizes the importance of respect for other faith traditions. The Pontifical Council for Interreligious Dialogue (PCID), established by Pope Paul VI in 1964, bears primary responsibility for interfaith relations. The PCID is charged specifically with three tasks: "1) to promote mutual understanding, respect and collaboration between Catholics and the followers of others religious traditions; 2) to encourage the study of religions; 3) to promote the formation of persons dedicated to dialogue."[109] The Commission for Religious Relations with Jews, a separate organization, is responsible for Catholic-Jewish relations. Since 2001, the PCID has attempted particularly to improve relations between Catholics and Muslims. A colloquium (the sixth in a series) held in April 2008 by the PCID and the Centre for Interreligious Dialogue of the Islamic Culture and Relations Organization resulted in a joint statement that read in part, "Christians and Muslims should go beyond tolerance, accepting differences, while remaining aware of commonalities and thanking God for them. They are called to mutual respect, thereby condemning derision of religious beliefs."[110]

In a war against a country in which the vast majority of the population was Muslim, their perceptions of Islam and its believers could not fail to affect the views of U.S. Christians. Evangelicals who regarded Islam as evil or wrong were much more likely to support the Bush administration's policies than were Mainline Protestants or Catholics who held a more benign view of that religion. Beyond this, as numerous studies have shown, human beings are more likely to favor war against peoples whom they regard as being unlike themselves—members of so-called outgroups or "the other"—than against peoples whom they consider to be fundamentally similar. The perceived "cultural distance" between Evangelical Protestants and Muslims in the first decade of the twenty-first century was much greater than the perceived distance between Mainline Protestants, Roman Catholics, and Muslims. It was in part for this reason that the latter Christian groups, particularly at the leadership and institutional levels, were much more reluctant to countenance the use of military force in the Persian Gulf.

Summary

As this chapter has demonstrated, Roman Catholics, Evangelical Protestants, and Mainline Protestants hold divergent views regarding the use of military force and associated foreign policy issues. In general, Mainline Protestants and Roman Catholics are much less supportive of the use of force—and of the building and deployment of various types of weapons systems—than Evangelical Protestants. These differences stem mainly from differences in views regarding the nature of God, the relationship between God and the United States, the amount of deference that should be given to governmental authority and civil institutions, the nature of Satan and the origin of evil, and—at least in the case of the Iraq War—the "validity" of Islam and, relatedly, the importance of converting Muslims to Christianity. These factors are summarized in Table 3.1.

How important have the views of U.S. Christians been in determining the course of U.S. policy? With the possible exception of U.S. policy in Central America during the 1980s and early 1990s, discussed in Chapter 2, it is probably fair to say that in no instance has pressure from religious groups been a major factor causing the U.S.

Table 3.1: Views of U.S. Christians Regarding the Use of Force

	Mainline Protestants	Evangelical Protestants	Roman Catholics
Use of Military Force	Laity often divided; generally unsupportive at the denominational level	Often supportive at both the institutional and rank-and-file levels	Laity often divided; generally unsupportive at the official level
View of God	Tends toward Distant or Benevolent; more likely to see God in gender-neutral terms	Tends toward Authoritarian; generally see God as masculine	Tends toward Distant or Benevolent; generally see God as masculine
Relationship between God and the United States	The United States not specially favored	The United States specially favored, endowed with God-given mission	The United States not specially favored
Deference to Governmental Authority	Lower level of deference	Higher level of deference	Lower level of deference
View of Satan	Mixed, but Satan widely regarded as metaphor for evil; evil of human origin	Satan generally regarded as actual supernatural being, source of evil	Satan generally regarded as metaphor for evil; evil of human origin
View of Other Religions (Islam)	Tend to see other religions as having elements of truth; considerable emphasis on interfaith cooperation	Tend to see other religions as false; not interested in interfaith dialogue	Tend to see other religions as false (and other versions of Christianity as lacking); nevertheless, emphasize ecumenical and interfaith cooperation and dialogue
Importance of Evangelizing and Converting Non-Christians	Relatively low	Very high	Higher than Mainline Protestants, but lower than Evangelical Protestants

government to refrain from taking military action against its preferences. It is also probably fair to say that in no instance has pressure from religious groups pushed the U.S. government into war against its will. At the same time, support from significant portions of the U.S. Christian community has made it easier for the government to threaten or to employ force in certain situations. Clearly, this was the case during the early years of the Cold War. More recently, it would have been much more difficult— perhaps politically impossible—for the administration of George W. Bush to take the United States into war with Iraq in 2003 without the support of Evangelical Protestants who constituted a large part of the Republican Party's political base. Finally, it can be argued, though not proved, that the evangelical views of George W. Bush and certain of his advisers inclined his administration toward war with Iraq to a degree that would not have been characteristic of a president who subscribed to views more typical of Mainline Protestants or Roman Catholics.

Notes

1. Stephen Bates, "'Godless Communism' and its Legacies," *Society* (March/April 2004): 30, www.springerlink.com/content/641a3blyhj5qma5l/.
2. George Sirgiovanni, *An Undercurrent of Suspicion: Anti-communism in America During the Cold War* (New Brunswick, NJ: Transaction Publishers, 1990), 27.
3. Bates, "'Godless Communism' and Its Legacies," 31; Sirgiovanni, *Undercurrent of Suspicion*, 26–27.
4. Dianne Kirby, "Harry Truman's Religious Legacy: The Holy Alliance, Containment and the Cold War," in *Religion and the Cold War*, ed. Kirby (New York: Palgrave/Macmillan, 2003), 77.
5. Bates, "'Godless Communism' and Its Legacies," 30.
6. Kirby, "Introduction," in *Religion and the Cold War*, ed. Kirby (New York: Palgrave/Macmillan, 2003), 2.
7. William Inboden III, *Religion and American Foreign Policy, 1945–1960: The Soul of Containment* (Cambridge: Cambridge University Press, 2008), 2.
8. H. W. Brands, "The Idea of the National Interest," in *The Ambiguous Legacy: U.S. Foreign Relations in the "American Century."* ed. Michael J. Hogan (New York: Cambridge University Press, 1999), 133–34.
9. Inboden, *Religion and American Foreign Policy*, 21.
10. Pew Forum, "Religion and Politics: Contention and Consensus." Evangelical Protestants were considerably more reluctant to vote for an atheist than either Mainline Protestants or Roman Catholics.
11. Bates, "'Godless Communism' and Its Legacies," 30.
12. Bates, "'Godless Communism' and Its Legacies," 32.
13. Quoted in Inboden, *Religion and American Foreign Policy*, 54.
14. Inboden, *Religion and American Foreign Policy*, 55.
15. Leo P. Ribuffo, "Religion in the History of U.S. Foreign Policy," in *The Influence of Faith: Religious Groups and U.S. Foreign Policy*, ed. Elliott Abrams (Lanham, MD: Ethics and Public Policy Center; Rowman & Littlefield, 2001), 16.
16. Ribuffo, "Religion in the History of U.S. Foreign Policy," 16.

17. A good, brief account is Scotty McLennan, "What Would Jesus Do? The Three Christian Positions on War," *Stanford Daily*, October 2, 2001; reprinted in PrayerinAmerica.org, "Prayer in America," www.prayerinamerica.org/wp-content/downloads/get-involved/themes/Armed-Conflict.pdf. McLennan was Dean for Religious Life at Stanford University.

18. Mt. 5.38–40.

19. Lk. 6.27–29.

20. Mt. 26.50–53.

21. Paul Christopher, *The Ethics of War and Peace: An Introduction to Moral and Legal Issues* (Englewood Cliffs, NJ: Prentice-Hall, 1994), 21–24.

22. Christopher, *Ethics of War and Peace*, 25–29, on Ambrose, and on Augustine, 30–48.

23. Just war thinking is not unique to Christianity. Early Christian theorists borrowed from Roman ideas of just war, especially as reflected in the writings of Cicero. Moreover, other cultures and religious traditions, both ancient and modern, have had and/or currently have notions of just war that are, in some cases, not terribly different from Christian notions. See Terry Nardin (ed.), *The Ethics of War and Peace: Religious and Secular Perspectives* (Princeton, NJ: Princeton University Press, 1996).

24. Michael Walzer, *Just and Unjust Wars: A Moral Argument with Historical Illustrations*, 4th ed. (New York: Basic Books, 2006), 54. On the difficulties in finding a solid foundation for notions of human rights, see Jack Donnelly, *Universal Human Rights in Theory and Practice*, 2nd ed. (Ithaca, NY: Cornell University Press, 2003), 18–21. Donnelly concludes that the provenance of human rights cannot be proved and that their existence in contemporary international society simply reflects a set of shared assumptions.

25. See, for example, Robert E. Williams, Jr., and Dan Caldwell, "*Jus Post Bellum*: Just War Theory and the Principles of Just Peace," *International Studies Perspectives*, 7, no. 4 (November 2006): 309–20, www3.interscience.wiley.com/cgi-bin/fulltext/118607018/HTMLSTART.

26. James Turner Johnson, "Just Cause Revisited," in *Close Calls: Intervention, Terrorism, Missile Defense, and "Just War Today,"* ed. Elliott Abrams (Washington, DC: Ethics and Public Policy Center, 1998), 3–4.

27. McLennan, "What Would Jesus Do?"

28. McLennan, "What Would Jesus Do?"

29. Quaker United Nations Office, "Quaker Service Agencies Statement on the Launching of War on Iraq," March 20, 2003, www.quno.org/newyork/Resources/LTR20030320QSA_Iraq.pdf.

30. Church of the Brethren, "Statement of the Church of the Brethren on War," www.cobannualconference.org/ac_statements/70War.htm.

31. Mennonite Church, *Confession of Faith in a Mennonite Perspective*, Article 22, www.mennolink.org/doc/cof/art.22.html.

32. UCC General Synod, "Pronouncement on Affirming the United Church of Christ as a Just Peace Church," www.ucc.org/justice/peacemaking/pdfs/Just-Peace-Church-Pronouncement.pdf.

33. Episcopal Church, "The Cross Before the Flag," www.episcopalchurch.org/50917_51103_ENG_HTM.htm?menupage=51102.

34. NCCB, *The Challenge of Peace*, iii.

35. The committee's report is at www.crcna.org/site_uploads/uploads/resources/synodical/2006_warandpeace.pdf.

36. Evangelical Lutheran Church in America [hereinafter ELCA], *For Peace in God's World*, August 20, 1995, www.elca.org/What-We-Believe/Social-Issues/Social-Statements/Peace.aspx.

37. United Methodist Church [hereinafter UMC], "Consequences of Conflict," *Book of Resolutions—2000*, http://archives.umc.org/interior.asp?ptid=1&mid=1410. "Consequences of Conflict" does not appear in the most recent versions of the UMC's *Book of Resolutions*.

38. Lester Kurtz and Kelly Goran Fulton, "Love Your Enemies? Protestants and United States Foreign Policy," in *The Quiet Hand of God: Faith-Based Activism and the Public Role of Mainline Protestantism*, ed. Robert Wuthnow and John H. Evans (Berkeley, CA: University of California Press, 2002), 366–69.

39. See Chapter 1.

40. A superb analysis of the evolution of Catholic, and especially U.S. Catholic thinking on war and peace is in George Weigel, Tranquillitas Ordinis: *The Present Failure and Future Promise of American Catholic Thought on War and Peace* (Oxford: Oxford University Press, 1987).

41. NCCB, *Harvest of Justice is Sown in Peace*, www.usccb.org/sdwp/harvest/shtml#theology.

42. NCCB, *The Challenge of God's Peace*, iii.

43. These documents can be accessed via the USCCB's website, www.nccbuscc.org/sdwp/international/warandpeaceind.shtml. They include, "Statement on New Nuclear Treaty and U.S. Nuclear Weapons Policy," May 24, 2002, www.nccbuscc.org/sdwp/international/may02fin.shtml; "Stop Funding for New Nuclear Weapons Research," September 30, 2005, www.nccbuscc.org/sdwp/international/actionalertrnep.shtml; "Sowing Weapons of War: A Pastoral Reflection on the Arms Trade and Landmines," June 16, 1995, www.usccb.org/sdwp/international/weaponsofwar.shtml.

44. NCCB, *Harvest of Justice is Sown in Peace*.

45. The text of the "Urgent Call" can be found at www.kycouncilofchurches.org/AnUrgentCall.html.

46. See RCA, "Church Leaders Sign 'Urgent Call to End the Nuclear Danger,'" www.rca.org/Page.aspx?pid=1539&srcid=1534. See also Disciples of Christ, "An Urgent Call to End the Nuclear Danger," www.disciples.org/Portals/0/PDF/ga/pastassemblies/2003/resolutions/0316.pdf. Among evangelical denominations, the Mennonite Church also urged its members to sign the petition circulating nationwide. See www.peace.mennolink.org/resources/actionnuke.pdf.

47. ELCA, *For Peace in God's World*.

48. UMC, "Support for the Land Mine Treaty," *Book of Resolutions–2004*, http://archives.umc.org/interior.asp?ptid=4&mid=1039.

49. Episcopal Church, "General Convention Resolutions, 1979–1988," www.episcopalchurch.org/5252_57271_ENG_HTM.htm, and "General Convention Resolutions, 1991–2003," www.episcopalchurch.org/5252_57290_ENG_HTM.htm.

50. Richard Land, "The So-Called 'Land Letter,'" October 3, 2002, SBC, Ethics and Religious Liberty Commission, http://erlc.com/article/the-so-called-land-letter.

51. Pew Forum, "Religious Landscape Survey," Report 2, 108.

52. Guth, "Militant and Cooperative Internationalism among American Religious Publics," 23, 8.

53. Reagan, speech delivered March 8, 1983, in Orlando, Florida, *RonaldReagan.com*, www.ronaldreagan.com/sp_6.html.

54. Quoted in Laurie Goodstein, "Seeing Islam as 'Evil' Faith, Evangelicals Seek Converts," *New York Times*, May 27, 2003, www.nytimes.com/2003/05/27/national/27ISLA.html?e x=1215144000&en=1fc28e95510c4a7b&ei=5070.

55. Carl W. Roberts argues that God is usually imagined or described along two dimensions: nurturance and discipline. See "Imagining God: Who is Created in Whose Image?" *Review of Religious Research*, 30, no. 4 (June 1989): 375–86, www.jstor.org/ stable/3511298.

56. PCUSA, "The Trinity: God's Love Overflowing," www.pcusa.org/theologyandworship/ issues/trinityfinal.pdf. See also K. Connie Kang, "Presbyterians and the Trinity: Let Us Phrase," *Los Angeles Times*, June 30, 2006, http://articles.latimes.com/2006/jun/30/ local/me-trinity30.

57. Leon J. Podles, "God Has No Daughters: Masculine Imagery in the Liturgy," *Catholic Culture*; previously published in *Homiletic & Pastoral Review* (November 1995): 20–27, www.catholicculture.org/library/view.cfm?recnum=613.

58. The text can be found at http://cba.cua.edu/crit.cfm.

59. "Blessed Be *the Name* of the Lord," *Christianity Today*, May 2008, www.christianitytoday.com/ct/2008/may/17.21.html.

60. LCMS, "Biblical Revelation and Inclusive Language: A Report of the Commission on Theology and Church Relations of the Lutheran Church—Missouri Synod," February 1998, www.lcms.org/graphics/assets/media/CTCR/biblrev.pdf.

61. SBC, "Resolution No. 4. On Today's New International Version." Resolution passed at the 2002 Annual SBC Meeting, June 11–12, 2002, www.sbcannualmeeting.net/sbc02/ resolutions/sbcresolution.asp?ID=4.

62. Albert Mohler, "There's Not Much Lord in this Church Service," www.albertmohler. com/blog_read.php?id=930.

63. "Blessed Be *the Name* of the Lord."

64. An early and excellent discussion is Nancy C. M. Hartsock, "Prologue to a Feminist Critique of War and Politics," in *Women's Views of the Political World of Men*, ed. Judith Stiehm (Dobbs Ferry, NY: Transnational Publishers, 1984), 123–50.

65. Baylor ISR, "American Piety in the 21st Century," 30.

66. Luis Lugo, Allen Hertzke, Richard Cizik, and Joel H. Rosenthal, "Evangelical Reflections on the U.S. Role in the World," Carnegie Council on Ethics and International Affairs, September 15, 2005, www.cceia.org/resources/transcripts/5230.html. John B. Judis has argued that the idea that the United States has been chosen by God to perform a special mission in the world is not unique to contemporary Evangelical Protestants, but has been a consistent theme throughout America's history. See Judis, "The Chosen Nation: The Influence of Religion on U.S. Foreign Policy," Policy Brief 37, Carnegie Endowment for International Peace, March 2005, www.carnegieendowment.org/files/PB37.judis. FINAL.pdf.

67. Pew Forum, "Americans Struggle with Religion's Role at Home and Abroad," 7.

68. Charles Babington, "Bush: U.S. Must 'Rid the World of Evil,'" *Washington Post*, September 14, 2001, www.washingtonpost.com/ac2/wp-dyn?pagename=article&node= &contentId=A30485-2001Sep14&notFound=true.

69. See note 13, above.

70. Quoted in Max Blumenthal, "Onward Christian Soldiers," *Salon.com*, April 15, 2003, http://dir.salon.com/story/news/feature/2003/04/15/in_touch/.

71. NPR, "Profile: Silent Evangelical Support Of Bush's Proposed War Against Iraq," *Morning Edition*, February 26, 2003, www.npr.org/programs/morning/transcripts/2003/feb/030226.hagerty.html.

72. LCMS, *MercyNotes*, 1, no. 1 (Winter 2003): 2, available for download at www.lcms.org/pages/internal.asp?NavID=14473.

73. Quoted in NPR, "Profile: Silent Evangelical Support Of Bush's Proposed War Against Iraq."

74. Quoted in NPR, "Profile: Silent Evangelical Support Of Bush's Proposed War Against Iraq."

75. Steven Waldman, "Why Evangelicals are Abandoning Bush," *Huffington Post*, November 2, 2006, www.huffingtonpost.com/steven-waldman/why-evangelicals-are-aban_b_33137.html.

76. Baylor ISR, "Religious Piety in the 21st Century," 37.

77. Assemblies of God [hereinafter AOG], General Council, "Spiritual Warfare (Attacks of Satan)," www.ag.org/top/Beliefs/sptlissues_spiritual_warfare.cfm.

78. SBC, "Resolution on the Necessity of Salvation," June 1988, www.sbc.net/resolutions/amResolution.asp?ID=446.

79. See Tim Ellsworth, "Baptists Adrift in Doctrinal Confusion," *SBC Life*, October/November 2001, www.sbclife.org/articles/2001/10/sla6.asp. Since the survey did not distinguish between Southern Baptists and other Baptists, including members of mainline denominations, the percentage of Southern Baptists who believe in the reality of Satan is undoubtedly higher than 34 percent.

80. See ELCA, "Satan," www.elca.org/questions/Results.asp?recid=25.

81. Ellsworth, "Baptists Adrift in Doctrinal Confusion."

82. Baylor ISR, "American Piety in the 21st Century," 37.

83. Ted G. Jelen, "Religion and Foreign Policy Attitudes: Exploring the Effects of Denomination and Doctrine," *American Politics Quarterly*, 22, no. 3 (July 1994): 382–400.

84. "Evangelical Views of Islam."

85. See Deborah Caldwell, "Despite Controversy, Iraq Beckons as Evangelical Mission Field," April 24, 2003, http://pewforum.org/news/display.php?NewsID=2186; Caldwell, "Poised and Ready," *Beliefnet*, April 2003, www.beliefnet.com/story/123/story_12365.html; Caldwell, "Why Iraq Beckons," *Beliefnet*, April 2003, www.beliefnet.com/story/124/story_12448.html; and Charles Duhigg, "Evangelicals Flock into Iraq on a Mission of Faith," *Los Angeles Times*, March 18, 2004, www.pipeline.com/~rougeforum/evangelicalsinvade.html.

86. Quoted in Duhigg, "Evangelicals Flock into Iraq," and Caldwell, "Why Iraq Beckons."

87. CNN Live Saturday, "Interview with Albert Mohler, Charles Kimball," *CNN.com*, May 10, 2003, http://edition.cnn.com/TRANSCRIPTS/0305/10/cst.11.html.

88. Quoted in Jeff Robinson, "No Country Off Limits for Missions, Mohler Says on Fox Radio Show," *Baptist Press*, April 14, 2004, www.bpnews.net/BPnews.asp?ID=18054.

89. Quoted in Robinson, "No Country Off Limits."

90. CNN Live Saturday, "Interview with Albert Mohler, Charles Kimball."

91. Quoted in Duhigg, "Evangelicals Flock into Iraq."

92. Quoted in Duhigg, "Evangelicals Flock into Iraq."

93. Quoted in Duhigg, "Evangelicals Flock into Iraq."

94. Goodstein, "Seeing Islam as 'Evil' Faith, Evangelicals Seek Converts."

95. Caldwell, "Why Iraq Beckons."
96. Quoted in Mark Kelly, "God Challenging Southern Baptists to Reach Muslims," SBC, International Mission Board, June 20, 2003, www.imb.org/main/news/details.asp?Language ID=1709&StoryID=942.
97. Christian Reformed World Missions, "The Scattered Ones," *Proclaim* (Summer 2004), www.crwm.org/wmre/wmre_proclaim_aug04_mali.htm. Many individual evangelicals do not hold this position. One survey found that 48 percent of "highly committed white evangelicals" believe that "many religions can lead to eternal life." Pew Forum, "Americans Struggle with Religion's Role at Home and Abroad."
98. "Evangelical Views of Islam."
99. Alan Cooperman, "Bush's Remark about God Assailed," *Washington Post*, November 22, 2003, A06, ProQuest National Newspapers Premier (Document ID: 463795401).
100. Quoted in Cooperman, "Bush's Remark about God Assailed."
101. Quoted in Cooperman, "Bush's Remark about God Assailed."
102. Goodstein, "Seeing Islam as 'Evil' Faith, Evangelicals Seek Converts."
103. Robert Buckley Farlee (ed.), *Honoring Our Neighbor's Faith* (Minneapolis, MN: Augsburg Fortress, 1999).
104. UMC, General Commission on Christian Unity and Interreligous Concerns, "Interreligious Relations," www.gccuic-umc.org/index.php?option=com_content&task=blogcategory&id=58&Itemid=222.
105. UMC, "Called to Be Neighbors and Witnesses: Guidelines for Interreligious Relationships," *Book of Resolutions–2008*, www.umc.org/site/apps/nlnet/content2.aspx?c=lwL4KnN1LtH&b=4951419&content_id={30D8D8C3-9E32-4465-B17F-6C1C7939532D}&notoc=1.
106. UMC, "Our Muslim Neighbors," www.gbgm-umc.org/interrelig/315%20Our%20Muslim%20Neighbors%202004.htm.
107. Goodstein, "Seeing Islam as 'Evil' Faith, Evangelicals Seek Converts."
108. "Pope: Other Christian Denominations Not True Churches," *FoxNews.com*, July10, 2007, www.foxnews.com/story/0,2933,288841,00.html.
109. The Vatican's website contains a full description of the PCID. See "The Pontifical Council for Interreligious Dialogue," www.vatican.va/roman_curia/pontifical_councils/interelg/documents/rc_pc_interelg_pro_20051996_en.html.
110. "Joint Declaration of the Pontifical Council for Inter-religious Dialogue (Vatican) and the Centre for Inter-religious Dialogue of the Islamic Culture and Relations Organization (Tehran, Iran)," Rome, April 28–30, 2008, www.vatican.va/roman_curia/pontifical_councils/interelg/documents/rc_pc_interelg_doc_20080430_rome-declaration_en.html.

CHAPTER 4

International Human Rights

That human beings enjoy, by virtue of being human, certain fundamental rights is an idea that dates back at least to the Western Enlightenment period. Thomas Jefferson famously wrote, in the *Declaration of Independence* (1776), that "all men are endowed by their Creator with certain unalienable rights" and that "among these are life, liberty, and the pursuit of happiness." The *Declaration of the Rights of Man*, approved by the French Assembly in 1789, asserted the rights to "liberty, property, security, and resistance to oppression."

Nevertheless, the concept of "human rights" is fundamentally a post-World War II phenomenon. The Holocaust and other atrocities committed by the governments and militaries of the Axis Powers during the 1930s and 1940s led the organizers of the Nuremburg War Crimes Tribunal to develop the idea of "crimes against humanity." Due in part to the heroic efforts of Eleanor Roosevelt, the United Nations General Assembly adopted the Universal Declaration of Human Rights in 1948. The rights enshrined in the Universal Declaration were, during the 1960s, codified in the International Covenant on Civil and Political Rights, and the International Covenant on Economic, Social, and Cultural Rights. Since that time, the international law of human rights has expanded dramatically, as has the network of international governmental and nongovernmental organizations intended to protect them.

At the rank-and-file level, Roman Catholics, Evangelical Protestants, and Mainline Protestants are deeply, and equally, committed to human rights. The 2004 study, "The American Religious Landscape and Political Attitudes," found that members of the three groups regarded human rights as the "best" foreign policy goal after national security in almost exactly the same proportions (46 percent, 47 percent, and 46 percent, respectively).[1] As subsequent sections of this chapter demonstrate, the situation is much the same at the institutional and leadership levels.

There is very little difference among major Christian denominations and organizations concerning the basis of their commitment to human rights. Christians, like Muslims and Jews, ground such rights in the notion of "human dignity," which itself derives from the belief that human beings are created in the image of God and are God's children. And, although in the past, Evangelical Protestants, Mainline Protestants, and Roman Catholics often differed considerably on the question of which rights should be given priority and on the desirability of various policy alternatives, recent years have seen an increasing convergence of views, due in large part to the growing engagement of Evangelical Protestants in issues outside their traditional areas of concern.

Evangelical Protestants

Until several decades ago, Evangelical Protestants, especially fundamentalists, evinced a relatively low level of concern for human rights. During the 1920s, the rise of theological liberalism in American Protestantism exacerbated an already existing split between "modernists" and "conservatives." Fundamentalists became what Allen Hertzke has described as "private" Protestants, concerned with defending their own moral and spiritual rectitude and, therefore, retreating from the public sphere in order to avoid the encroachment of sinful societal norms.[2]

By the late 1970s, however, fundamentalists, and evangelicals more generally, were becoming increasingly involved in the social and political realm. Much of this was the consequence of the increasing membership in—and hence the greater potential influence of—evangelical churches and other organizations. The late 1960s and early 1970s witnessed the Civil Rights movement, the Vietnam War, the growth of feminism, increasing drug use, and the Sexual Revolution. Many U.S. Christians, feeling adrift in the turmoil of the time, sought certainty and security in more conservative denominations that emphasized a return to the fundamentals of the faith and traditional moral values.[3] The increasing involvement of the Christian Right in the public sphere was also a result of the rise of new leaders, such as Jerry Falwell, founder of the Moral Majority, who were not concerned solely with their own personal piety, but with the values and practices of U.S. society as a whole.

The interest of Evangelical Protestants in human rights initially centered on two issues that remain among their core concerns: religious freedom and the right to life of unborn children. A 2000 survey of several hundred evangelical leaders found that 75 percent believed that efforts to end religious persecution should be a priority for evangelicals in terms of civic engagement.[4] As Hertzke notes,

> Since Christianity is the largest and most widely dispersed religious faith on the globe, with the cutting edge of its growth occurring outside of the West, numerous indigenous Christians live in hostile places without the protection of democratic rights. It has been estimated that some 200 million Christians live in countries where they face serious persecution, while another 400 million face nontrivial restrictions on their religious freedom. Probably thousands are killed annually, victims of despotic regimes or communal violence, an astonishing figure vastly underplayed by the Western press.[5]

Spurred on by stories of the destruction of Bibles in China, the arrest and imprisonment of Christians in certain countries and the murder of Christian clergy in others, evangelicals during the 1990s mobilized in support of religious freedom.[6] In 1996, the National Association of Evangelicals issued a "Statement of Conscience

Concerning Worldwide Religious Persecution." It called on the U.S. government to undertake a variety of measures, including "public acknowledgement of today's widespread and mounting anti-Christian persecution," "issuance by the State Department's Human Rights Bureau and related government agencies of more carefully researched, more fully documented, and less politically edited reports of the facts and circumstances of anti-Christian and other religious persecution," and "cessation of the indifferent and occasionally hostile manner in which the Immigration and Naturalization Service often treats the petitions of escapees from anti-Christian persecution."[7] Evangelical leaders lobbied members of Congress to pass legislation that would demonstrate the commitment of the United States to religious freedom. Major evangelical organizations including the NAE, the Southern Baptist Convention, the National Coalition of Religious Broadcasters, the Christian Coalition, the Family Research Council, and Concerned Women for America offered their support.[8]

Aided by the Roman Catholic Church—whose assistance was critical to countering charges that religious freedom was an issue only to the religious right—and by other religious groups, including Jews and Tibetan Buddhists, evangelical pressure succeeded in convincing Congress to pass the 1998 International Religious Freedom Act (IRFA), which was subsequently signed into law by then-president Bill Clinton.[9] The Act provided for the establishment of an Office of International Religious Freedom within the U.S. Department of State. It requires the State Department to report annually to Congress on the state of religious freedom in every foreign country, to identify especially egregious violators as "countries of particular concern," and to explain what measures the administration is undertaking to enhance religious freedom abroad. Understandably, evangelicals were (and are) concerned primarily with preventing the persecution of fellow Christians. During the campaign for the IRFA, they were careful to couch their calls for religious freedom in broad terms. The NAE's 1996 Statement of Conscience expressed "deep concern for the religious freedom of . . . people of every faith." Still, each of the thirteen "incidents" of religious persecution listed in the document referred to the persecution of Christians and/or their churches.[10]

Over the past several decades, evangelicals have also sought to influence U.S. foreign policy in the area of family planning and reproductive rights. They have supported the so-called Mexico City Policy initiated by President Ronald Reagan in 1984 and continued by every Republican administration thereafter. This policy denies family planning monies from the United States Agency for International Development (USAID) to any foreign nongovernmental organization (NGO) that funds abortions or provides advice, counseling, or information regarding them. Evangelicals have also favored the Kemp-Kasten Amendment to the 1985 Supplemental Appropriations Act, which prohibits the disbursement of USAID funds to any organization that the president of the United States determines is involved in coercive abortion or involuntary sterilization. Except during the presidencies of Bill Clinton and Barack Obama, the Kemp-Kasten Amendment has been consistently invoked to deny U.S. contributions to the United Nations Population Fund.[11] In 1998, with the support of evangelicals, conservatives in the U.S. House of Representatives "nearly blocked $18 million in funding for the [International Monetary Fund]" because they believed the IMF provided monies to "countries and organizations that regard abortion as an acceptable part of family planning or population control."[12]

Recently, evangelical institutions and leaders, as well as evangelicals more generally, have broadened the scope of their human rights efforts to include such issues as slavery and human trafficking, genocide, and torture. In 1999, a group of evangelical leaders, including Chuck Colson, Richard Cizik, and Richard Land, met with others in Washington to discuss strategy for promoting legislation to address the problem of sex-slavery. They agreed to back a bill that had previously been introduced by Republican Representative Chris Smith, rather than a competing bill being pushed by liberal Democratic Senator Paul Wellstone, fearing that Wellstone's bill lacked enforcement provisions and addressed other issues, including sweat-shop wages and labor conditions.[13] After the meeting, as Hertzke notes, "the top leadership of the evangelical world swiftly mobilized their networks in support of the legislation."[14] In June 2000, the Southern Baptist Convention passed a resolution, "On Condemning the Trafficking of Women and Children for Sexual Purposes." The resolution asked "Congress to pass legislation increasing criminal penalties for the perpetrators, providing assistance for the victims, and urging worldwide action to eliminate this particularly vile form of human trafficking."[15] Likewise, the National Association of Evangelicals adopted a resolution expressing its support for "appropriate federal legislation that would seek to end sex trafficking by punishing those responsible." Said the NAE, "Penalties should be considered that punish violators in a just manner and to serve as a deterrent. Such legislation may also include incentives to countries to take appropriate actions (e.g., criminalizing and punishing offenders)."[16] The Salvation Army, which also took up the cause, later assumed leadership of the Initiative Against Sexual Trafficking (IAST), "a partnership of faith-based, human rights, child and women's rights advocacy organisations."[17]

In addressing the issue of human trafficking, as in the case of religious persecution, evangelicals worked closely with other groups. Equality Now, a feminist organization headed by Gloria Steinem, came on board, as did a number of Jewish leaders. Eventually, Paul Wellstone was convinced to support the Smith bill and served as Senate cosponsor along with conservative Republican Samuel Brownback of Kansas. In October 2000, the Trafficking Victims Protection Act (TVPA) cleared Congress and was signed by President Clinton. Over the next several years, supporters of the TVPA became increasingly frustrated by what they perceived as lack of adequate enforcement by the Bush administration. According to Hertzke, in the summer of 2002 "there was serious talk among evangelicals about how to embarrass their president to get action." Under pressure, the director of the State Department's Trafficking in Persons (TIP) Office, Nancy Ely-Raphael, was replaced by former Congressman John Miller, who proved to be a much more vigorous enforcer of the law.[18]

Since 2002, evangelical leaders have expanded their campaign against sex-slavery to encompass other forms of servitude. Focus on the Family and the National Association of Evangelicals, which have been at odds on such issues as climate change (see Chapter 7), both support "The Amazing Change" campaign, which seeks to end "bonded labor, human trafficking, and military recruitment of children."[19] Initiated by Bristol Bay Productions, the makers of the film, *Amazing Grace: The William Wilberforce Story*, a tale of the nineteenth century British abolitionist, the campaign had, by early 2008, garnered 127,000 signatures. Together with Stop the Traffick, a worldwide coalition of more than 1,000 organizations, Amazing Change presented petitions containing 1.5 million signatures to the conference of the United Nations Global Initiative to Fight Trafficking (UNGIFT) in February of that year.[20]

Evangelical Protestants pushed the Bush administration to act to end the humanitarian crisis in Darfur. Shortly before George W. Bush was elected president, Franklin Graham told him, "Governor, if you become president, I hope you put Sudan on your radar."[21] Not long after Bush took office, Charles Colson delivered the same message. According to one observer, this "quiet diplomacy, tinged with religious fervor, helped elevate Sudan to a top foreign policy priority for the Bush administration."[22] Sam Brownback, speaking to a meeting of the Christian Coalition, congratulated evangelicals on their efforts, noting that previously, "This wasn't on anybody's foreign policy agenda."[23] Initially, many evangelicals, regarding the issue as one of religious freedom, favored addressing the situation in Darfur by having the United States government provide arms to Christian groups in Southern Sudan in order to assist them in their efforts to break away from the Islamic government in Khartoum. This position, which placed them at odds with the United States Conference of Catholic Bishops and the National Council of Churches, each of which was promoting talks with all the parties to the conflict, was eventually altered, in part because of the Bush administration's reluctance to involve itself militarily.[24] With strong evangelical support, Bush appointed John Danforth, a former Missouri senator, as special envoy to the region. Negotiations conducted by Danforth and diplomats from other nations culminated in the Comprehensive Peace Agreement (CPA) of January 2005. Although the CPA subsequently unraveled, without evangelical support it might never have been concluded.

In 2007, the National Association of Evangelicals endorsed "An Evangelical Declaration Against Torture," a document prepared by the newly formed organization, Evangelicals for Human Rights (EHR). Authors of the declaration, responding to instances of extraordinary rendition and maltreatment of prisoners at places such as Abu Ghraib and Guantanamo Bay, placed themselves in at least implicit opposition to the Bush administration, writing that we "affirm our support for detainee human rights and opposition to any resort to torture." Noting that "documented cases of torture and inhumane and cruel behavior have occurred at various sites in the war on terror" and that "current law opens procedural loopholes for more to continue," the statement urged that a ban on torture "extend to every sector of the United States government without exception, including our intelligence agencies."[25]

Evangelicals and evangelical organizations have recently demonstrated interest in issues that have long been of far greater concern to secular liberals and Mainline Protestants as well as freestyle evangelicals. In spring 2005, Rick Warren, pastor of the Saddleback Church in Lake Forest, California, and author of the best-selling book, *The Purpose-Driven Life*, sent an open letter to President Bush asking that the U.S. government step up its efforts to combat global poverty. The letter urged the president to "help the poorest people of the world fight poverty, AIDS and hunger at a cost equal to just ONE percent of the U.S. budget," to "cancel 100% of the debts owed by the poorest countries," and to "reform trade rules so poor countries can earn sustainable incomes." Appealing to fellow evangelicals to support the campaign, Warren wrote that combating global poverty "is a moral issue, a compassion issue, and because Jesus commanded us to help the poor, it is an obedience issue. . . . I deeply believe that if we as evangelicals remain silent and do not speak up in defense of the poor, we lose our credibility and our right to witness about God's love for the world."[26]

The National Association of Evangelicals, in its 2004 document, *For the Health of the Nation: An Evangelical Call to Civic Responsibility*, had previously signaled a broadening of its concerns beyond the traditional human rights focus on religious freedom and abortion, as well as the preservation of traditional moral values, noting that "the Bible makes it clear that God cares a great deal about" many matters, including "justice for the poor." Wrote the NAE, "While individual persons and organizations are at times called by God to concentrate on one or two issues, faithful evangelical civic engagement must champion a biblically balanced agenda."[27] Evidencing this new approach, in June 2005, NAE leaders joined other religious leaders in urging countries participating in a Group of Eight economic summit to "dramatically increase aid and trade benefits to impoverished nations."[28] In a 2008 essay, "Evangelicals a Liberal Can Love," *New York Times* columnist Nicholas Kristof noted that "a recent CBS News poll found that the single issue that white evangelicals most believed they should be involved in was fighting poverty. The traditional issue of abortion was a distant second."[29] Indeed, Jim Wallis, head of the freestyle evangelical organization Sojourners, predicts in his book, *The Great Awakening*, that issues of social justice will be increasingly important to evangelicals in coming years.

Mainline Protestants

Mainline Protestant organizations have adopted positions similar to those of Evangelical Protestants on many, if not most, human rights issues. They have opposed torture and pushed the Bush administration to end abuses by the American military and intelligence services. The Presbyterian Church (USA), in 2004, adopted a resolution that affirmed the support of the denomination for "human rights and the Geneva Convention relative to the Treatment of Prisoners of War" and rejected "torture and abuse as methods of interrogation and treatment of prisoners." In 2006, the church called for "a formal congressional inquiry into how torture came to be used in U.S. military and other prisons," and endorsed "remedies for the use of torture and illegal detention by agencies of the U.S. government, such as the appointment of a special counsel, open hearings, appropriate investigation, and legislation outlawing the use of 'extraterritorial rendition' and extraterritorial prison facilities."[30] Commenting in 2005 on anti-torture legislation making its way through the U.S. Congress, legislation that was opposed by Bush administration officials, the National Council of Churches (NCC) declared that "we find any and all use of torture unacceptable and contrary to U.S. and international legal norms" and that "we find it particularly abhorrent that our nation's lawmakers would fail to approve the pending legislation disavowing the use of torture by an entity on behalf of the United States government." The NCC asked the Senate to follow the House of Representatives in passing the legislation and urged the president and other members of his administration to support it.[31]

Mainline Protestant churches were active on the matter of genocide in Southern Sudan. The NCC and other members of the Save Darfur Coalition called on members of the United Nations Security Council to sponsor a resolution that would "mandate peace enforcement operations in Darfur."[32] Mainline denominations also condemned human trafficking and advocated policies to address it. The United Methodist Church issued a resolution, "The Abolition of Sex Trafficking," which pledged the church to employ "education, financial resources, publication, lobbying, and the use of every relevant gift of God" to end "the modern-day enslavement of humans for commercial sexual exploitation."[33] The Presbyterian Church (USA) adopted a resolution calling for "safe housing, medical and psychological help for trafficked persons," "efforts to provide appropriate documentation" (which would allow them to remain in the United States), and/or assistance for "trafficked persons, especially women, in safely returning to their country of origin." The PCUSA directed its Washington and United Nations Offices to "partner with ecumenical and interfaith entities to build coalitions against trafficking and participate in activities such as the National Day of Human Trafficking Awareness and the Global Initiative to Fight Human Trafficking (UN)."[34]

Mainline Protestants have, like their evangelical counterparts, been concerned with issues of religious persecution. The United Methodist Church's "Resolution on Religious Liberty," adopted in 1988 and then readopted in 2000, "declares religious liberty, the freedom of belief, to be a basic human right that has its roots in the Bible" and states that the UMC "places a high priority on the struggle to maintain freedom of religious belief and practice in the world."[35] The National Council of Churches, in November 1997, issued a statement expressing appreciation of "the new energy from both evangelical Christian groups and Congress which calls attention to the pain of this issue and the need to seek fresh solutions."[36] In a June 1998 statement, the NCC referred to religious persecution as a "scourge that has afflicted humankind for most of its history" and noted that the National Association of Evangelicals "deserve[s] credit for placing the issue of religious persecution at the top of the nation's moral agenda."[37] The Episcopal Church, under the leadership of Tom Hart, head of the denomination's Washington Office, was an integral part of the evangelical-led coalition working toward passage of the International Religious Freedom Act. According to one observer, "None of the groups were more active or strategic in pushing for IRFA than the Episcopal Church."[38]

It may seem surprising then, that with the exception of the Episcopal Church, no major Mainline Protestant organizations supported the IRFA. Why was this the case? The reasons had mainly to do with disagreements regarding the methods by which religious liberty should be promoted. While the IRFA authorized the U.S. government to act on its own initiative, the NCC argued that "violations of human rights abroad are best addressed by multilateral efforts." The NCC was also concerned that the imposition of economic sanctions, as called for in the legislation, "should be a matter of thoughtful last resort, not automatic first resort." The NCC was particularly worried that the IRFA, with its focus on the persecution of Christians, and the potential sanctioning of governments responsible, would damage both interfaith relations and the relations of the United States with predominantly non-Christian countries:

> Care should be exercised so that traditions and cultures of other nations are respected. Although we cherish and affirm the principles of the First Amendment as the best mechanism for protecting religious liberty, we recognize that they are rooted in western philosophical, political and religious thought. We should not seek to impose the American arrangement on others. This includes respecting the traditions of established religions and churches common to European as well as Islamic nations. America's response to religious persecution must not be perceived as "anti-Islamic."[39]

An NCC analysis of the IRFA concluded that, if enacted, it would probably harm relations with Muslim states and that the legislation was unnecessary in view of the "increased investigation of and reporting on religious persecution as well as the new training of government personnel" to confront the problem.[40]

Perhaps the major difference between Mainline and Evangelical Protestants on matters of human rights revolves around the question of U.S. foreign aid and family planning. Mainline Protestant organizations have vigorously opposed the Mexico City Policy, the Kemp-Kasten Amendment, and other efforts to link aid to the issue of abortion. Part of the reason, discussed below, is that Mainline Protestants do not view abortion as an unmitigated evil. Part of it is that they regard family planning programs as being essential to human rights. The Religious Coalition for Reproductive Choice (RCRC), to which most mainline denominations belong, considers reproductive freedom—the decision whether or not to have children, and if so, when—to be a basic right.[41] Moreover, mainline denominations argue, cutting funds to organizations that provide family planning services is destructive of other rights, including freedom from poverty and the right to life. Family planning, contends the

Evangelical Lutheran Church in America, helps to control population growth and thereby ease pressures on scarce resources.[42] Its absence, mainline churches claim, not only results in higher mortality among women of childbearing age, but, by increasing the number of unwanted pregnancies, increases the number of abortions. James Winkler, general secretary of the United Methodist Church's General Board of Church and Society, wrote to President Bush in early 2002 to protest the president's return to the Mexico City Policy:

> In the developing world, one woman dies every minute of every day in childbirth or from pregnancy complications. . . . Access to reproductive planning and education are the two most important determinants of whether these women and their children will live or die. . . . You have imposed on the poorest women of the world a halt to information that women in the United States are guaranteed. The poorest women and men around the globe will no longer have access to basic means "to limit their fertility" as The Social Principles [of the UMC] affirm, or to safely plan pregnancies to enhance the potential that both mothers and their babies will thrive. The U. S. Agency for International Development has found that in every nation where information about contraception and access to methods of birth control are available, abortion rates decline. Far from pro-life, your action ensures that more poor women and their children will perish.[43]

At approximately the same time, the Presbyterian Church (USA), in 2002, reaffirmed its opposition to "legislative efforts that reduce foreign aid for comprehensive family planning programs." It urged President Bush "to reverse his order to ban U.S. assistance to international family planning programs agencies that use non-U.S. funds for abortion information or services, because reductions in the availability of family planning services impede the urgently needed stabilization of the human population, while leading to an actual increase in the number of abortions, including those that endanger a woman's life."[44]

Although there has been a discernable shift in the evangelical focus on human rights issues over the past decade or more, it is probably fair to say that Mainline Protestants still attach greater importance to a broader range of human rights, including political, social, economic, and cultural rights, than do their evangelical counterparts. The United Methodist Church's *Book of Discipline* states, "We hold governments responsible for the protection of the rights of the people to free and fair elections and to the freedoms of speech, religion, assembly, communications media, and petition for redress of grievances without fear of reprisal; to the right to privacy; and to the guarantee of the rights to adequate food, clothing, shelter, education, and health care."[45] The Division of Global Mission of the Evangelical Lutheran Church in America expresses its adherence to the

> International Bill of Human Rights (consisting of the Universal Declaration of Human Rights, the International Covenant on Civil and Political Rights, and the

International Covenant on Economic, Social and Cultural Rights), and the Beijing Declaration and Platform for Action, adopted at the 1995 UN Fourth World Conference on Women, which articulate specific aspects of the definition of, call to, and struggle for human rights for all women, men, and children.[46]

The Episcopal Church has adopted resolutions on a variety of human rights issues ranging from racism and discrimination to health and human needs.[47]

Mainline Protestant organizations are particularly interested in issues of "economic and social justice." The Evangelical Lutheran Church in America, for example, in its statement, *Sufficient, Sustainable Livelihood for All*, argues that "Human impoverishment, excessive accumulation and consumerism driven by greed, gross economic disparities, and the degradation of nature are incompatible" with Christian teaching. The ELCA notes that "in many countries, the problem is not the lack of resources, but how they are shared, distributed, and made accessible within society. Justice seeks fairness in how goods, services, income, and wealth are allocated among people so that they can acquire what they need to live." It contends that people should have enough, but not too much.[48] The United Methodist Church, in "Economic Justice for a New Millennium," expresses dismay at the fact that "Worldwide, poverty and hunger have increased, especially among women and children. Human rights have become untenable. Homelessness remains rampant in major cities, while many rural communities are in rapid decline as family farms go bankrupt in record numbers. In developing countries, shanty-towns surround major cities as people leave rural areas in search of jobs."[49]

Evangelical Protestants, as noted above, are not uninterested in addressing poverty, hunger, and related issues. Evangelicals and the institutions that represent them contribute huge sums of money to humanitarian causes. In 2005, evangelical organizations accounted for nearly half of all private voluntary organizations (PVOs) engaged in international relief and development efforts, as well as 40 percent of the total revenues of such organizations. Figures for Mainline Protestant and Roman Catholic PVOs were much lower.[50] Samaritan's Purse, an organization headed by Franklin Graham, son of famed evangelist Billy Graham and one of today's leading evangelicals, provides in excess of $150 million per year in food and medical care to some of the world's poorest regions.[51] Unlike Mainline Protestants, however, evangelicals tend not to see poverty, malnutrition, and disease as a denial of "rights," and they call more for "charity" than for "justice." The difference is subtle, but potentially important. Charity imposes less of a moral obligation than justice (or denial of rights) on those persons and institutions in a position to confront humanitarian problems. Moreover, charity tends to be a private obligation rather than a public one; hence, evangelicals generally do not regard the government of the United States (or other governments) as being responsible for addressing international social and economic concerns to the same degree that Mainline Protestants do.

Mainline Protestants, more than evangelicals, tend to regard economic and social injustice as a function of structural factors inherent in the nature of the contemporary international system and especially in capitalism as a mode of economic organization. In this respect, their position resembles the criticism often leveled by radical or neo-Marxist analysts of world affairs. The United Church of Christ has criticized the International Monetary Fund (IMF), the World Bank, and the World Trade Organization (WTO) for implementing globalization in such a way that it has "failed to live up to its potential to improve the lives of billions of people." In general, writes the UCC, "Neo-liberal policies tend to advance and protect the interests of multinational corporations and elites around the world more than the interests of individuals, workers, local communities, or the environment."[52] The Evangelical Lutheran Church in America argues that any assessment of economic practices must acknowledge "the moral imperative to seek sufficient, sustainable livelihood for all." Noting that "Market-based thought and practices dominate our world today," the ELCA contends that these are often in conflict with Christian principles:

> While a market economy emphasizes what individuals want and are willing and able to buy, as people of faith we realize that what human beings *want* is not necessarily what they *need* for the sake of life. While a market economy assumes people will act to maximize their own interests, we acknowledge that what is in our interest must be placed in the context of what is good for the neighbor.[53]

The ELCA thus supports "just arrangements to regulate the international economy."[54] The United Methodist Church condemns "structures of injustice" in the world economy, contending that injustices

> are imposed upon the people of the world by economies characterized by a concentration of wealth and power, an export-based development, heavy indebtedness, and reliance on a militarized national security system. The belief that competition results in greater economic growth underlies much of the emerging global economic order. In the production and consumption of goods, corporations are to compete with corporations, individuals with one another, and societies with other societies. The central value is "more." Greed and the corporate culture of materialism, of "more is better," have permeated our world. It is a culture that has little use for those who lack the means to consume.[55]

Like the UCC, the UMC takes to task the IMF and the World Bank for imposing structural adjustment programs on developing countries that "have placed the burden of debt repayment squarely on the shoulders of poor and working people by devaluing currencies, freezing wages, curbing government price subsidies (on rice, cooking oil, beans, and other essential items), and cutting subsidized credits in rural areas."[56]

Mainline denominations advocate a variety of measures to achieve greater economic and social justice. These include the expansion of foreign aid. While evangelicals tend to emphasize humanitarian assistance, mainline organizations place equal or greater stress on aid for purposes of economic development. The ELCA, for example, notes that

> While the United States has been generous in providing humanitarian aid, our nation dramatically trails the rest of the industrialized world in providing development assistance relative to our production of wealth. We support continued and increased assistance by the United States, and call for its gradual realignment toward more development assistance and a proportional reduction in subsidies to purchase weapons.[57]

Most mainline churches favor some form of debt relief for the developing world. The ELCA advocates "reduction of overwhelming international debt burdens in ways that do not impose further deprivations on the poor, and cancellation of some or all debt where severe indebtedness immobilizes a country's economy."[58] The United Church of Christ calls for the debt of the world's poorest countries to be forgiven "completely and unequivocally."[59] Tom Hart, director of governmental relations for the Episcopal Church, has declared that "we should remedy the HIPCs' [Heavily Indebted Poor Countries] debt crisis like any bankruptcy. We should write off their debts, then help them avoid getting back into debt by providing grants. It's the only sensible long-term solution."[60]

Roman Catholics

Roman Catholic positions on human rights strongly resemble Evangelical and Mainline Protestant positions. On issues where Protestants have tended to ally with one another, the Catholic Church has expressed similar views. On issues concerning abortion and its linkage to foreign aid and family planning, Catholics have aligned themselves with evangelicals. On matters of social and economic justice, the Roman Catholic Church has adopted stances more consistent with those of Mainline Protestants.

Until the late 1800s, the Catholic Church was largely hostile to human rights. Indeed, as one author has written, "the idea of human rights was regarded with deep suspicion by the nineteenth century papacy."[61] But during the twentieth century, the position of the Church underwent a radical change. According to Zachary Calo, "One of the most significant of the twentieth-century revolutions was the transformation of the Roman Catholic church from entrenched defender of the anciène

[sic] regime into one of the world's leading advocates of social and political justice, democratic governance, and human rights."[62]

This transformation began in 1891, when Pope Leo XIII's encyclical, *Rerum Novarum*, articulated "the concept of the dignity of the human person made in the image and likeness of God."[63] The most dramatic development, however, occurred at the Second Vatican Council (Vatican II). In 1965, assembled bishops representing a church that had conducted the Spanish Inquisition, fought the Protestant Reformation, and executed heretics overwhelmingly approved a Declaration on Religious Freedom (*Dignitatis Humanae*), which was subsequently promulgated by Pope Paul VI. According to George Weigel, the acceptance of a right to religious freedom was "the crucial breakthrough to the Catholic human rights revolution."[64] Calo observes, "In the years following Vatican II, the Catholic church emerged as a leading voice in the human rights movement."[65] It remains so today.

As the preceding paragraph indicates, the Roman Catholic Church shares with both Mainline and Evangelical Protestants a deep concern for religious liberty. The U.S. Catholic bishops, through the National Conference of Catholic Bishops (NCCB), the United States Catholic Conference (USCC), and, beginning in 2001, the United States Conference of Catholic Bishops (USCCB), have, since the 1970s, been working to end religious persecution. In 1997, Drew Christiansen, Director of the USCC's Office of International Justice and Peace, appeared before Congress to express the bishops' support for the Wolf-Specter bill, which eventually became the International Freedom of Religion Act. The USCC and NCCB were strong supporters of the IRFA, and several bishops have served on the U.S. Commission on International Religious Freedom established by that legislation.[66] The bishops continue, on a regular basis, to offer testimony regarding the U.S. Department of State's Annual Report on Religious Freedom and Annual Human Rights Report, to send letters to members of Congress, and to issue "background" reports detailing the Church's position and its activities on behalf of religious freedom.[67]

The U.S. Catholic Church also shares with Mainline and Evangelical Protestant organizations opposition to torture, a commitment to preventing genocide and other humanitarian crises, and a desire to end human trafficking. Like the NCC, the USCCB is a member of the Save Darfur Coalition, "an alliance of more than 150 faith-based, humanitarian and human rights organizations" that has sponsored rallies and engaged in a variety of other activities to bring attention to the humanitarian crisis in Southern Sudan.[68] In September 2005, the chairman of the USCCB's Committee on International Policy, joined others in calling for a "National Day of Action for the People of Darfur," stating that "We cannot stand idly by while human life is threatened. The United States and the international community can and must do more to end this moral and humanitarian crisis."[69] The USCCB advocated vigorously for the Darfur Peace and Accountability Act of 2006, which denied visas to and froze the assets of those determined by the president to be "responsible for acts of genocide, war crimes, or crimes against humanity" in Sudan, urged the president to seek expanded NATO support for the African Union peacekeeping forces in the region, and sought to deny the Sudanese government oil revenues by prohibiting ships carrying Sudanese oil from docking and unloading at U.S. ports.[70]

On the issue of torture and the treatment of detainees by the U.S. government, the Catholic bishops aligned themselves with mainline denominations and the National Association of Evangelicals. In 2005, the chairman of the USCCB's Committee on International Policy, Bishop John H. Ricard, urged Congress to include, in the fiscal year (FY) 2006 Defense Appropriations Act, "provisions prohibiting cruel, inhuman and degrading treatment of persons under custody or control of the United States government," and to "provide uniform standards for the interrogation of persons under detention of the Department of Defense."[71] The following year, Ricard's successor, Bishop Thomas G. Wenski, wrote to Secretary of Defense Donald Rumsfeld to express concern that the Defense Department was preparing to issue a directive regarding the treatment of detainees that would not incorporate the standards of Common Article 3 of the Geneva Conventions, which prohibits "cruel treatment and torture" of prisoners of war. Wenski argued that, in addition to undermining U.S. efforts to defeat terrorism, mistreatment of prisoners "compromises human dignity. A respect for the dignity of every person, ally or enemy, must serve as the foundation of the pursuit of security, peace, and justice. There can be no compromise on the moral imperative to protect the basic human rights of any individual incarcerated for any reason."[72]

The Catholic bishops pushed hard for the FY 2008 Intelligence Authorization Act, which would have extended the prohibition on cruel, inhuman, and degrading treatment of persons in U.S. custody beyond the U.S. military to U.S. intelligence agencies, particularly the CIA. In a January 2008 letter to senators, Bishop Wenski repeated much of the language he had employed in his letter to Rumsfeld.[73] In February 2008, the USCCB issued an action alert, "Urge Your Senators to Expand the Ban on Torture," asking Catholics to contact certain senators and ask them to support the anti-torture provisions of the bill.[74] The bill, including the anti-torture provisions, passed the Senate later that month, at which time the USCCB, reacting to a threatened veto by President Bush, issued a second action alert, encouraging Catholics to call the White House or e-mail the president in an effort to change his mind.[75] Together with other religious leaders, including Michael Kinnamon, the general secretary of the National Council of Churches, and David Saperstein, director of the Religious Action Center of Reform Judaism, Bishop Wenski circulated an op-ed piece, "End the Torture Nightmare," which stated that "torture is an intrinsic evil" and that "'enhanced' interrogation practices—waterboarding, hypothermia, long-time standing, sleep deprivation and the use of psychotropic drugs—contradict our democratic values as well as essential principles of morality and faith."[76] On March 5, 2008, Cardinal Francis George, archbishop of Chicago and president of the USCCB, sent a letter to President Bush, urging him to sign the Intelligence Authorization Act, including the anti-torture provisions. Three days later, Bush vetoed the bill, arguing that it would undermine the efforts of the U.S. Government to combat terrorism and otherwise protect American citizens.[77] A subsequent effort by Congress to override the veto failed.

The Roman Catholic Church, primarily through the Migration and Refugees Services (MRS) division of the USCCB, has been a staunch supporter of efforts to end human trafficking. Bishop Gerald Barnes, chairman of the USCCB Committee on Migration, forcefully articulated the Church's position:

> Human trafficking is a horrific crime against the basic dignity and rights of the human person and all efforts must be expended to end it. In the end, we must work together—church, state, and community—to eliminate the root causes and markets that permit traffickers to flourish; to make whole the survivors of this crime; and to ensure that one day soon trafficking in human persons vanishes from the face of the earth.[78]

The Catholic bishops advocated vigorously for the Trafficking Victims Protection Act. In May 2000, Bishop Nicholas DiMarzio, head of the NCCB's Committee on Migration, issued a statement welcoming "congressional efforts to address, in a comprehensive manner, the heinous and growing practice of trade in human persons."[79] When Congress passed the TVPA and President Clinton signed it into law, the bishops hailed the event as a "huge legislative victory."[80] The USCCB strongly supported 2005 legislation reauthorizing the TVPA, although it found that the bill, as signed into law by President Bush, did not adequately protect the rights of children.[81]

With regard to U.S. funding of international family planning programs, the USCCB has taken positions similar if not identical to most Evangelical Protestant organizations. In 1989 testimony before the Foreign Operations Subcommittee of the House Committee on Appropriations, Bishop James T. McHugh argued in favor of the Reagan administration's Mexico City Policy. It was, he said, "in the area of foreign assistance, the most significant policy initiative on abortion taken by the United States in the last five years."[82] When, in 2001, President Bush reinstated the policy, which had been abandoned by the Clinton administration, Gail Quinn, executive director of the NCCB's Secretariat for Pro-Life Activities, sent a letter to members of Congress urging them to oppose legislation that would overturn it.[83] Cathleen Cleaver, director of Planning and Information in the Secretariat for Pro-Life Activities, testified before the Senate Foreign Relations Committee on the importance of the Mexico City Policy and commended President Bush for rein-stating it.[84] Bills in both the House and Senate aimed at reversing Bush's decision failed to come to a vote.

In 2007, similar legislation made its way through Congress. On June 18, Cardinal Justin Rigali, archbishop of Philadelphia and chairman of the USCCB's Committee for Pro-Life Activities, sent a letter to members of the House of Representatives asking them to remove language from the State Department Foreign Operations Authorization Bill that would have negated the Mexico City Policy.[85] On September 6, the Cardinal sent a follow-up letter to members of the Senate.[86] The House complied with the USCCB's request, but the Senate did not, voting on September 7 to overturn the policy. The House and Senate bills then went to joint committee, where, faced with the promise from President Bush to veto any legislation that would weaken official U.S. policies on abortion, the offending language was removed from the legislation.

The U.S. Catholic bishops have also fought to deny federal assistance, under the terms of the 1985 Kemp-Kasten Amendment, to any international organization that, as determined by the president, "supports or participates in the management of programs of coercive abortion or involuntary sterilization." In 2002, President Bush cut off all U.S. funding for the United Nations Population Fund (UNPF), citing the UNPF's participation in forced sterilizations in China. Bishop Wilton Gregory, president of the USCCB, wrote to the president thanking him for withholding the monies, which totaled $34 million.[87] The following May, House member Joseph Crowley (D-NJ) moved in committee to amend the State Department Authorization Bill to earmark $50 million for the UNPF, effectively reversing Kemp-Kasten. Crowley's language also sought to make the application of Kemp-Kasten more difficult by allowing funds to be cut off only if the UNPF "knowingly and intentionally" sought to promote coercive abortion or forced sterilization or played a "primary and essential role" in the "coercive or involuntary aspect" of the population program it was managing. When the committee approved the amendment by a narrow margin, the USCCB sought to have it removed on the House floor. In a letter to members of both Houses of Congress, Cardinal Anthony Bevilacqua, archbishop of Philadelphia and chairman of the USCCB's Committee for Pro-Life Activities, asked Congress to "stand in the defense of the freedom and dignity of women and their unborn children" and to "strike the Crowley Amendment."[88] The amendment was struck. A similar pattern occurred in 2007, when a Senate committee approved language deleting Kemp-Kasten from the 2008 State Department Foreign Operations Appropriations Bill. Cardinal Rigali sent a letter to members of the Senate requesting that they restore Kemp-Kasten.[89] On September 6, the Senate approved an amendment offered by Sam Brownback that did so.

Although Roman Catholic leaders in the United States have aligned themselves with Evangelical Protestant organizations on funding for international family planning programs, their views on social and economic justice are closer to those of Mainline Protestant institutions. In 1967, Pope Paul VI issued an encyclical, *Populorum Progressio* (On the Development of Peoples), in which he lamented the widening differences between the world's rich and poor and condemned "oppressive social structures, whether due to the abuses of ownership or to the abuses of power, to the exploitation of workers or to unjust transactions."[90] The 1970s saw the rise, particularly in Latin America, of "liberation theology," which emphasized Jesus' affinity for the poor and oppressed, and which argued that the Catholic

Church should become an active agent of social and political change. Although the Vatican rejected much of this theology, particularly its adoption of certain Marxist ideas, the basic notion that Christians had an obligation to seek justice and resist oppression continued to gain acceptance. In its 1986 pastoral letter, *Economic Justice for All*, the National Conference of Catholic Bishops wrote that "every economic decision and institution must be judged in light of whether it protects or undermines the dignity of the human person." The bishops distinguished among commutative justice, which "calls for fundamental fairness in all agreements and exchanges between individuals or private social groups," distributive justice, which "requires that the allocation of income, wealth, and power in society be evaluated in light of its effects on persons whose basic material needs are unmet," and social justice, which "implies that persons have an obligation to be active and productive participants in the life of society and that society has a duty to enable them to participate in this way." And, the bishops stated, "Economic conditions that leave large numbers of able people unemployed, underemployed, or employed in dehumanizing conditions fail to meet the converging demands of these three forms of basic justice."[91]

In the pursuit of justice, the NCCB called for "a fundamental reform in the international economic order." The bishops asked that the U.S. government significantly increase development assistance, noted that "developing nations have a right to receive a fair price for their raw materials," and urged the United States to "seek effective special measures under the General Agreement on Tariffs and Trade (GATT), to benefit the poorest countries." Offering a critique of international economic institutions echoing that of Mainline Protestant denominations, they wrote, in reference to the International Monetary Fund's structural adjustment programs, that it was a "scandal" that "it is the poorest people who suffer most from the austerity measures required when a country seeks the IMF 'seal of approval.'"[92]

Since 1986, the U.S. Catholic bishops have continued to advocate for fundamental changes in the way the international economy operates. In 1991, during negotiations on the North American Free Trade Agreement (NAFTA), they wrote U.S. Trade Representative Carla Hills to ask that NAFTA be designed in such a way as to achieve just wages and working conditions, to address unemployment and underemployment, and to respect the right of workers to organize. These "questions of economic and social justice," the bishops stated, should "receive priority attention" and should not be considered "side issues or peripheral matters."[93] In 1989, the USCC issued "Relieving Third World Debt: A Call for Co-Responsibility, Justice, and Solidarity," and a decade later, a "Jubilee Call for Debt Forgiveness." While the bishops did not call for universal, complete forgiveness of developing countries' external debt, they did note that "our faith and our Church call us to stand with the poor in their just call and urgent hope for debt relief."[94] In the past two decades, the Catholic bishops have, through letters, action alerts, and other measures, continued to press the U.S. government to enact legislation and support international initiatives that would provide the world's poorest countries with relief from foreign indebtedness.[95]

Explaining the Differences

As the preceding sections reveal, Evangelical Protestants, Mainline Protestants, and Roman Catholics share a strong commitment to human rights. Each group is concerned with a broad range of rights. And the positions of the three groups are becoming increasingly similar as Evangelical Protestants temper their formerly near-exclusive emphasis on religious freedom and the right to life. This convergence, and the growing ecumenical cooperation that it is likely to engender, may portend increasing influence for Christian organizations and institutions as they seek to influence U.S. human rights policy in the future.

Still, for the present, there remain important differences in three areas. First, Evangelical Protestants and Roman Catholics are more concerned with religious freedom than are Mainline Protestants. Second, Mainline Protestants, unlike Roman Catholics and Evangelical Protestants, do not favor the restrictions placed on U.S. funding of international family planning organizations that are associated with abortion. Third, Roman Catholics and Mainline Protestants tend to see poverty, hunger, and related problems as a denial of basic human rights caused, at least in part, by flaws in the international economic system. Evangelical Protestants, for the most part, do not. What accounts for these differences?

With respect to the question of international family planning, the position of each group is largely an extension of its position on abortion (right to life). The Roman Catholic Church has long been known for its opposition to family planning. Although it is widely ignored by individual believers, the official position of the Church is still to forbid all forms of contraception except for the so-called rhythm method, which requires abstaining from sex when the woman is most fertile. According to Catholic doctrine, human life begins at conception. Abortion is thus regarded as being particularly vile. Indeed, according to the USCCB, "Abortion does not plan a family. It kills a member of the family."[96] The USCCB explicitly rejects the argument, offered by Mainline Protestant denominations, that the availability of contraceptives and other methods of family planning serves to reduce abortions.[97]

Evangelicals likewise tend to believe that human life begins at the moment of conception. Citing God's words in the book of Jeremiah—"Before I formed you in the womb I knew you, before you were born I set you apart"—and other biblical passages, the Lutheran Church—Missouri Synod holds that "the living but unborn are persons in the sight of God from the time of conception."[98] If human life begins at conception, terminating a pregnancy kills a child. Abortion is murder. Given the large number of abortions performed worldwide every year, it is not difficult to understand the urgency felt by those seeking to end the practice.

Mainline Protestants are less likely to believe that human life begins at conception, or at least to be more uncertain about the point at which an embryo or fetus becomes a child. The Episcopal Church, the Presbyterian Church (USA), the United Methodist Church, and the United Church of Christ are all members of the Religious Coalition for Reproductive Choice (RCRC).[99] The RCRC notes that the common understanding, in biblical times, was that human life began at birth. Thus, "Jewish and biblical tradition defined a human being with the word 'nephesh'—the breathing one."[100] Advances in medicine have, of course, subsequently made human fetuses viable long before they would ordinarily be born. But, the RCRC argues, "Modern science has reminded us that the brain is the essence of our existence and no human person can exist without a brain, which does not begin to take shape until the formation of the neocortex, or no earlier than the second half of gestation."[101] If one accepts viability outside the womb as the point at which a fetus can be said to have become a child, then abortions as late as the midpoint of the second trimester of pregnancy do not take a human life.

Compared to evangelical denominations and the Roman Catholic Church, mainline churches place more emphasis on the rights of the pregnant woman and less on those of the child she carries. The United Methodist Church states, "Our belief in the sanctity of unborn human life makes us reluctant to approve abortion. But we are equally bound to respect the sacredness of the life and well-being of the mother and the unborn child."[102] The UMC has, however, become increasingly pro-life, voting only narrowly in 2008 to retain its membership in the RCRC, and it would be wrong to suggest that mainline denominations favor abortion or take it lightly. The Evangelical Lutheran Church in America advises that abortion is a morally responsible choice only under very limited circumstances: pregnancies that threaten the life of the mother, those that result from rape or incest, and those that involve "extreme fetal abnormality."[103] Like the UMC, The Episcopal Church holds that any abortion has a "tragic dimension," while the Presbyterian Church (USA) has expressed its dismay at abortions that are "chosen as a convenience or to ease embarrassment," agreeing with the UMC that "abortion should not be used as a method of birth control."[104] Mainline denominations tend to regard whether or not to terminate a pregnancy as a matter of personal conscience, and their preferred strategy for reducing the number of abortions is not to outlaw the practice, but to focus on education, contraception, and other efforts to reduce the number of unwanted pregnancies, and on changing values and circumstances that make abortion seem desirable or even necessary. For this reason, they consider defunding, because of their association with abortion, UN programs and NGOs that provide a broad range of family planning services to be counterproductive.

The emphasis of Evangelical Protestants, and of Roman Catholics, on religious freedom has origins that are more theological in nature. As noted in the preceding chapter, Evangelical Protestants tend to believe that Christianity is the one true faith, the only path to salvation. The Roman Catholic Church continues to maintain that its particular version of Christianity is the only correct one, that other Christian "faith communities" are deficient in certain respects. Given these views, it is not surprising that evangelicals and Catholics are strongly guided by the "Great Commission," Jesus' commandment at the end of the book of Matthew to go and "make disciples of all the nations, baptizing them into the name of the Father and of the Son and of the Holy Spirit." Christians who hold that Christianity is the one true religion believe that only those who have accepted Jesus as their Lord and Savior will go to heaven; everyone else will be consigned to hell. For such persons, religious freedom is of paramount importance. Without it, missionaries find it more difficult to win converts, and Christian believers find it more difficult to practice and hold on to their faith. Although opponents of evangelism often regard proselytizing as offensive and reflecting a lack of respect for nonbelievers, those who engage in it often—perhaps usually—do so out of a genuine and profound concern for those they seek to convert.

In the book of John, Jesus refuses to chastise Mary for purchasing an expensive bottle of perfume with which to anoint him instead of giving the money to the poor, telling the disciples that the poor would always be with them.[105] Critics of evangelicals sometimes suggest that this passage causes evangelicals to be skeptical about the possibility of improving people's lives in the here-and-now. But there is little evidence for this, and much against it. Evangelicals, as noted previously, are *not* unconcerned with bettering the material conditions in which people live. They *are* more likely than Mainline Protestants or Roman Catholics to regard humanitarian and related human rights efforts as a component of missionary work, as a means to gain converts. An essay by Byron Klaus, president of the Assemblies of God Theological Seminary in Springfield, Missouri, is quite clear on this: "The empowerment of the baptism in the Holy Spirit is truly the sole source of hope and the possibility of meaningful life to so many in the non-Western world. . . . Any program of social concern must point people to the central message of redemption through the blood of Jesus Christ."[106]

Mainline Protestants and, among the laity, Roman Catholics, are, as has been noted, more likely than Evangelical Protestants to regard other religions as being at least partly valid and to believe that there are multiple paths to salvation. For this reason, they tend to feel less urgency in fulfilling the "Great Commission." Instead, they place equal or greater emphasis on the "Second Great Commandment," Jesus' admonition, in the book of Matthew, to love one's neighbor as oneself. Mainline Protestant denominations in particular frequently articulate a "Social Gospel" orientation, which deemphasizes personal piety and the salvation of souls and stresses instead the importance of addressing people's material and other needs. The Social Gospel movement dates back to the late nineteenth and early twentieth century, at which time theologians, church leaders, and clergy began to emphasize the societal role that might be played by the Christian church. It was in many respects a reaction to the poverty, child labor, abysmal working conditions, and other ill effects produced by industrial capitalism, effects chronicled by many observers, including Karl Marx and Charles Dickens.[107] Social Gospel theology refers explicitly to the example set by Christ in his life on Earth: healing the sick, feeding the hungry, and assisting those at the margins of society, including tax collectors and prostitutes. And it takes its cues in part from the account, in the book of Matthew, of a story told by Jesus concerning God's judgment:

> Then the King will say to those on his right, "Come, you who are blessed by my Father; take your inheritance, the kingdom prepared for you since the creation of the world. For I was hungry and you gave me something to eat, I was thirsty and you gave me something to drink, I was a stranger and you invited me in, I needed clothes and you clothed me, I was sick and you looked after me, I was in prison and you came to visit me."
>
> Then the righteous will answer him, "Lord, when did we see you hungry and feed you, or thirsty and give you something to drink? When did we see you a stranger and invite you in, or needing clothes and clothe you? When did we see you sick or in prison and go to visit you?"
>
> The King will reply, "I tell you the truth, whatever you did for one of the least of these brothers of mine, you did for me."

For these reasons, then, Evangelical Protestants are interested more in conversion and addressing the spiritual needs of people, while Mainline Protestants are dedicated more to addressing their material needs. And, for these reasons, as Hertzke writes, Roman Catholics are somewhere in the middle.[108]

Summary

On one issue, there exists a stark divide among Roman Catholics, Evangelical Protestants, and Mainline Protestants concerning U.S. human rights policy. Evangelical Protestants and Roman Catholics tend to regard unborn children as human beings with an absolute right to life, and they therefore oppose U.S. government funding of international governmental and nongovernmental organizations that provide family planning services, including abortion information and counseling. Most Mainline Protestant denominations also consider unborn children to have a right to life, but they contend that this right is not absolute and must be weighed against the rights of the mother and sometimes against the prospects for the child to have a healthy, meaningful life. Many of them subscribe to the notion of "reproductive rights." They generally view family planning counseling as essential to upholding these rights and as essential to reducing the number of unwanted pregnancies and, thus, abortions. Hence, mainline churches typically support government funding of international organizations that provide these services, even if those services include abortion itself.

On most other dimensions of human rights policy, the differences among the groups are primarily differences of emphasis. Although Evangelical Protestants have tended to focus most heavily on religious freedom and the right to life of unborn children, during the 1990s and 2000s, they expanded dramatically the scope of their concerns to include, among other issues, slavery, human trafficking, genocide, and torture. Mainline Protestants have been actively engaged on these same issues, as have Roman Catholics. It is true that with the important exception of the Episcopal Church, Mainline Protestant denominations generally opposed the International Religious Freedom Act. But this was not because of a lack of commitment to religious freedom. Rather, it was due to fears that the legislation would prove counterproductive by damaging U.S. relations with Muslim countries. In this instance, the two Protestant camps disagreed on the proper strategy, but not on the ultimate goal.

All three groups of U.S. Christians are dedicated to meeting the material needs of human beings around the globe. Mainline Protestants and Roman Catholics tend to regard these needs as rights and view fulfilling them as a matter of social and economic "justice." They frequently identify economic liberalization, market capitalism, free trade, and globalization as the sources of existing injustices and call for fundamental reform of the international economic order. Evangelical Protestants, for reasons that are explored briefly in Chapter 7, are much more deeply committed to free enterprise and market capitalism. They do not generally see problems, for example, of poverty, malnutrition, and the inequitable distribution of wealth as products of "the system." They tend to regard the alleviation of human misery as a matter more of charity than of justice, and, more frequently than either Mainline Protestants or Roman Catholics, they view it as a means to conversion and the saving of souls rather than an end in itself. The differences (and similarities) among the three groups of U.S. Christians on human rights policy, and the reasons for them, are summarized in Table 4.1.

The realm of human rights is one in which the advocacy of religious organizations has clearly affected the foreign policy of the U.S. government. Much of the impetus for the International Religious Freedom Act came from U.S. Christian groups.[109] The same was true of the Trafficking Victims Protection Act and the anti-torture provisions of the 2008 Intelligence Authorization Act, which passed Congress but was vetoed by President Bush. Prodding by these groups encouraged the Bush administration to become more engaged in the crisis in Southern Sudan. It is in part the shared commitment to human rights and the similarity of many of the positions taken by Roman Catholic, Evangelical Protestant, and Mainline Protestant leaders and institutions that have made them effective advocates in this area. While differences on abortion-related matters (e.g., international family planning programs) will almost certainly persist, convergence on other issues appears likely to continue. If this proves to be the case, then the impact of Christians and their organizations on U.S. human rights policy may be even greater in the future than in the past.

Table 4.1: Views of U.S. Christians Regarding Human Rights Policy

	Mainline Protestants	Evangelical Protestants	Roman Catholics
Human Rights	Support broad range of human rights, political, social, and economic. Support family planning and reproductive rights. Somewhat concerned with religious freedom. See meeting the material needs of humans as inherently important. Tend to regard poverty, hunger, and other problems as denial of rights caused by the nature of the international economic system.	Have traditionally placed most emphasis on religious freedom and right to life of the unborn, but increasingly support a broad range of human rights. Often see meeting the material needs of humans as being less important than meeting their spiritual needs. Often regard material assistance as a means to conversion. More emphasis on charity than on justice.	Support broad range of human rights. Place considerable emphasis on religious freedom and right to life of the unborn. See meeting the materials needs of humans as being inherently important. Tend to regard poverty, hunger, and other problems as denial of rights caused by the nature of the international economic system.
When Does Human Life Begin?	At birth, or at point of viability outside the womb	At conception	Officially, at conception; views among the laity vary
View of Other Faiths	Often believe that other faiths have some validity	Tend to regard other faiths as false	Church regards other faiths as false; laity often believes that other faiths have some validity
Biblical Teaching Emphasized	The "Second Great Commandment," leading to "Social Gospel" orientation	The "Great Commission"—to make all people disciples of Jesus	Relatively equal emphasis on the "Second Great Commandment" and the "Great Commission"
View of Laissez-Faire Economics and the International Economic Order	Tend to believe that capitalism and free trade produce inherent injustices	Favor capitalism and free trade policies; tend to regard material want as a product of individual failure rather than of systemic failure	Tend to believe that capitalism and free trade produce inherent injustices

Notes

1. Green, "American Religious Landscape and Political Attitudes," 38.
2. Hertzke, *Representing God in Washington*, 29.
3. Hertzke, *Representing God in Washington*, 32.
4. John C. Green, "Evangelicals and Civic Engagement: A View from (near) the Top," www.eppc.org/programs/ecl/conferences/eventID.29,programID.31/conf_detail.asp.
5. Allen D. Hertzke, *Freeing God's Children* (New York: Rowman & Littlefield, 2004), 59.
6. Hertze, *Freeing God's Children*, 59–61.
7. NAE, "1996 Statement of Conscience Concerning Worldwide Religious Persecution," www.pcahistory.org/pca/3–476.pdf.
8. Hertzke, *Freeing God's Children*, 194–95.
9. A fascinating and detailed account of the movement of this legislation through Congress is found in Hertzke, *Freeing God's Children*. See chapter 6, "The Hand of Providence in Congress."
10. NAE, "1996 Statement of Conscience Concerning Worldwide Religious Persecution."
11. Caity Brown, "America's Flawed Policies toward International Family Planning: The Mexico City Policy and the De-funding of UNFPA" (unpublished manuscript, 2005).
12. William Martin, "The Christian Right and American Foreign Policy," *Foreign Policy*, no. 114 (Spring 1999): 74, www.jstor.org/stable/1149591.
13. Hertzke, *Freeing God's Children*, 324–25.
14. Hertzke, *Freeing God's Children*, 325.
15. SBC, "On Condemning The Trafficking Of Women And Children For Sexual Purposes," www.sbc.net/resolutions/amResolution.asp?ID=626.
16. NAE, "Trafficking in Women and Children," www.nae.net/government-affairs/policy-resolutions/337-trafficking-in-women-and-children-1999-.
17. Salvation Army, "The Army's History in Fighting Sexual Trafficking," www.salvation-army.org/ihq%5Cwww_sa.nsf/vw-sublinks/0E27816C599D728580256E550016A130?openDocument.
18. Hertzke, *Freeing God's Children*, 330–32.
19. Ed Stoddard, "Slavery Campaign Closes Gap among Evangelicals," *Boston Globe*, April 1, 2007, www.boston.com/news/nation/articles/2007/04/02/slavery_campaign_closes_gaps_among_evangelicals/.
20. See the Amazing Change website at http://theamazingchange.com/.
21. Quoted in Farah Stockman, "Christian Lobbying Finds Success: Evangelicals Help to Steer Bush Efforts," *Boston Globe*, October 14, 2004, www.boston.com/news/nation/articles/2004/10/14/christian_lobbying_finds_success/.
22. Stockman, "Christian Lobbying Finds Success."
23. Quoted in Stockman, "Christian Lobbying Finds Success."
24. Jane Perlez, "The World: Suddenly in Sudan, A Moment to Care," *New York Times*, June 17, 2001, 4, www.nytimes.com/2001/06/17/weekinreview/the-world-suddenly-in-sudan-a-moment-to care.html?scp=1&sq=Suddenly%20in%20Sudan&st=cse.
25. Evangelicals against Torture, "An Evangelical Declaration Against Torture: Protecting Human Rights in an Age of Terror," www.evangelicalsforhumanrights.org/storage/mhead/fullstatement.pdf.

26. "The ONE Campaign: An Advocacy Letter from Rick Warren," *Beliefnet*, www.beliefnet.com/Faiths/Christianity/2005/06/The-ONE-Campaign-An-Advocacy-Letter-From-Rick-Warren.aspx.
27. NAE, *For the Health of the Nation: An Evangelical Call for Civic Responsibility*. Available for download at www.nae.net/government-affairs.
28. Nina J. Easton, "With Antipoverty Call, Evangelicals Seek New Tone," *Boston Globe*, July 5, 2005, www.boston.com/news/nation/washington/articles/2005/07/05/with_antipoverty_call_evangelicals_seek_new_tone/.
29. Nicholas D. Kristof, "Evangelicals a Liberal Could Love," *New York Times*, February 3, 2008, www.nytimes.com/2008/02/03/opinion/03kristof.html?_r=1&th&emc=th&oref=slogin.
30. PCUSA, "The Presbyterian Church Speaks on Torture," www.pcusa.org/peacemaking/actnow/tortureinsert.pdf.
31. NCC, "NCC General Assembly Declares 'Any and All Use of Torture is Unacceptable,'" www.ncccusa.org/torture.html.
32. NCC, "NCC and NGO's in U.S., U.K. and France Urge UN Resolution on Darfur," www.ncccusa.org/news/072105Darfur.html.
33. UMC, "Abolition of Sex Trafficking," *Book of Resolutions–2004*, http://archives.umc.org/interior.asp?mid=11942.
34. PCUSA, "A Resolution to Expand the Church's Ministry with and Advocacy Against Human Trafficking," www.pc-biz.org/Explorer.aspx?id=1539&promoID=7.
35. "United Methodist Church Resolution on Religious Liberty," www.vwc.edu/academics/csrf/links/umc_resolution.ph.
36. NCC, "An NCC Statement: Elements Needed in Any Legislation Authorizing the United States Government to Address Religious Persecution Globally," www.ncccusa.org/assembly/elements.html.
37. NCC, "NCC Statement on Proposed Federal Legislation Addressing Religious Persecution," June 2, 1998, www.ncccusa.org/assembly/june2.html.
38. Hertzke, *Freeing God's Children*, 224–25.
39. NCC, "NCC Statement on Proposed Federal Legislation Addressing Religious Persecution."
40. NCC, "NCC Analysis of 'International Religious Freedom Act of 1998,'" www.ncccusa.org/assembly/irfa.html.
41. Religious Coalition for Reproductive Choice [hereinafter RCRC], "Words of Choice: Countering Anti-Choice Rhetoric," 2, www.rcrc.org/pdf/Words_of_Choice.pdf.
42. ELCA, *Sufficient, Sustainable Livelihood for All*, www.elca.org/socialstatements/economiclife.
43. UMC, General Board of Church and Society, Press Statement, January 31, 2002, quoted in "Church exec objects to Bush's order on family planning," www.wfn.org/2001/02/msg00026.html.
44. PCUSA, Washington Office, "Saving Women's Lives," www.pcusa.org/washington/issuenet/wf-020313.htm.
45. UMC, "Basic Freedoms and Human Rights," *Book of Discipline—2004*, http://archives.umc.org/interior.asp?mid=1824.
46. ELCA, "Guiding Principles and Commitments: Human Rights," www2.elca.org/globalmission/policy/hr.html.

47. Documents and reports on activities of the Episcopal Church's Peace and Justice Ministries can be found at www.episcopalchurch.org/peace_justice.htm.

48. ELCA, *Sufficient, Sustainable Livelihood for All.*

49. UMC, "Economic Justice for a New Millennium," *Book of Resolutions–2004,* http://www.umc-gbcs.org/site/apps/nlnet/content3.aspx?c=frLJK2PKLqF&b=2954221&ct=4838943&notoc=1.

50. Rachel M. McCleary, *Global Compassion: Private Voluntary Organizations and U.S. Foreign Policy since 1939* (Oxford: Oxford University Press, 2009), 16, 22.

51. Nicholas D. Kristof, "Giving God a Break," *New York Times,* June 10, 2003, www.nytimes.com/2003/06/10/opinion/10KRIS.html?

52. UCC, "A Faithful Response: Calling for a More Just, Humane Direction for Economic Globalization," available for download at www.ucc.org/synod/resolutions/past-general-synod.html.

53. ELCA, *Sufficient, Sustainable Livelihood for All.*

54. ELCA, *Sufficient, Sustainable Livelihood for All.*

55. UMC, "Economic Justice for a New Millennium."

56. UMC, "Economic Justice for a New Millennium."

57. ELCA, *For Peace in God's World.*

58. ELCA, *Sufficient, Sustainable Livelihood for All.*

59. UCC, "A Faithful Response."

60. Episcopal Church, "Episcopal Church Urges Further Debt Cancellation for Poorest Countries," *Episcopal News Service,* February 18, 2002, www.episcopalchurch.org/3577_20513_ENG_HTM.htm.

61. Anthony F. Lang, Jr., "The Catholic Church and American Foreign Policy," Carnegie Council, October 11, 2002, www.cceia.org/resources/articles_papers_reports/79.html.

62. Zachary R. Calo, "Catholic Social Thought, Political Liberalism, and the Idea of Human Rights," www4.samford.edu/lillyhumanrights/papers/Calo_Catholic.pdf.

63. Allen D. Hertzke, "Roman Catholicism and the Faith-Based Movement for Global Human Rights," *Review of Faith and International Affairs,* 3, no. 3 (Winter 2005): 19, www.rfiaonline.org/archives/issues/3–3/93-faith-based-movement.

64. George Weigel, "The Catholic Human Rights Revolution," *Crisis,* July/August 1996, www.ewtn.com/library/CHISTORY/HRREVOLU.TXT.

65. Calo, "Catholic Social Thought, Political Liberalism, and the Idea of Human Rights," 21.

66. USCCB, Office of International Peace and Justice, "Background on Religious Liberty," February 2008, www.txcatholic.org/documents/usccb/200802rellibbck.pdf.

67. Many of these documents are available at www.usccb.org/sdwp/international/libertyind.shtml.

68. "U.S. Bishops Urge Action Now to End Darfur Crisis as Negotiation Ongoing," *Catholic Online,* May 5, 2006, www.catholic.org/national/national_story.php?id=19646.

69. USCCB, "Chairman Urges Action on Darfur Crisis," September 20, 2005, www.usccb.org/comm/archives/2005/05–211.shtml.

70. The text of the bill is at www.govtrack.us/congress/billtext.xpd?bill=h109–3127&show-changes=0.

71. John Ricard, "Letter to U.S. Senators against torture," October 4, 2005, www.usccb.org/sdwp/international/senateletterretorture100405.pdf.

72. Thomas G. Wenski, "Letter to Donald Rumsfeld on Ethical Standards in Treatment of Detainees," June 16, 2006, www.usccb.org/sdwp/international/2006Juneletterretorture.pdf.

73. Thomas G. Wenski, "Letter to U.S. Senators urging support of HR 2082, a ban on torture," January 30, 2008, www.usccb.org/sdwp/international/wenski_jan30–2008_ltr_on_torture_final.pdf.

74. USCCB, "Action Alert: Urge Your Senators to Expand the Ban on Torture," February 7, 2008, www.usccb.org/sdwp/international/action_alert_on_hr_2082_2-7-08_with_hdr.pdf.

75. USCCB, "Action Alert: Urge President Bush to Sign Anti-Torture Provisions," February 28, 2008, www.usccb.org/sdwp/international/action_alert_on_hr_2082_2–28-08_with_op-ed_on_veto.pdf.

76. "End the Torture Nightmare: An Op-Ed," February 28, 2008, www.usccb.org/sdwp/international/action_alert_on_hr_2082_2-28-08_with_op-ed_on_veto.pdf.

77. The text of Bush's veto message is at www.govtrack.us/congress/record.xpd?id=110-h20080310–10&bill=h110–2082.

78. USCCB, "Statement of Most Reverend Gerald R. Barnes, Bishop of San Bernardino, California, Chairman, USCCB Committee on Migration on Human Trafficking," September 12, 2007, www.usccb.org/mrs/traffickingstatement.pdf.

79. Nicholas DiMarzio, "Statement on Trafficking in Persons," May 16, 2000, www.usccb.org/mrs/traffickers.shtml.

80. USCC/MRS, "Legislative Outcome: The Victims of Trafficking and Violence Protection Act of 2000," November 14, 2000, www.usccb.org/mrs/tra1000.shtml.

81. "Human Trafficking Bill Lacking, Says USCCB," *Catholic News Service*, January 12, 2006, www.catholic.org/national/national_story.php?id=18297.

82. James T. McHugh, "Testimony of Bishop James T. McHugh before the House Appropriations Subcommittee on Foreign Operations," April 24, 1989, www.usccb.org/prolife/issues/abortion/McHugh1989.pdf.

83. Gail Quinn, "Letter to Congress on the Mexico City Policy," April 18, 2001, www.usccb.org/prolife/issues/abortion/mexcit418.shtml.

84. Cathleen A. Cleaver, "Testimony before the Senate Foreign Relations Committee," July 19, 2001, www.usccb.org/prolife/issues/abortion/mexcity71901.shtml.

85. Justin Rigali, "Letter to House of Representatives," June 18, 2007, www.usccb.org/prolife/issues/abortion/mexicocity2007.pdf.

86. Justin Rigali, "Letter to Senate supporting the Kemp-Kasten Amendment," September 6, 2007, www.usccb.org/prolife/issues/abortion/foreignops2008.pdf.

87. Wilton Gregory, "Letter to President Bush thanking him for the UNFPA Decision," July 23, 2002, www.usccb.org/prolife/issues/abortion/unfpa072302.shtml.

88. Anthony Bevilacqua, "Vote for the Smith/Oberstar/Hyde Amendment," July 10, 2003, www.usccb.org/prolife/issues/abortion/unfpa703.pdf.

89. Rigali, "Letter to Senate."

90. The text of the encyclical is at www.osjspm.org/majordoc_populorum_progressio_official_text.aspx.

91. NCCB, *Economic Justice for All*, a Pastoral Letter on Catholic Social Teaching and the U.S. Economy Issued by the National Conference of Catholic Bishops, www.usccb.org/sdwp/international/EconomicJusticeforAll.pdf.

92. NCCB, *Economic Justice for All*.

93. Robert N. Lynch, "Letter on NAFTA to USTR Clara [sic] Hills," June 4, 1991, www.usccb.org/sdwp/international/hills.shtml.

94. United States Catholic Conference [hereinafter USCC], "A Jubilee Call for Debt Forgiveness," April 1999, www.usccb.org/sdwp/international/adminstm.shtml.

95. Documents pertaining to the NCCB/USCC/USCCB's activities promoting debt forgiveness may be accessed at www.usccb.org/sdwp/international/debtindex.shtml.

96. Rigali, "Letter to House of Representatives."

97. Rigali, "Letter to House of Representatives."

98. LCMS, "What About . . . Abortion?" www.lcms.org/graphics/assets/media/LCMS/wa_abortion.pdf.

99. The Coalition's website is at www.rcrc.org.

100. RCRC, "Words of Choice," 6.

101. RCRC, "Words of Choice," 6.

102. UMC, "The Nurturing Community," Social Principles, ¶161. II. J., www.umc-gbcs.org/site/c.frLJK2PKLqF/b.3713149/k.BC0/182161_II_The_Nurturing_Community/apps/nl/newsletter.asp.

103. ELCA, "Abortion" (1991), www.elca.org/What-We-Believe/Social-Issues/Social-Statements/Abortion.aspx.

104. Quoted in RCRC, "We Affirm: Religious Organizations Support Reproductive Choice," www.rcrc.org/issues/questions.cfm.

105. For an interesting analysis of this story, see Bryant Myers, "Will the Poor Always be with Us?" *Sojourners Magazine*, June 15, 2005, www.sojo.net/index.cfm?action=news.display_article&mode=C&NewsID=4847.

106. Byron D. Klaus, "Compassion Rooted in the Gospel that Transforms," *Enrichment Journal*, http://enrichmentjournal.ag.org/200402/200402_016_compassion.cfm. It should be noted that, in this essay, Klaus calls on the Assemblies of God to re-evaluate its traditional emphasis on evangelism at the expense of social concern.

107. Hertzke, *Representing God in Washington*, 29.

108. Hertzke, *Representing God in Washington*, 110.

109. Despite IRFA, the former director of the State Department's Office of International Religious Freedom argues that the U.S. government has not actively or effectively pursued religious freedom. See Thomas F. Farr, *World of Faith and Freedom: Why International Religious Liberty is Vital to American National Security* (Oxford: Oxford University Press, 2008), 17.

CHAPTER 5

Middle East Policy

The Middle East has been, for more than half a century, one of the most world's troublesome areas for makers of U.S. foreign policy. The formation of the state of Israel in 1948 sparked the first of a series of Arab–Israeli Wars, as Arab states attempted to destroy the fledging country. Subsequent conflicts occurred during the Suez Crisis (1956), the Six Days' War (1967), and the Yom Kippur War (1973). As a result of its military victories, particularly in the Six Days' War, Israel not only survived but took control of territories owned or previously occupied by neighboring states: the Sinai Peninsula (Egypt), the Golan Heights (Syria), the West Bank of the Jordan River, including East Jerusalem (Jordan), and the Gaza Strip (Egypt). Meanwhile, hundreds of thousands of Palestinian Arabs were driven out of Israel or left of their own accord.

Recurrent efforts to secure peace in the Middle East have met with some success. The most notable achievement has been the Camp David accords. In 1978, under the prodding of U.S. president Jimmy Carter, Egyptian president Anwar Sadat and Israeli prime minister Menachem Begin agreed that Israel would return the Sinai Peninsula to Egypt, while Egypt would accept Israel's right to exist, establish diplomatic relations, and live in peace with its neighbor.[1] The Camp David accords fundamentally altered the political and strategic dynamics of the region. With the most powerful Arab state on good terms with Israel, other Arab states were forced to recognize the futility of confronting Israel militarily. In 1994, Israel and Jordan signed a peace treaty, further enhancing the stability of the Middle East.

Progress on resolving the "Palestinian problem," however, has been minimal. In 1993, representatives of Israel and the Palestine Liberation Organization (PLO) concluded the so-called Oslo Accords. Under the terms of the "Declaration of Principles on Interim Self-Government Arrangements" (DOP), Palestinians were to be granted self-rule in the West Bank and Gaza over a period of five years.[2] In return, Palestinian leader Yasser Arafat acknowledged the right of Israel to exist, renounced terrorism, and pledged to remove from the Palestinian Covenant sections that were inconsistent with these commitments.[3]

To reach agreement in Oslo, Israeli and Palestinian negotiators postponed addressing the thorniest problems confronting them. According to the DOP, "permanent status" issues—the drawing of borders, the status of Jerusalem, Jewish settlements in Palestinian territories, Palestinian refugees and their right to return to Israel, and security arrangements, among others—were to be negotiated and resolved in talks beginning no later than May 1996. Permanent status arrangements were to take effect by May 1999.

Permanent status negotiations have occurred on and off since Oslo, without success. The issues are extraordinarily difficult. The government of Israel has declared Jerusalem to be its capital and has expressed its intent to keep the entire city in Israeli possession, while the Palestinian Authority hopes to make largely Arab East Jerusalem the capital of a Palestinian state. Jewish settlements in the West Bank, thanks in part to periodic encouragement from the Israeli government, are now quite numerous. Many of the settler groups are well armed and have expressed their determination to remain where they are. Presumably Israeli Defense Forces (IDF) could remove them if necessary, but doing so might be bloody and politically very damaging. Leaving them in place, on the other hand, is not acceptable to the Palestinian leadership, and, in any event, the presence of Jewish enclaves within a Palestinian state would seem to be a recipe for ethno-religious violence. Palestinian negotiators continue to insist that Palestinian refugees and their descendents enjoy an absolute right to return to the homes and land they once owned in what is now Israel. But the Israeli government cannot admit this right because if large numbers of Palestinians were to return, then mainly Muslim Arabs would outnumber Israeli Jews and Israel would cease to be a Jewish state. Compromise is, of course, possible in principle, but in practice has proved elusive. In July 2000, thanks in part to efforts by the Clinton administration, Palestinian president Yasser Arafat and Israeli prime minister Ehud Barak appeared close to an agreement, but their talks collapsed amid mutual recriminations.

In April 2003, Israel and the Palestinian leadership, in negotiations conducted under the auspices of the United Nations, European Union, United States, and Russia, agreed to a "Performance-Based Roadmap to a Permanent Two-State Solution to the Israeli-Palestinian Conflict."[4] The Roadmap laid out a three-stage process to a permanent settlement. In Phase I, which was to end in May 2003, terrorism and violence would cease, Palestinian–Israeli security cooperation would resume, Palestinians would prepare for the eventual establishment of a Palestinian state, and Israel would withdraw IDF forces from Palestinian areas occupied since September 28, 2000. Israel also pledged to take steps to improve the humanitarian situation in Palestinian territories.

Phase II, the transition phase, was to run from June 2003 to December 2003. During this period, Palestinian elections would be held, a Palestinian constitution would be approved, a Palestinian government would be formed, and an independent Palestinian state, with provisional borders, would be established. Phase III, to be completed no later than 2005, would see Israel and Palestine reach a permanent status agreement resolving questions of borders, refugees, Jerusalem, and settlements. The two countries would establish normal diplomatic relations with one another.

Although both sides continue to express their support for the Roadmap, progress has been much slower than planned. Terrorist activities have continued. Israel fought a war with the Syrian-backed terrorist organization Hezbollah in Southern Lebanon in 2006. The Israeli government has constructed portions of a "separation wall" cordoning off Jewish areas that it says are intended to protect Israeli citizens, but which Palestinians have interpreted as an effort to establish final borders unilaterally. The peace process has been complicated enormously by internal conflict among the Palestinians. In January 2006, Hamas, a Palestinian group that is still committed to the destruction of Israel, won a surprise victory in Palestinian elections. The following June, Palestinian president Mahmoud Abbas declared a state of emergency, dissolved the government, and dismissed the prime minister, appointing a new one in his place. Fighting in Gaza between Hamas and Fatah, the Palestinian faction previously in control of the government, ensued. By the end of June, Hamas had defeated Fatah. As a consequence, the Palestinian National Authority (PNA), the Palestinian government recognized by Israel, the United States, and most other countries, now controls only the West Bank. There are, in fact, two Palestinian governments, each of which claims to be the legitimate government of all Palestine. At this writing, prospects for a resolution of the Israeli–Palestinian conflict any time soon appear dim.

The government of the United States has attempted on numerous occasions to play a constructive role in facilitating peace in the Middle East.[5] But it has not been, for the most part, impartial. Israel since 1976 has been the single largest annual recipient of U.S. foreign aid. Unlike other aid recipients, which receive their assistance in quarterly installments, Israel is given a lump sum at the beginning of each year. It is the only recipient of U.S. aid that is not required to account for how the aid is spent. In addition to economic support, the United States has provided Israel with considerable diplomatic support. The U.S. government has vetoed more than thirty United Nations Security Council resolutions condemning Israel. It has blocked Arab efforts to place Israel's nuclear arsenal on the Security Council agenda at the same time it has vigorously opposed nuclear proliferation elsewhere in the world.[6] While U.S. administrations have sometimes criticized the government of Israel for policies—e.g., encouraging Jewish settlements in the West Bank—that are in violation of either international law or of undertakings agreed to by Israel in negotiations with Palestinians, such criticism has been rare and relatively muted. No punitive actions, such as a suspension of aid to Israel, have been taken or even seriously considered.

It is not the purpose of this chapter to argue that such partiality is unwarranted. While John Mearsheimer and Stephen Walt have claimed that favoritism toward Israel is inimical to U.S. interests on a variety of fronts, others contend that it is justified for a range of cultural, political, and strategic reasons. Whatever the merits, it is clear that the United States has been an uncommonly strong supporter of Israel. And, not surprisingly, various groups of U.S. Christians have adopted quite different positions concerning this support.

Evangelical Protestants

Within the U.S. Christian community, Evangelical Protestants are by far the most enthusiastic advocates for Israel. The connection between Israel and the religious right in the United States dates to the late 1960s and early 1970s. According to Donald Wagner, what has become known as "Christian Zionism" sprang from a number of causes. Most important was the place of Israel in evangelical, especially fundamentalist, eschatology, the branch of theology that deals with the so-called end times and the Second Coming of Jesus. This factor is discussed in detail below. Other factors included the growth of evangelical churches and other organizations relative to Mainline Protestant denominations and the Roman Catholic Church; reaction to the posture of U.S. president Jimmy Carter; alienation of Israel from Mainline Protestant, Catholic, and Orthodox Christian communities as a consequence of Israel's occupation of Arab territories after the 1967 war, and the election in 1977 in Israel of a conservative and more religiously oriented government headed by Prime Minister Menachem Begin. Supporters of Begin's Likud Party, among them settlers and small Orthodox parties, employed the biblical terms "Judea and Samaria" to refer to portions of the occupied West Bank, and argued that since God had given these lands to the Jewish people, they had a right to control and live within what they termed "Eretz," or "Greater" Israel.[7]

Jimmy Carter had announced in March 1977 that he favored Palestinian rights, including the "right to a homeland." When Likud took power in Israel in May, it decided to attempt to "split evangelical and fundamentalist Christians from Carter's political base and rally support among conservative Christians for Israel's opposition to the United Nations' proposed Middle East Peace Conference."[8] The Institute for Holy Land Studies, an evangelical organization in Jerusalem, purchased full-page advertisements in leading U.S. newspapers stating that "The time has come for evangelical Christians to affirm their belief in biblical prophecy and Israel's divine right to the land. . . . We would view with grave concern any effort to carve out of the Jewish homeland another nation or political entity."[9] During the 1980 U.S. presidential campaign, evangelical and Jewish groups worked hard to oust Carter in favor of Ronald Reagan, and Carter's abandonment by evangelical voters contributed to his defeat in November of that year.[10] Since that time, Evangelical Protestants, especially fundamentalists, have been staunch supporters of Israel. In January 1998, Begin's successor, Prime Minister Benjamin Netanyahu, arrived in the United States to discuss delays in the Middle East peace process with U.S. president Bill Clinton, whose administration was concerned that Israel was dragging its feet on the implementation of the Oslo Agreements. Netanyahu's first visit was to the Mayflower Hotel in Washington, where fundamentalist leader Jerry Falwell was addressing Voices United for Israel, a coalition of conservative Jewish and Christian organizations. According to one observer, Netanyahu entered the ballroom at the hotel to "thunderous applause" and was introduced by Falwell as "the Ronald Reagan of Israel." The Israeli prime minister told the several hundred people in attendance that Jerusalem would "never be divided" and that it was necessary that Israel retain the West Bank and other territories that had been "regained by Israel."[11] Following closed-door meetings with Netanyahu, Falwell announced that he, Morris Chapman, and Richard Lee, leaders of the Southern Baptist Convention, as well as John Hagee, televangelist and pastor of the Cornerstone Church in San Antonio, Texas, would mobilize evangelicals to "'tell President Clinton to refrain from putting pressure on Israel' to comply with the Oslo accords."[12] Said Falwell, "There are about 200,000 evangelical pastors in America, and we're asking them all through e-mail, faxes, letters, telephone, to go into their pulpits and use their influence in support of the state of Israel and the Prime Minister."[13]

Falwell's influence, and the influence of evangelicals more generally, was demonstrated in 2001, when President George W. Bush, whose administration was usually very supportive of Israel, called on the government of Israeli prime minister Ariel Sharon to withdraw Israeli tanks from Palestinian towns on the West Bank. Falwell sent a letter to the White House in protest. More than 100,000 emails from Christian conservatives subsequently arrived. As Bob Simon of CBS News noted, "Israel did not move its tanks. Bush did not ask again."[14] Falwell subsequently boasted of evangelical Christians: "There are 70 million of us. And if there's one thing that brings us together quickly it's whenever we begin to detect our government becoming a little anti-Israel."[15]

Evangelical leaders have continued to express support for Israel. In 2004, televangelist Pat Robertson warned his audience on the Christian Broadcasting Network that dividing Jerusalem would be "suicide" for the United States. Said Robertson,

> If the United States, and I want you to hear me very clearly, if the United States takes a role in ripping half of Jerusalem away from Israel and giving it to Yasser Arafat and a group of terrorists, we are going to see the wrath of God fall on this nation that will make tornadoes look like a Sunday school picnic.[16]

In February 2006, John Hagee founded Christians United For Israel (CUFI).[17] According to the organization's website, CUFI's purpose "is to provide a national association through which every pro-Israel church, parachurch organization, ministry or individual in America can speak and act with one voice in support of Israel in matters related to Biblical issues." CUFI now claims to be "the largest pro-Israel organization in the United States and one of the leading Christian grassroots movements in the world." Every year, the organization "holds hundreds of pro-Israel events in cities around the country. And each July, thousands of pro-Israel Christians gather in Washington, DC to participate in the CUFI Washington Summit and make their voices heard in support of Israel and the Jewish people." Boasts CUFI, "Our impact has been immediate. Our growth has been phenomenal. And we've only just begun."[18]

The administration of President George W. Bush recognized the difficulty of proceeding with the Roadmap to Peace in the face of opposition from the evangelical community, a major base of political support for the administration and the Republican Party more generally. In July 2003, the White House Office of Public Liaison convened a meeting of forty evangelical leaders who were briefed by National Security Adviser Condoleezza Rice in an effort to convince them of the wisdom of the plan. The attempt at persuasion did not succeed, and criticism of the Roadmap from evangelical quarters continued unabated.[19] It is hard to imagine that evangelical opposition to the Roadmap was not at least partly responsible for the failure of the Bush administration to pursue more than halfhearted efforts to secure peace in the Middle East. Indeed, as discussed below, the administration eventually countenanced unilateral initiatives undertaken by the Israeli government that violated the same Roadmap that the administration had helped to negotiate.

To be fair, it must be noted that not all evangelicals are pro-Israel. In 2002, several dozen evangelical leaders sent a letter to President Bush asking him to pursue "an even-handed U.S. policy toward Israelis and Palestinians," noting that such a policy would include support for a Palestinian state with 1967 borders. Signers of the letter included Ron Sider, president of Evangelicals for Social Action, Richard Mouw, president of Fuller Theological Seminary, and Tony Campolo, founder of Evangelicals for Education.[20] But an answering letter was written the following year by Gary Bauer, Jerry Falwell, Richard Land, and 21 others that termed even-handedness in the Middle East "morally reprehensible."[21] While the evangelical community is clearly not a monolith with respect to Middle East policy, support for Israel is much stronger among evangelicals, and especially among fundamentalists, than among other U.S. Christian groups. One study found that 47 percent of fundamentalist Christians favored Israeli control of Jerusalem and 67 percent supported Israeli settlements in the West Bank and Gaza. Forty-five percent believed that the United States should take Israel's side in the Middle East dispute. By contrast, only 21 percent of other Protestants and 17 percent of Catholics favored Israeli control of Jerusalem. Only 40 percent of other Protestants and 37 percent of Catholics supported Israeli settlements in the West Bank and Gaza. And only 16 percent of other Protestants and 16 percent of Catholics believed the United States should side with Israel in the Middle East dispute.[22] Data such as these, along with the pronouncements and activities of evangelical leaders, confirm the declaration of one prominent analyst that, within the U.S. Christian community, evangelicals are "Israel's best friend."[23]

Mainline Protestants

As the preceding paragraph suggests, Mainline Protestants generally take a more balanced, or more pro-Palestinian position than evangelicals. Mainline denominations typically support a Palestinian state, oppose Israeli settlements in the Occupied Territories, reject Israeli annexation of East Jerusalem, and oppose the construction of a "separation wall." While they sympathize with the plight of the Israeli people, who have been subjected to Palestinian terrorism, they also sympathize with the Palestinian population, which they see as having rights that are frequently violated by Israeli policy. A 2002 resolution of the Episcopal Church's Executive Council condemned both "the violence of the suicide bombers and the violence of the Occupation." The resolution went on to express support for a Palestinian State and to call for an end to Jewish settlement activities because "the Israeli policy of building settlements in the Occupied Territories thwarts the peace process." Although the Council called for "the guarantee of an Israel secure and at peace with her neighbors," the resolution concluded with a critique of Israeli policy that laid most of the blame for ongoing problems in the Middle East at the feet of the Israeli government:

> The Occupation of the West Bank, including East Jerusalem, and Gaza, has been the single most aggravating source of tension in this long conflict and has resulted in the humiliation of the Palestinian people. The decades old policy of Israel to build settlements on this land for Israelis greatly exacerbates the Occupation, taking prime land from Palestinians and populating them with Israelis protected by Israeli Defense Forces. Roads built for settlers connecting them to Israel sever ties between Palestinian villages and towns, resulting in severe travel restrictions on the Palestinian people and isolation of local communities into virtual cantons. The consequence is further humiliation and dislocation of the Palestinian people.[24]

In April 2004, the presiding bishop of the Episcopal Church, Frank T. Griswold, wrote a letter to President Bush, noting that "the Episcopal Church has a long record of support for a just peace that guarantees Israel's security and Palestinian aspirations for a viable sovereign state with Jerusalem as the shared capital of both Israel and Palestine." He conveyed his concern at the president's apparent willingness to abandon the "Road Map to Peace" and to accept unilateral Israeli actions, including the construction of a wall separating Israel from Palestinian areas.[25] Two months later, the Church's Executive Council expressed its unhappiness at "the positions taken by President Bush to concede some West Bank settlements to Israel and negates [sic] the right of return of Palestinian refugees."[26] In November 2006, the Council adopted a resolution calling for "an end to the isolation of East Jerusalem and Bethlehem from the West Bank created by the continued construction of Israeli settlements, settler roads and the barrier," and "removal of the barrier by Israel where it violates Palestinian territory."[27] A second resolution called for "the recognition of Jerusalem as the shared capital of the two [Israeli and Palestinian] states" and "the withdrawal by Israel from all occupied Palestinian territories."[28]

Other Mainline Protestant denominations have articulated similar views. The United Methodist Church adopted a resolution expressing its opposition to "continued military occupation of the West Bank, Gaza, and East Jerusalem, the confiscation of Palestinian land and water resources, the destruction of Palestinian homes, the continued building of illegal Jewish settlements, and any vision of a 'Greater Israel' that includes the occupied territories and the whole of Jerusalem and its surroundings." The UMC asked that the United States redistribute the large amount of aid given Egypt and Israel to "support economic development efforts of nongovernmental organizations throughout the region, including religious institutions, human rights groups, labor unions, and professional groups within Palestinian communities." The UMC also called upon the U.S. government, in cooperation with the United Nations and other countries, to urge the state of Israel to

> 1. cease the confiscation of Palestinian land and water for any reason; 2. cease the building of new, or expansion of existing, settlements and/or bypass roads in the occupied territories including East Jerusalem; 3. lift the closures and curfews on all Palestinian towns by completely withdrawing Israeli military forces to the Green Line (the 1948 ceasefire line between Israel and the West Bank); 4. disman-tle the segment of the Wall of Separation constructed since May 2002 that is not being built on the Green Line but on Palestinian land.[29]

Likewise, the Evangelical Lutheran Church in American has called for "the immedi-ate cessation of construction of the Israeli separation wall and removal of all existing portions of this wall on Palestinian land."[30]

The National Council of Churches, not surprisingly, has expressed similar senti-ments. In its 2003 Resolution on Conflict in the Middle East, the NCC articulated "deep distress" at "the building of the Separation Wall by Israel." The NCC noted "that the Wall is resulting in the de facto imprisonment of the Palestinian popula-tion, the denial of access by Palestinians to emergency services, health care, food, employment, schools and water resources, the curtailment of freedom of movement among the Palestinian people, and the exacerbation of suffering," and it called upon the Israeli government to tear it down. The NCC also reiterated its "long-standing support for the establishment of a Palestinian State" and its "call for the preservation of the City of Jerusalem as an open, shared city where free access to holy places and freedom of worship are assured for people of all faiths."[31]

Roman Catholics

With respect to Middle East policy, Roman Catholic leaders have tended to employ more muted, and more balanced, language than Mainline Protestant denominations, but their stances on the issues are closer to those of the mainline churches than to those of evangelicals. The relationship between the Roman Catholic Church and Israel has not always been a smooth one. Indeed, the Vatican, or Holy See, did not establish diplomatic relations with Israel until 1993, 45 years after the founding of the Jewish state. The U.S. Catholic bishops have since that time, written on several occasions to the Israeli government to protest delays in implementing certain aspects of the Fundamental Agreement between Israel and the Holy See. Of particular con-cern have been the rights of the Catholic Church in connection with its properties in Israel. The USCCB has expressed its dismay at what it considers "arbitrary taxation policies by the government of Israel against Church properties and the government's denial of access to due process through Israeli courts to settle property disputes," holding that the Israeli government is violating "international law and the history of the prior rights of the Church." According to the USCCB, maintaining its properties in Israel is "key to the mission and ministry of the Church in the Holy Land and thus its religious freedom."[32]

The USCCB's predecessor organization, the National Conference of Catholic Bishops (NCCB) issued policy statements on the Middle East in 1973, 1978, and 1989. In the 1989 statement, *Toward Peace in the Middle East: Perspectives, Principles, and Hopes*, the bishops wrote, in regards to the Israeli–Arab–Palestinian question, that any settlement should be based on "recognition of Israel's right to existence within secure borders" and "recognition of Palestinian rights," including the right to "an independent homeland." Although they did not exclude the possibility that sovereignty over Jerusalem might be exercised by a single civil power (e.g., Israel), the bishops stressed that "the sacred character of Jerusalem as a heritage for the Abrahamic faiths [Judaism, Christianity, and Islam] should be guaranteed," that "religious freedom of persons and of communities should be safeguarded," that "the rights acquired by various communities regarding shrines, holy places, educational and social institutions must be ensured," and that "the Holy City's special religious status and the shrines proper to each religion should be protected by 'an appropriate juridical safeguard' that is internationally respected and guaranteed." Importantly, they wrote, "Clearly the ultimate status of the city cannot be settled by unilateral measures."[33]

In 2001, the Catholic bishops issued a statement on the Israeli–Palestinian situation that articulated what they considered to be the necessary steps toward peace in the Middle East: "real security for the State of Israel, a viable state for Palestinians, just resolution of the refugee problem, an agreement on Jerusalem which protects religious freedom and other basic rights, an equitable sharing of resources, especially water, and implementation of relevant UN resolutions and other provisions of international law." Noting that each side had "deep, long-standing, and legitimate grievances" that had to be addressed, the bishops wrote that "Palestinians rightly insist on an end to Israel's three-decade-long occupation of the West Bank and Gaza and to the continued establishment and expansion of settlements." While Israel, they stated, had "a fundamental right to security," they emphasized that "security will not be won by ongoing annexation of Palestinian land, blockades, air strikes on cities, destruction of crops and homes, and other excessive use of force." At the same time, however, the USCCB stressed that "Israelis rightly see the failure of Palestinians to demonstrate full respect for Israel's right to exist and flourish within secure borders as a fundamental cause of the conflict. Palestinian leaders," they wrote, "must clearly renounce violence and terrorist attacks against innocent civilians, take effective steps to stop them, and bring to justice those responsible."[34] The following year, the bishops reiterated their stance: "Israeli occupation cannot be sustained— militarily or morally—nor can the indiscriminate use of force in civilian areas. Palestinian attacks on innocent civilians cannot be tolerated—both because they are morally indefensible and because they undermine the legitimate claims of the Palestinian people."[35]

The USCCB has lobbied the U.S. government to maintain what it considers to be a balanced approach to Middle East policy. It commended President Bush, who had been critical of the Clinton administration's engagement in the Middle East, on his decision to involve himself personally in negotiations leading to the 2003 Roadmap to Peace.[36] It also criticized the Bush administration when it accepted unilateral Israeli actions that violated the Roadmap. In April 2004, Israeli Prime Minster Ariel Sharon announced the closing of Israeli settlements in Gaza and the withdrawal of Israeli troops from that territory, along with the construction of a security wall and expansion of Jewish settlements on the West Bank. In response, Wilton B. Gregory, president of the USCCB, wrote to President Bush to express "grave concerns about developments in the Holy Land, and our hope that you and your Administration will take new steps to reverse a seriously deteriorating situation and to revive the peace process between Israelis and Palestinians. . . . A just and lasting peace will not be possible," Gregory stated, "if the United States acquiesces in unilateral initiatives that undermine" efforts to achieve it.[37]

Gregory's letter did not produce the desired effect; on April 14, the Bush administration expressed its approval of Sharon's initiatives. A few days later, Gregory responded with a statement on behalf of the USCCB that criticized U.S. policy in unusually harsh terms. Wrote the bishop, "President Bush's recent announcement of support for the unilateral Israeli policy toward Gaza and the West Bank is deeply troubling. The President's acquiescence in Prime Minister Ariel Sharon's unilateral approach risks undermining the Roadmap for Peace and prospects for a negotiated settlement of this conflict." Gregory argued that "in accepting Israeli-created 'facts-on-the-ground,' which were established in defiance of long standing US policy regarding Israeli settlements and the right of return, the United States has set a worrying precedent that will make it extremely difficult to create a viable, independent Palestinian state, especially if the West Bank settlements are enlarged and the security wall proceeds as planned." Worried that Israeli policy would do nothing but "feed the fires of resistance" among Palestinians, he urged

> the Bush administration to return to the traditional U.S. role of "honest broker" by working with the international community and Palestinians and Israelis to develop trust-building measures and to pursue peaceful means to negotiate their differences, in accord with international law and existing UN Resolutions. In that way, they can build together a culture of peace that respects the rights of all.[38]

The Catholic bishops have continued to press the U.S. government to remain committed to the Roadmap to Peace. In March 2006, following the victory of Hamas in Palestinian parliamentary elections, the Committee on International Relations of the U.S. House of Representatives took up legislation, the Palestinian Anti-Terrorism Act, that would have denied aid to the Palestinian Authority. Thomas Wenski, chairman of the USCCB's Committee on International Policy, sent a letter to Henry Hyde, chair of the House Committee, opposing the bill, because it would not be "wise or just to withhold aid to the Palestinian people at large or punish them for the possible actions of their political leaders." Wrote Wenski, "Poverty and unemployment are still far too prevalent and a significant loss of funds for help for the Palestinian people can only add to their desperate plight."[39] The legislation was amended by the House Committee on International Relations to allow aid necessary to "meet basic human health needs," but the bishops found the exception too narrow. In a second letter to Hyde, Wenski wrote that meeting health needs was insufficient, that "the basic human needs of the Palestinian people as they fall into deeper poverty include: 'education, job training, psycho-social counseling and other humanitarian needs.'" The bishops also objected to provisions in the amended bill that forbad contact with the Palestinian Council and restricted travel and representation in the United States by officials of the PLO because they would "curtail contact with moderate Palestinian leaders whose support and cooperation are crucial for pursuing a two state solution."[40] Accompanying Wenski's missive was a page of proposed amendments to the legislation.

In May 2006, the USCCB issued an action alert warning Catholics of an impending House vote on the Palestinian Anti-Terrorism Act and urging them to phone their Congressional representatives and ask them to oppose the bill.[41] On May 23, however, the House passed the legislation. As a consequence, the USCCB shifted the focus of its efforts to the U.S. Senate, which was considering a similar bill. On May 25, Wenski faxed a letter to Richard Lugar, chair of the Senate Committee on Foreign Relations, with copies to the members of that committee and Mitch McConnell, Senate majority leader. Noting that the Senate version of the legislation had a less restrictive definition of the aid that could be provided to Palestinians by nongovernmental organizations, Wenski nevertheless urged Lugar to ensure that the bill specifically "define a broader range of essential assistance including, but not limited to, food, water, medical services, sanitation services, education, job training, psycho-social counseling, agricultural development, and other assistance to meet basic human needs." He also reiterated the bishops' objections to the restrictions on travel for officials of the PLO and other limitations on contact with moderate Palestinian leaders.[42]

The final version of the Palestinian Anti-Terrorism Act was passed by the Senate on June 23, 2006. The Senate version was then approved by the House on December 7 and signed into law by President Bush on December 21. The law did not incorporate all the changes advocated by the USCCB, but it did include some of them. Among the exceptions to the ban on aid to Palestinians were (1) "assistance to meet food, water, medicine, health, or sanitation needs, or other assistance to meet basic human needs," (2) "assistance to promote democracy, human rights, freedom of the press, non-violence, reconciliation, and peaceful co-existence, provided that such assistance does not directly benefit Hamas or any other foreign terrorist organization," and (3) "assistance, other than funding of salaries or salary supplements, to individual members of the Palestinian Legislative Council who the President determines are not members of Hamas or any other foreign terrorist organization, for the purposes of facilitating the attendance of such members in programs for the development of institutions of democratic governance, including enhancing the transparent and accountable operations of such institutions, and providing support for the Middle East peace process." The act also permitted the issuance of visas to "(1) the President of the Palestinian Authority and his or her personal representatives, provided that the President and his or her personal representatives are not affiliated with Hamas or any other foreign terrorist organization; and (2) members of the Palestinian Legislative Council who are not members of Hamas or any other foreign terrorist organization." The latter exception was lacking in both the House version and the original Senate version of the law.[43]

In the summer of 2006, while the Palestinian Anti-Terrorism Act was making its way through Congress, war broke out in Southern Lebanon between Hezbollah and Israel. Lesser hostilities occurred in Gaza between Israeli forces and those of Hamas. The USCCB condemned the actions of both the Israeli government and the Palestinian factions involved. A statement issued by Bishop Wenski acknowledged the "harsh realities of occupation and the yearning for a viable state" on the part of Palestinians, but said "we cannot support rocket barrages and suicide bombings against innocent Israeli civilians and cross-border attacks and abductions. Such actions violate the principle of civilian immunity and undermine the possibility of a negotiated resolution of the Israeli-Palestinian conflict." Similarly, Wenski recognized that "Israel has a right to defend itself," but stated that the bishops could not "support its sweeping counterattacks on civilian areas, civilian infrastructure, blockades and other acts of war in Gaza and Lebanon. Punishment of an entire population for the indefensible acts of extreme armed factions," he wrote, "is wrong and causes unjustified harm to noncombatants."[44] A subsequent letter from Wenski to members of Congress repeated these themes. It blamed Hamas and Hezbollah, and their allies in Syria and Iran, for initiating the violence, but contended that "Israel's response has been in some instances militarily disproportionate and indiscriminate." Importantly, Wenski urged the U.S. government to become actively involved in the crisis, calling on Congress and the administration to "exercise greater leadership to end the current cycle of violence, condemn all attacks on civilians, secure an effective and immediate ceasefire, open humanitarian corridors, oppose disproportionate and indiscriminate actions, and move toward negotiations between Israelis and Palestinians to advance a two state solution, and ensure the independence of Lebanon."[45] An action report issued by the USCCB on August 1 asked Catholics to phone the White House and to speak to their senators and representatives during the August Congressional recess, in an effort to reinforce the message.[46]

In the past several years, the Roman Catholic hierarchy has continued to push the U.S. government toward increased diplomatic involvement in the Middle East. Often, it has coordinated its efforts with those of Orthodox and Mainline Protestant denominations, as well some freestyle evangelical leaders. A January 2007 letter to President Bush composed by Bishop Wenski, the head of the Diocese of the Armenian Church in America, the ecumenical officer of the Greek Orthodox Archdiocese of America, the presiding bishop of the Evangelical Lutheran Church in America, and the presiding bishop of the Episcopal Church was signed by a number of other Christian leaders, including representatives of the Moravian Church in American, the Alliance of Baptists, the United Methodist Church, the Church of the Brethren, the Presbyterian Church (USA), and the Reformed Church in America. The letter asked the president to "make Israeli-Palestinian peacemaking, in the context of a comprehensive Arab-Israeli peace initiative, an urgent priority for your Administration." It commended Bush for his "vision of a viable, contiguous Palestinian state living as a peaceful neighbor alongside the state of Israel" and stated that "with your active engagement, this vision could reignite a passion for peace that can overcome the appeal of violence, vengeance and exclusivity."[47]

Since 2003, two Roman Catholic bishops, as well as the president of the USCCB, have been among the leaders of the National Interreligious Leadership Initiative for Peace in the Middle East (NILI). Other Christian members of NILI include the primates of the Greek Orthodox and Armenian Apostolic Churches, the heads of most of the major Mainline Protestant denominations—the Evangelical Lutheran Church in America, the Presbyterian Church (USA), the Episcopal Church, the United Methodist Church, the United Church of Christ, and the Christian Church (Disciples of Christ)—and the president of the National Council of Churches. Several prominent evangelicals belong, though not, it should be noted, the leaders of any major evangelical denominations or the National Association of Evangelicals. A genuine interfaith effort, NILI also has as members a number of U.S. Jewish and Muslim leaders.[48]

Shortly after its founding, NILI adopted a statement outlining "twelve urgent steps for peace" in the Middle East. Based on full implementation of the Roadmap, these steps included democratic reform and increased financial accountability on the part of the Palestinian Authority, the halting of Palestinian attacks on Israelis and the punishment of those responsible for them, and cooperation by the Palestinian Authority with regional and international efforts to deny financial assistance to anti-Israeli terrorist groups. They also included the dismantling of all unauthorized Jewish settlements in the occupied territories established since March 2002 with no further expansion of other settlements, the lifting of curfews and restrictions on movement of Palestinians in the West Bank and Gaza, the end to construction of the security fence or wall of separation "in areas which require confiscation of more Palestinian land and threaten the viability of a future Palestinian state," and the withdrawal of Israeli Defense Forces from Palestinian areas occupied after September 2000.[49] NILI has engaged in a variety of advocacy efforts, holding press conferences, issuing statements, meeting with U.S. Secretary of State Colin Powell, and writing letters to Powell and his successor Condoleezza Rice, as well as to President Bush.[50] "An Urgent Appeal to the President" in January 2005 received widespread media coverage and was listed by Google as the top story of the day.[51] As of this writing, those efforts appear to have had little influence on U.S. policy. They reflect, however, the relatively high level of cooperation and the general correspondence in views regarding the Middle East between U.S. Catholics on the one hand and Mainline Protestant denominations on the other.

Explaining the Differences

Analysts agree that the key to understanding the differences among various groups of U.S. Christians on Middle East policy lies in the realm of eschatology, or theology of the end times. Many evangelicals, especially more fundamentalist ones, subscribe to an eschatological doctrine known as "premillennial dispensationalism" (or, alternatively, "dispensational premillennialism"). This doctrine was first popularized in Great Britain by John Nelson Darby in the nineteenth century, and later in the United States by William Blackstone, author of *Jesus is Coming* (1882), and Cyrus Scofield. The so-called Scofield Bible, an annotated version published in the early years of the twentieth century, became, quite literally, the premillennial dispensationalists's Bible.[52]

For purposes of clarity, it may be helpful to discuss dispensationalism and premillennialism in turn. Dispensationalism holds that human history consists of a series of stages, or dispensations. Each of these eras is defined according to "the manner in which God deals with humanity" and especially in which human beings are brought into relationship with God.[53] There does not exist a single dispensational scheme. Some envision as many as seven dispensations; others, as few as three. According to many dispensationalists, we are currently living in the dispensation of "Grace," in which people are reconciled to God through their faith in Jesus Christ. This dispensation is sometimes called the "Church Age," because, according to dispensational doctrine, it began with the establishment of the Christian Church on Pentecost. Dispensationalists generally agree that the final stage of human history will be the "Millennial Kingdom" dispensation: a thousand-year period in which the rule of Jesus will be established on Earth. This prediction is grounded in Rev. 20.1–6:

> Then I saw an angel coming down from heaven, holding the key of the abyss and a great chain in his hand. And he laid hold of the dragon, the serpent of old, who is the devil and Satan, and bound him for a thousand years; and he threw him into the abyss, and shut it and sealed it over him, so that he would not deceive the nations any longer, until the thousand years were completed; after these things he must be released for a short time.
>
> Then I saw thrones, and they sat on them, and judgment was given to them. And I saw the souls of those who had been beheaded because of their testimony of Jesus and because of the word of God, and those who had not worshiped the beast or his image, and had not received the mark on their forehead and on their hand; and they came to life and reigned with Christ for a thousand years. The rest of the dead did not come to life until the thousand years were completed. This is the first resurrection. Blessed and holy is the one who has a part in the first resurrection; over these the second death has no power, but they will be priests of God and of Christ and will reign with Him for a thousand years.

Premillennialism holds that the predicted Second Coming of Jesus will occur before the millennial kingdom, or at its beginning. Christ will physically return to Earth, where he will then rule for a thousand years. By contrast, postmillennialism contends that Jesus will return after the millennial kingdom has been established by the church "through its faithful and Spirit-empowering preaching of the Gospel." The third major school of thought concerning the millennium, amillennialism, regards the thousand-year rule of Jesus as being a figurative rather than a literal prophecy. The millennial kingdom is a spiritual, not an earthly kingdom. It exists, and has existed since the first coming of Christ, in his church and in the hearts of believers. Jesus will reign in and through his church until the Second Coming, at which time all those who believe will enter into eternal life with him.[54]

According to premillennial dispensationalists, a specific series of events must occur before Christ returns to Earth and the millennial kingdom is established. Most crucially, from the standpoint of this chapter, the nation of Israel must be refounded. The Jewish people must return to the Holy land and take possession of it. The temple in Jerusalem must be rebuilt.[55] In the Old Testament book of Daniel, chapter 9, the angel Gabriel reveals to the prophet that

> Seventy weeks are decreed for your people and for your holy city: Then transgression will stop and sin will end, guilt will be expiated, everlasting justice will be introduced, vision and prophecy ratified, and a most holy will be anointed. Know and understand this: From the utterance of the word that Jerusalem was to be rebuilt until one who is anointed and a leader, there shall be seven weeks. During sixty-two weeks it shall be rebuilt, with streets and trenches, in time of affliction.

Sometime after Jerusalem and particularly the temple on Mt. Zion are rebuilt, what premillennialists call "the Rapture" will occur. The Apostle Paul, in his first letter to the church at Thessolonika, told his readers that "the Lord himself, with a word of command, with the voice of an archangel and with the trumpet of God, will come down from heaven, and the dead in Christ will rise first. Then we who are alive, who are left, will be caught up together with them in the clouds to meet the Lord in the air."[56] In the Rapture, then, true Christians will suddenly be taken up into heaven, while the rest of humanity remains on Earth. There will be seven years of "tribulation," marked by famine, war, and other catastrophic events. A false Christ, or Anti-Christ, will gain many adherents who mistakenly believe him to be Jesus. The forces of evil and an army of Christians will engage in a final, climactic struggle, the Battle of Armageddon, in which good triumphs and Satan is taken captive. Following the Battle of Armageddon, Jesus will return to Earth to begin his thousand-year reign.[57] At the end of the Millennium, Satan will be released and the Day of Judgment will occur.

Evidence of premillennial dispensationalist beliefs is widespread in contemporary U.S. culture. They have been reflected in a number of best-selling books. First among these was *The Late Great Planet Earth*, by Hal Lindsey. Published in 1970, Lindsey's book was a sensation, in large part because he interpreted specific real-world events and people as the fulfillment of certain dispensationalist predictions. As Weber notes,

> The Antichrist's revived Roman Empire was the European Common Market. The northern confederacy was the Soviet Union and the Eastern Bloc. The southern confederacy was an Arab-African coalition headed by Egypt. The kings of the east were the Chinese Communists. He [Lindsey] translated "fire and brimstone" into nuclear explosions and showed the chaos of the sixties as signs of the times.[58]

On the basis of what he observed, Lindsey predicted that the Rapture would occur, at the latest, in 1988.[59]

Lindsey's mantle was subsequently assumed by evangelical authors Tim LaHaye and Jerry Jenkins. The 16 volumes in their *Left Behind* series—so-named because those not taken into heaven at the Rapture would be left behind—have sold over 60 million copies in the United States and more than 700 million around the world.[60] Nearly 10 percent of adult Americans and nearly 20 percent of evangelicals in the United States have read one or more of the works.[61] Bearing titles such as *Tribulation Force, Glorious Appearing, The Regime, The Rapture,* and *Kingdom Come: The Final Victory,* the novels provide a fictional, premillennial dispensationalist account of the end times. Although, unlike Lindsey, Jenkins and LaHaye do not explicitly tie real-world persons and events to biblical prophecies, astute readers find it easy to do so. For example, the Anti-Christ, the Supreme Potentate of the Global Community, is the secretary-general of the United Nations in not-so-subtle disguise.[62]

The implications of premillennial dispensationalism for Middle East policy are obvious. For evangelicals eagerly awaiting the arrival of Christ and the establishment of his kingdom, the health and survival of Israel are crucial. A Palestinian state that would endanger Israel's security must be opposed. Settlements that might ultimately expand the territory of the Jewish state into the biblical areas of Samaria and Judea must be supported. Jerusalem must remain under Israel's control. At best, the Palestinian people and their aspirations are irrelevant. At worst, they are enemies of God and God's plan.

Evangelical leaders sometimes offer other biblical reasons why Israel must be supported so strongly. One is that aiding Israel is necessary if the United States is to earn God's favor. Ed McAteer, founder of the Moral Majority, along with Jerry Falwell and others, once noted that God promised Abraham, "I will bless them who bless you and curse them who curse you."[63] Falwell himself stated that "God had been kind to America only because 'America has been kind to the Jews.'"[64] A more important reason is the land promised to Abraham and his descendents in the Abrahamic Covenant. As recounted in Gen. 13.15: "The Lord said to Abram: 'Look about you, and from where you are, gaze to the north and south, east and west; all the land that you see I will give to you and your descendants forever.'" And in Gen. 15.18–21: "On that day the Lord made a covenant with Abram and said, 'To your descendants I give this land, from the river of Egypt to the great river, the Euphrates—the land of the Kenites, Kenizzites, Kadmonites, Hittites, Perizzites, Rephaites, Amorites, Canaanites, Girgashites and Jebusites.'"

Leaders within the evangelical community have been outspoken in advancing these views, often in combination with premillennial dispensationalism. Pat Robertson told his 700 Club audience that the land occupied by Israel is

> a permanent possession given by God to Abraham, and all of this territory is the land of Israel. There is no such thing as a Palestinian state, nor has there ever been. Now we're going to make something that never happened before in contravention to Scripture. God may love George Bush. God may love America. God may love us all. But if we stand in the way of prophecy and try to frustrate what God said in his immutable Word, then we're in for a heap of trouble. And I think this is a warning we all should take.
>
> The road map, as it is set up now, with the United Nations, with the European Union, and with the Russians coming together in the so-called quartet, these are all enemies of Israel. If we ally ourselves with the enemies of Israel, we will be standing against God Almighty.[65]

Similarly, John Hagee has written, in his book, *Final Dawn over Jerusalem*, that

> there can be no compromise regarding the city of Jerusalem, not now, not ever. We are racing toward the end of time, and Israel lies in the eye of the storm. . . . Israel is the only nation created by a sovereign act of God, and He has sworn by His holiness to defend Jerusalem, His holy city. If God created and defends Israel, those nations that fight against it fight against God.[66]

In February 2002, Hagee announced that his Cornerstone Church was giving more than $1 million to Israel to finance the settlement of Jews from the former Soviet Union in Jerusalem and the West Bank. Said Hagee, "We feel like the coming of Soviet Jews to Israel is a fulfillment of biblical prophecy." When asked whether he was concerned that his initiative might be illegal because it contradicted official U.S. policy in opposition to such settlements, Hagee replied, "I am a Bible scholar and a theologian and from my perspective, the law of God transcends the law of the United States government and the U.S. State Department."[67] Jerry Falwell, in July 2006, wrote that Americans needed to support Israel in part because "the founding of Israel as a nation in 1948 was ordained of God to provide a homeland for the Jewish people and to prepare for the future return of Jesus Christ."[68] Such pronouncements and activities—as of this writing, Hagee's ministries have contributed more than $3.7 million toward the resettlement of roughly 6,000 Jews—together with the war in Iraq led some observers to conclude that fundamentalist evangelicals had become "Armageddonites," moving "from forecasting Armageddon to actually trying to bring it about."[69]

The belief that Israel was and is God's gift to the Jewish people is by no means universal among evangelicals. But it is widespread. A 2006 survey found that nearly as many White Evangelical Protestants (71.6 percent) as Jews (73.7 percent) subscribed to the view that God gave the land of Israel to the Jews. Numbers for Non-Latino Catholics (30.7 percent), Latino Catholics (15.7 percent), and White Mainline Protestants (24.6 percent) were much lower.[70] The same is true of pre-millennial dispensationalism. According to one 1999 poll, nearly three-quarters of Evangelical Protestants are convinced "that Armageddon will unfold as described by the book of Revelation."[71] A 2003 Pew survey found that more than 60 percent of evangelicals believe that the emergence of the state of Israel in 1948 fulfills the biblical prophecy that Israel must be refounded before the Second Coming can occur.[72]

At the denominational level, the picture is complicated. Some Evangelical Protestant denominations explicitly reject premillennial dispensationalism. The Christian Reformed Church and the Lutheran Church—Missouri Synod are two of these, reflecting their Reformed and Lutheran traditions, respectively (see below). Other evangelical denominations officially accept the doctrine. The Evangelical Free Church of America (EFCA) believes "in the personal, bodily and premillennial return of our Lord Jesus Christ."[73] Still other denominations take no position. Premillennial dispensationalist thinking pervades the Southern Baptist Convention. Historian Timothy Weber has labeled the SBC dispensationalism's "biggest success story."[74] Language suggestive of premillennialist eschatology can be found in some of the SBC's denominational documents. For example, the resolution, "On Praying for Peace in the Middle East," expresses support for the 1947 decision by the international community to "re-establish" the nation of Israel.[75] Nevertheless, in 2000, the SBC adopted a "judiciously written" statement on "Last Things" that, according to one Baptist theologian, "provides insight into some of the most significant events in the future and at the same time can be embraced by believers from various millennial perspectives."[76]

Among the largest Evangelical Protestant denominations, the Assemblies of God (AOG) are the strongest proponents of premillennial dispensationalist theology. According to the church, "Israel has an important role to play in the end-times. . . . When the modern nation of Israel was founded in 1948, and Jews began returning from all over the world, Bible scholars knew that God was at work and that we were very likely living in the last days." While the AOG are in sentiment pro-Israel, the denomination does not offer its unconditional support for the Jewish state. Declares the church, "Though we have emotional ties and affections with Israel, we cannot endorse and approve every action of a particular country whether right or wrong." Rather than involve itself in Middle East policy, the historically apolitical denomination focuses on the Great Commission and the Christian duty to bring the message of salvation to Muslim and Jew alike: "We must remember that millions on both sides of this end-times conflict need to come to a faith in Jesus Christ."[77]

Conclusive links between end-times theology and Middle East policy preferences can be hard to establish at the official, denominational level, but they are clear among denominational clergy. James Guth's analysis of data from the Cooperative Clergy Study Project found that "the strongest support for Israel appears in denominations most influenced by dispensationalism and premillennialism: the Assemblies of God, the Evangelical Free Church and the Southern Baptist Convention." This pattern also prevailed among the laity. Eighty-five percent of those regularly attending services of the Assemblies of God favored Israel in the Arab–Israeli conflict, while only 35 percent of United Methodist parishioners and 19 percent of Presbyterians did so. Differences between Evangelical and Mainline Protestant laypersons were even starker among those who had heard their pastor speak on the Middle East. At the extremes, 92 percent of those attending services in churches of the Assemblies of God favored Israel, as compared to a mere 1 percent of Presbyterians.[78] An earlier statistical analysis by Guth and others revealed that premillennial dispensationalism consistently "predicts positive assessments of Israel" within each Christian tradition and at every level, from clergy to laity— even among the mass public.[79] Also testing the theological connection, John Green found that among those who believed that Israel was the fulfillment of biblical prophecy, nearly two-thirds favored Israel in its dispute with the Palestinians, while fewer than 40 percent of those who did not believe Israel was the fulfillment of prophecy took the same position. He discovered that the belief that Israel was God's gift to the Jewish people had a similar impact on attitudes. Among those who accepted this view, 63 percent expressed support for Israel, while among those who did not accept it, support for Israel dropped to only 38 percent.[80]

Because premillennial dispenstionalism rests on a literal interpretation of the Bible, and particularly of the prophecies on which it is based, Christians and Christian denominations that tend to read the Bible figuratively or allegorically are much less likely to subscribe to the doctrine. Since the time of Augustine, the Roman Catholic Church has adhered to an amillennialist position. Like other Christians, Catholics believe that, following his death and resurrection, Jesus ascended into heaven. It was this event, more than 2,000 years ago, which according to Catholic theology, marks the establishment of his kingdom. *The Cathechism of the Catholic Church* states:

> Being seated at the Father's right hand signifies the inauguration of the Messiah's kingdom, the fulfillment of the prophet Daniel's vision concerning the Son of man: "To him was given dominion and glory and kingdom, that all peoples, nations, and languages should serve him; his dominion is an everlasting dominion, which shall not pass away, and his kingdom one that shall not be destroyed."[81]

Most Mainline Protestant denominations also subscribe to amillennialism. As Paul Boyer has noted, Martin Luther initially dismissed the book of Revelation as "neither apostolic nor prophetic," and the Augsburg Confession, which constitutes the basis of much of Lutheran theology, condemned millennialism as "Jewish doctrine." John Calvin was more charitable, but he, too, had little use for premillennialism. "Both the Lutheran and the Reformed theological traditions, then, began with a strong amillennial bias and suspicion of end-times speculation that they retain to this day."[82] Although Charles Wesley, brother of Methodism's founder, John Wesley, seems to have had premillennialist leanings, the United Methodist Church also espouses an amillennial viewpoint. In their Episcopal Address to the 2000 General Conference of the UMC, the Council of Bishops proclaimed that

> The Kingdom of God is already at hand and at work. The age to come has already broken through. Already the crucified Christ has been raised as the first fruits of those who have died and now reigns as Lord. Already the ungodly are justified by faith, both those under and outside the Law. Already they are in Christ and form his body. Already the Spirit has been poured and shed abroad and the community of faith may already receive the gift and bear the fruits of the Spirit. Already a new future has dawned![83]

Because they are mainly amillennialists, Roman Catholics and Mainline Protestants do not attach any particular eschatological significance to Israel. In terms of the Second Coming, it is immaterial whether or not Israel continues to exist as a state, whether or not Jerusalem is divided, or whether or not Jews continue to live on the West Bank of the Jordan River.

Israel's lack of importance in Roman Catholic and Mainline Protestant eschatology may also be attributable to the long history of supersessionist doctrine in both the Catholic and Protestant traditions. Although the doctrine takes various forms, supersessionism—sometimes termed replacement theology or fulfillment theology—in essence holds that the Mosaic Covenant made by God with the Jewish people in the time of Moses was replaced or superseded by a New Covenant promising salvation through faith in the risen Christ. God's favor and his promises, in this view, were transferred from Jews to Christians and particularly the Christian church, the "new Israel." Evangelical Protestants, of course, like their mainline counterparts, are heirs to the Protestant tradition of supersessionism. Among evangelicals, however, this doctrine has been to a considerable degree supplanted by dispensationalism, with which it is largely incompatible. As Michael Vlach writes, replacement theology "rules out any future restoration of national Israel."[84]

In part because of the doctrine's anti-Semitic overtones, the Roman Catholic Church, at Vatican II, began to distance itself somewhat from supersessionism; a number of Mainline Protestant denominations also have done so. "Two-covenant theology," which holds that God's promises to the Jewish nation remain in effect alongside the New Covenant, has become increasingly influential in some quarters.[85] But two-covenant theory, like supersessionism, attaches little or no significance to Israel in terms of end-times theology.

Since eschatology does not drive their views on Middle East policy, the Roman Catholic Church and Mainline Protestant denominations are influenced more heavily by other considerations. In addition to their concern for justice and human rights, the historical interactions between these churches and Arab Christians may have an important effect. The Christian church originated in the Middle East, and there has been a strong Catholic (and Orthodox) presence ever since. Today, there are seven Catholic Churches in the Middle East, most of which are Arabic. The Latin Patriarchate of Jerusalem (Archdiocese of Jerusalem) is a formal division of the Roman Catholic Church operating in Israel, Jordan, Palestine, and Cyprus. The Maronite Church in Lebanon is also a part of the Roman Catholic Church. The other Catholic Churches in the region have organizations separate from Rome, and from one another, but they remain within what the Vatican calls the Universal Church and participate in a variety of common activities.

Protestant churches began, during the nineteenth century, to send missionaries to the region, and there are now at least 13 Protestant denominations in the Middle East. Many of these are part of or closely associated with large international and generally mainline churches. The Episcopal Diocese of Jerusalem, for example, which encompasses Israel, Jordan, Lebanon, Syria, and Palestine, is an arm of the same worldwide Anglican communion as the Episcopal Church in the United States. The Presbyterian Church of the Sudan, which was founded by American missionaries, has a close relationship with the Presbyterian Church (USA). The Evangelical Lutheran Church in Jordan and the Holy Land cooperates with the Evangelical Lutheran Church in America, but not with the Lutheran Church—Missouri Synod.

Most of the Catholic, Orthodox, and Protestant churches in the Middle East belong to the Middle East Council of Churches (MECC), a regional affiliate of the World Council of Churches, to which nearly all Mainline Protestant churches in the United States belong. Today, roughly 14 million Arab Christians live in the Middle East. Both the Roman Catholic Church and Mainline Protestant denominations have histories of cooperation with and institutional ties to this important, though often unappreciated element of the Arab world. These connections almost certainly help to explain the greater sympathy for Palestinians and other Arabs expressed by these churches, as compared to Evangelical Protestant ones.

Summary

There exist significant differences on Middle East policy among groups of Christians in the United States. These differences, and the reasons for them, are summarized in Table 5.1.

Evangelical Protestants, and especially fundamentalists, tend to be strongly pro-Israel and anti-Palestinian. The reasons for this have mainly to do with eschatology, and particularly with the importance attached to Israel in the sequence of events leading to the Second Coming of Jesus. Because Roman Catholic and Mainline Protestant end-times theology does not assign Israel any particular significance, these denominations and their believers are generally much more critical of the policies of the Israeli government and supportive of efforts to create a Palestinian state.

Since the election of Ronald Reagan in 1980, evangelical support for Israel has influenced U.S. policy in the Middle East. Although it seems doubtful that Reagan and subsequent Republican presidents, including George W. Bush,

Table 5.1: Views of U.S. Christians Regarding Middle East Policy

	Mainline Protestants	Evangelical Protestants	Roman Catholics
Middle East Policy	Balanced, perhaps leaning toward a pro-Palestinian position; often critical of Israeli government policy and U.S. support for it; also critical of Palestinian terrorism; favor two-state solution, strong concern for rights of Palestinians	Markedly pro-Israel, especially among fundamentalists; tend to condemn Palestinian terrorism but not Israeli policy in the Occupied Territories; oppose two-state solution	Balanced; critical of both Israeli government policy and Palestinian terrorism; support Israeli security, but not punitive anti-Palestinian measures; Church has pushed U.S. government to oppose Israeli actions violating the Roadmap to Peace; favor two-state solution
Eschatology	Mostly amillennialist; do not believe state of Israel has eschatological significance	Often premillennialist and dispensationalist, especially among fundamentalists; believe formation of state of Israel is a fulfillment of biblical prophecy and heralds the Second Coming of Jesus; survival of the state of Israel is crucial to further fulfillment of biblical prophecy	Officially amillennialist; do not believe state of Israel has eschatological significance
Non-Eschatological Reasons to Support Israel	None; tend to believe that the covenant between God and Abraham has been superseded by the "new covenant" embodied in Jesus' death and resurrection; historical and institutional ties to Arab Christians	Often believe that those who favor Israel will be blessed by God; also that the covenant between God and Abraham, granting Israel the land of Palestine, is still in effect	None; tend to believe that the covenant between God and Abraham has been superseded by the "new covenant" embodied in Jesus' death and resurrection; historical and institutional ties to Arab Christians

themselves subscribed to a fundamentalist eschatology, it is clear that the need to maintain, if not increase, the support of their conservative Christian political base made them reluctant to criticize Israeli policy or to put pressure on the Israeli government to pursue a permanent settlement in the region. Evangelical opposition to the Roadmap to Peace, for example, contributed to the lukewarm commitment of the Bush administration to the very agreement that it had helped negotiate. While the Roman Catholic bishops and many Mainline Protestant denominations have consistently pushed both Congress and the executive branch of the U.S. government to adopt a more balanced Middle East policy, their efforts have thus far been largely unsuccessful.

Notes

1. "Camp David: The Framework for Peace in the Middle East," September 17, 1978, www.usembassy-israel.org.il/publish/peace/campdav.htm; and "Camp David: Annex to the Framework Agreements," www.usembassy-israel.org.il/publish/peace/cdappend.htm.
2. "Declaration of Principles on Interim Self-Government Arrangements," www.usembassy-israel.org.il/publish/peace/decprinc.htm.
3. Arafat to Rabin, September 9, 1993, www.usembassy-israel.org.il/publish/peace/isplorec.htm.
4. "A Performance-Based Roadmap to a Permanent Two-State Solution to the Israeli-Palestinan Conflict," www.un.org/media/main/roadmap122002.html.
5. A good history of these efforts is William B. Quandt, *Peace Process: American Diplomacy and the Arab-Israeli Conflict since 1967*, 3rd ed. (Washington, DC: Brookings Institution, 2005).
6. Mearsheimer and Walt, "The Israel Lobby."
7. Donald Wagner, "Evangelicals and Israel: Theological Roots of a Political Alliance," *Christian Century*, November 4, 1998, www.religion-online.org/showarticle.asp?title=216.
8. Wagner, "Evangelicals and Israel."
9. Quoted in Wagner, "Evangelicals and Israel."
10. Wagner, "Evangelicals and Israel."
11. Steven Erlanger, "Netanyahu, In U.S., Woos Conservatives," *New York Times*, January 20, 1998, www.nytimes.com/1998/01/20/world/netanyahu-in-us-woos-conservatives.html.
12. Wagner, "Evangelicals and Israel."
13. Quoted in Laurie Goodstein, "Falwell to Mobilize Support for Israel," *New York Times*, January 21, 1998, www.nytimes.com/1998/01/21/world/falwell-to-mobilize-support-for-israel.html.
14. Bob Simon, "Zion's Christian Soldiers: The '60 Minutes' Transcript," *Washington Report on Middle East Affairs*, December 2002, www.wrmea.com/archives/december02/0212068.html.
15. Mary Jayne McKay, "Falwell Brands Mohammed a 'Terrorist,'" *CBS News*, October 6, 2002, www.cbsnews.com/stories/2003/06/05/60minutes/main557187.shtml.
16. Pat Robertson, "Israel and the Road Map to Peace," www.patrobertson.com/Teaching/TeachingonRoadMap.asp.
17. Sarah Posner, "Pastor Strangelove," *The American Prospect*, May 21, 2006, www.prospect.org/cs/articles?articleId=11541.
18. CUFI, "About CUFI," www.cufi.org/site/PageServer?pagename=about_AboutCUFI.
19. Robert O. Smith, "Between Restoration and Liberation: Theopolitical Contributions and Responses to U.S. Foreign Policy in Israel/Palestine," *Journal of Church and State,* 36, no. 4 (Autumn 2004): 846, *Expanded Academic ASAP*. Web.

20. "Evangelicals Ask Bush for Even Mideast Tack," *The Christian Century*, 119, no. 16 (July 31, 2002): 2, www.proquest.com.
21. Peggy L. Shriver, "Evangelicals and World Affairs," *World Policy Journal*, 23, no. 3 (Fall 2006): 54, *Expanded Academic ASAP*. Web.
22. Jeremy D. Mayer, "Christian Fundamentalists and Public Opinion toward the Middle East: Israel's New Best Friends?" *Social Science Quarterly*, 85, no. 3 (September 2004): 695–712, www3.interscience.wiley.com/cgi-bin/fulltext/118763830/HTMLSTART.
23. Timothy P. Weber, "How Evangelicals Became Israel's Best Friend," *Christianity Today*, October 5, 1998, www.christianitytoday.com/ct/8tb/8tb038.html.
24. Episcopal Church, "Executive Council Resolution: Urging Israeli/Palestinian Negotiations Based on UN Resolutions 242 + 338," Executive Council Resolution 022, June 18, 2002, www.episcopalchurch.org/1866_70067_ENG_HTM.htm.
25. Frank T. Griswold, "Presiding Bishop's Letter to Bush on Middle East Crisis," *Episcopal News Service*, April 21, 2004, www.episcopalchurch.org/3577_37591_ENG_HTM.htm.
26. Episcopal Church, "Response to the Treatment of Detainees, the Situation in Iraq, and Palestine/Israel Peace Proposals," Executive Council Resolution INC 024, June 18, 2004, www.episcopalchurch.org/1866_70811_ENG_HTM.htm.
27. Episcopal Church, "Executive Council Resolution: On Israeli-Palestinian Relations," Executive Council Resolution INC 007, November 27, 2006, www.episcopalchurch.org/1866_81178_ENG_HTM.htm.
28. Episcopal Church, "Executive Council Resolution: On Israeli-Palestinian Relations," Executive Council Resolution INC 006, November 27, 2006, www.episcopalchurch.org/1866_81177_ENG_HTM.htm.
29. UMC, "Opposition to Israeli Settlements on Palestinian Land," *Book of Resolutions–2004*, http://archives.umc.org/interior_print.asp?ptid=4&mid=6855.
30. ELCA, "Separation Wall in Palestine," Council Action CC05.04.19, http://archive.elca.org/socialpolicyresolutions/resolution.asp?id=167&ref=rrt.
31. NCC, "Resolution on the Conflict in the Middle East," www.ncccusa.org/news/03separationwall.html.
32. William S. Skylstad, "Letter to Ambassador Daniel Ayalon on Negotiations between Israel and the Holy See," January 18, 2005, www.usccb.org/sdwp/international/ayalon011805.shtml.
33. NCCB, *Toward Peace in the Middle East: Perspectives, Principles, and Hopes*, November 1989, www.usccb.org/sdwp/international/TowardPeaceintheMiddleEast.pdf.
34. USCCB, "Resolution on the Israeli-Palestinian Crisis," June 15, 2001, www.usccb.org/sdwp/international/resolution.shtml.
35. USCCB, "Statement on Israeli-Palestinian Violence," March 13, 2002, www.usccb.org/sdwp/international/mideastind/stat302.shtml.
36. Wilton B. Gregory, "Letter to President Bush on the Road Map for Peace in the Middle East," May 30, 2003, www.usccb.org/sdwp/international/bush503.shtml.
37. Wilton B. Gregory, "Letter to President Bush on Deteriorating Situation in the Holy Land," April 13, 2004, www.usccb.org/sdwp/international/bush404.shtml.
38. Wilton B. Gregory, "A Statement Concerning U.S. Support for Sharon Initiative," www.usccb.org/sdwp/international/ricard404.shtml.
39. Thomas G. Wenski, "Letter to Henry Hyde on U.S. Policy in Palestine," March 1, 2006, www.usccb.org/sdwp/international/letterMarch1rehearingonpalestineaidfinal.pdf.

40. Thomas G. Wenski, "Letter to Chairman Henry Hyde on the Amendment to the Palestinian Anti-Terrorism Act of 2006," April 6, 2006, www.usccb.org/sdwp/international/2006–04 -HydeLetter.pdf.

41. USCCB, "Action Alert: Palestinian Aid and Engagement for Peace Ask Representatives to Oppose HR 4681," May 8, 2006, www.usccb.org/sdwp/international/aa050806.shtml.

42. Thomas G. Wenski, "Letter to Richard Lugar on the Palestinian Anti-Terrorism Act," May 25, 2006, www.usccb.org/sdwp/international/2006–05Lugarletter.pdf.

43. For the final version of the bill, see www.govtrack.us/congress/billtext.xpd?bill=s109–2370. The original Senate version is at www.govtrack.us/congress/billtext.xpd?bill=s109–2370&version=is. The version initially passed by the House is at www.govtrack.us/congress/billtext.xpd?bill=h109–4681.

44. Thomas G. Wenski, "Break the Cycle of Violence in the Holy Land," July 17, 2006, www.usccb.org/sdwp/international/2006July17HolyLandstatement.pdf.

45. Thomas G. Wenski, "Letter to Congress on Cycle of Violence in the Middle East," July 20, 2006, www.usccb.org/sdwp/international/2006 July 19 cover note to congress.pdf.

46. USCCB, "Action Report on Middle East Crisis: Request U.S. Leadership to Achieve an Immediate Ceasefire, Deliver Humanitarian Aid and Seek Political Solutions," August 1, 2006, www.usccb.org/sdwp/international/MiddleEastCrisis080106.pdf.

47. The text of the letter is at www.usccb.org/sdwp/international/2007-01Ecumenical-Letter pdf.

48. NILI's website is at www.nili-mideastpeace.org.

49. NILI, "Twelve Urgent Steps for Peace," December 2, 2003, nili-mideastpeace.org/downloads/2003_12TwelveUrgentSteps.pdf.

50. A list of the major documents produced by NILI, with links to each of them, is at www.nili-mideastpeace.org/advocacy.html.

51. NILI, "Highlights," www.nili-mideastpeace.org/highlights.html.

52. Wagner, "Evangelicals and Israel"; Jody C. Baumgartner, Peter L. Francia, and Jonathan Morris, "A Clash of Civilizations? The Influence of Religion on Public Opinion of U.S. Foreign Policy in the Middle East," *Political Research Quarterly*, 61, no. 2 (June 2008): 173, www.jstor.org/stable/20299723.

53. Wagner, "Evangelicals and Israel."

54. Timothy P. Weber, *Living in the Shadow of the Second Coming: American Premillennialism, 1875–1982* (Chicago, Il: University of Chicago Press, 1987), 9.

55. Tony Campolo, "The Ideological Roots of Christian Zionism," *Tikkun*, 20, no. 1 (January–February 2005): 19–20, www.tikkun.org/article.php/Campolo-roots-of-christian-zionism.

56. 1 Thess. 4.16–17.

57. Campolo, "Ideological Roots of Christian Zionism," 19–20.

58. Weber, "How Evangelicals Became Israel's Best Friend."

59. Campolo, "Ideological Roots of Christian Zionism," 20.

60. Campolo, "Ideological Roots of Christian Zionism," 20.

61. Baumgartner, Francia, and Morris, "Clash of Civilizations?" 173.

62. The *Left Behind* series has an official website at www.leftbehind.com.

63. Quoted in Doug Bandow, "Crackpot Theology Makes Bad Foreign Policy," June 4, 2002, www.cato.org/dailys/06-04-02.html.

64. Quoted in Doug Bandow, "Crackpot Theology Makes Bad Foreign Policy."

65. Robertson, "Israel and the Road Map to Peace."
66. Quoted in Paul S. Boyer, "When U.S. Foreign Policy Meets Biblical Prophecy," *Alternet*, February 20, 2003, www.alternet.org/story/15221.
67. Wagner, "Evangelicals and Israel." See also Smith, "Between Restoration and Liberation," 855.
68. Falwell's remarks are at www.falwell.com/index.cfm?PID=13838.
69. Jon Basil Utley, "America's Armageddonites," *Antiwar.com*, October 11, 2007, www.antiwar.com/utley/?articleid=11735.
70. John C. Green, "The American Public and Sympathy for Israel: Present and Future," *Journal of Ecumenical Studies*, 44, no. 1 (Winter 2009): 7.
71. Baumgartner, Francia, and Morris, "Clash of Civilizations?" 173.
72. Shriver, "Evangelicals and World Affairs," 54.
73. EFCA, "Statement of Faith," adopted June 26, 2008, www.efca.org/about-efca/statement-faith.
74. Quoted in Cory J. Hailey, "SBC is 'Biggest Success Story' of Dispensationalism, Prof Says," *Baptist Press*, February 11, 1999, www.bpnews.net/bpnews.asp?id=1216.
75. SBC, "On Praying for Peace in the Middle East," June 2002, www.sbc.net/resolutions/amResolution.asp?ID=1116
76. William F. Cook, "Baptist Faith and Message, Article 10: Last Things," *Baptist Press*, August 28, 2002, www.bpnews.net/BPnews.asp?ID=14124.
77. AOG, "Israel—the Church's Response," http://ag.org/top/Beliefs/sptlissues_israel.cfm.
78. James L. Guth, "Religious Leadership and Support for Israel: A Study of Clergy in Nineteen Denominations." Presented at the annual meeting of the Southern Political Science Association, January 3–7, 2007.
79. James L. Guth, Cleveland R. Fraser, John C. Green, Lyman A. Kellstedt, and Corwin E. Smidt, "Religion and Foreign Policy Attitudes: The Case of Christian Zionism," in *Religion and the Culture Wars: Dispatches from the Front*, ed. Green, Guth, Smidt, and Kellstedt (Lanham, MD: Rowman & Littlefield, 1996), 353.
80. Green, "American Public and Sympathy for Israel," 9, 8.
81. *Catechism of the Catholic Church*, Part 2, 664, www.usccb.org/catechism/text/pt1sect2chpt2art6.shtml.
82. Paul Boyer, *When Time Shall Be No More: Prophecy Belief in Modern American Culture* (Cambridge, MA: Belknap/Harvard University Press, 1992), 60–61.
83. UMC, "Discipleship at the Turn of the Ages," The Episcopal Address, The General Conference, 2000, Cleveland, Ohio, www.gc2000.org/articles/episcopal_address.htm.
84. Michael J. Vlach, "Defining Supersessionism," www.theologicalstudies.org/articles/article/1546226/17515.htm.
85. Kenneth A. Myers, "CT Classic: Do Jews Really Need Jesus?" *Christianity Today*, August 2002 (web only), www.christianitytoday.com/ct/2002/augustweb-only/8-12-52.0.html.

CHAPTER 6

International Law and Institutions

George Washington, in his farewell address, famously advised his countrymen to "have as little political connection as possible" with foreign states. In 1796, this meant with Europe. And "Europe," Washington declared,

> has a set of primary interests, which to us have none, or a very remote relation. Hence she must be engaged in frequent controversies, the causes of which are essentially foreign to our concerns. Hence therefore it must be unwise to implicate ourselves, by artificial ties, in the ordinary vicissitudes of her politics, or the ordinary combinations and collisions of her friendships, or enmities.[1]

Why should the United States, asked the first president rhetorically, "by interweaving our destiny with that of any part of Europe, entangle our peace and prosperity in the toils of European ambition, rivalship, interest, humor, or caprice?"[2]

Washington warned only against political connections with other states and in fact advocated "extending our commercial relations" with them.[3] Moreover, this "great rule of conduct," as he referred to it, was intended to be temporary, "to buy time for American political institutions, and a distinctive American character, to mature." Washington believed that after a relatively short period—perhaps two decades or so—"a strong, self-sufficient America would be in a position to dictate its future political, strategic, and economic relationship with the European powers, rather than the other way around. In the meantime, and perhaps thereafter, the United States could rely on temporary alliances to see them through emergencies."[4]

Nevertheless, Washington's words were interpreted long thereafter as recommending isolationism as the appropriate posture for the United States in world affairs. More than a century later, they were in part responsible for the inability of Woodrow Wilson to lead the United States into the League of Nations following World War I, as well as for the failure of the United States, during the 1930s, to enter into alliances with Britain and the Soviet Union that might conceivably have prevented war with Nazi Germany and Imperial Japan. President Harry Truman recounted in his memoirs that "throughout my years in the Senate I listened each year as one of the senators would read Washington's Farewell Address . . . for the isolationists this address was like a biblical text."[5]

Changing international conditions and especially the coming of World War II meant the end of American isolation. For the second half of the twentieth century and the early years of the twenty-first, the United States has been actively engaged in international affairs. In the 1940s, it was a founding member of the United Nations.

Its leadership was essential to the conclusion of the General Agreement on Tariffs and Trade, the establishment of the Bretton Woods monetary system, and the formation of the North Atlantic Treaty Organization. Today, the United States participates in a large number of international organizations and is signatory to a vast array of international accords ranging from the North American Free Trade Agreement to various human rights conventions. Interest in international cooperation and the respect for international law and institutions demonstrated by the U.S. government has varied somewhat over the years. The administration of President George W. Bush, which withdrew the United States from the Anti-Ballistic Missile (ABM) Treaty with Russia, invaded Iraq in defiance of the United Nations Security Council, and tortured suspected terrorists in violation of the Geneva Conventions, was less inclined toward multilateralism than most. But the United States is now, and will continue in the future to be, engaged globally on a massive scale.

Christian groups in the United States have somewhat different views concerning international cooperation and participation in it by the United States. Mainline Protestants and Roman Catholics generally encourage collaboration among states and support the institutionalization of this cooperation in the form of international law and institutions. They regard movement in the direction of greater global community as a positive development. In particular, they view the United Nations as an important and potentially powerful, though imperfect, source of good in the world. Evangelical Protestants, on the other hand, tend to take a dimmer view of international cooperation and its institutional manifestations.

Mainline Protestants

During the 1930s and early 1940s, many Mainline Protestant leaders, still distressed by the terrible carnage of World War I, clung to a pacifist and hence largely isolationist position. Others, the so-called Christian Realists, most notably Reinhold Niebuhr, argued that the United States must actively oppose the Axis Powers. In any event, as World War II progressed, most mainline denominations became strong supporters of efforts at international cooperation, and of U.S. participation in these efforts. John Foster Dulles, son of a Presbyterian minister and later secretary of state under President Dwight Eisenhower, headed the Commission to Study the Bases of a Just and Durable Peace (CJDP) established by the Federal Council of Churches (FCC) to formulate a plan for postwar cooperation based on Christian principles. Under his direction, the FCC issued its famous "Six Pillars of Peace" in March 1943:

1. The peace must provide the political framework for a continuing collaboration of the United Nations and, in due course, of neutral and enemy nations.
2. The peace must make provision for bringing under international supervision those economic and financial acts of national governments that have widespread international repercussions.
3. The peace must make provision for an organization to adapt the treaty structure of the world to changing underlying conditions.

4. The peace must proclaim the goal of autonomy for subject people, and it must establish international organization to assure and to supervise the realization of that end.
5. The peace must establish procedures for controlling military establishments everywhere.
6. The peace must establish in principle, and seek to achieve in practice, the right of individuals everywhere to religious and intellectual liberty.[6]

The appearance of the Six Pillars of Peace marked the beginning of a well organized, highly orchestrated public relations campaign intended to swing popular opinion behind an internationalist foreign policy. Copies of the document were sent to Protestant churches across the country, as well as to Protestant chaplains in the U.S. armed services. Articles promoting it appeared in more than 100 U.S. newspapers.[7] The major mainline denominations—Methodists, Presbyterians, Congregationalists, Northern Baptists—"mobilized massive numbers of churchgoers to write letters to Congress and the White House urging 'international cooperation' in organizing the post-war world." Washington was flooded with mail.[8]

It is difficult to know whether or not the influence of Mainline Protestant leaders and organizations was decisive in causing the U.S. public and members of Congress to abandon the isolationism of the 1930s and embrace international organization. What is clear is that, as William Inboden writes, "America's mainline Protestant leaders, or the 'churchmen' as they were widely known, enjoyed considerable success during the war years in generating popular support for the United Nations."[9] And this was not the extent of their influence. Through the FCC and the Foreign Missions Conference of North America (FMCNA), the mainline churches played an important role in the development of the U.N. Charter and the organization itself.[10] Following the Dumbarton Oaks Conference in Washington in August 1944, the U.S. State Department, seeking to sway public opinion in favor of the draft agreement for the formation of the United Nations, arranged meetings to discuss the draft with a number of civic and religious groups, including the Rotary Club, the League of Women Voters, the American Bar Association, and the National Association for the Advancement of Colored People (NAACP). Among these groups was the Federal Council of Churches. A review of the draft by the FCC's Commission to Study the Bases of a Just and Durable Peace in January 1945 produced nine proposed amendments to the Dumbarton Oaks agreement. These called for

an explicit statement of intent to develop and codify international law, and create an agency for hastening decolonization; provisions for prompt disarmament, the protection of smaller nations against subjection to the mighty, and for membership eventually to be universal; establishment of a Commission on Human Rights and Fundamental Freedoms in addition to the proposed Economic and Social Council to uphold the sacred worth of the individual and protect the free exercise of religion; and above all, a declaration in the preamble that the purpose of the international body was to promote human welfare and worldwide justice.[11]

These amendments were brought to the United Nations Conference on International Organization (UNCIO, the San Francisco Conference), which began in late April of 1945, by the U.S. delegation, to which John Foster Dulles served as an adviser. Four were adopted and became part of the U.N. Charter. "These included language in the preamble stating the moral purposes of the UN, a commitment to developing customary international law, the formation of the Trusteeship Council to assist colonial peoples' transition to democratic rule, and a declaration of universal human rights."[12]

More than half a century later, the commitment of Mainline Protestants to international cooperation remains strong. The forces of globalization—economic, social, and political—they contend, demand the formation of a world community because in its absence the problems generated by increasing global interconnectedness cannot be addressed successfully. The United Methodist Church holds that

> God's world is one world. The unity now being thrust upon us by technological revolution has far outrun our moral and spiritual capacity to achieve a stable world. The enforced unity of humanity, increasingly evident on all levels of life, presents the Church as well as all people with problems that will not wait for answer: injustice, war, exploitation, privilege, population, international ecological crisis, proliferation of arsenals of nuclear weapons, development of transnational business organizations that operate beyond the effective control of any governmental structure, and the increase of tyranny in all its forms. This generation must find viable answers to these and related questions if humanity is to continue on this earth. We commit ourselves as a Church to the achievement of a world community that is a fellowship of persons who honestly love one another. We pledge ourselves to seek the meaning of the gospel in all issues that divide people and threaten the growth of world community.[13]

The UMC regards the United Nations, as well as other international organizations, as essential to the formation of world community and the achievement of many goals to which the Church aspires:

> We endorse the United Nations, its related bodies, the International Court of Justice and the International Criminal Court as the best instruments now in existence to achieve a world of justice and law. . . . We urge acceptance for membership in the United Nations of all nations who wish such membership and who accept United Nations responsibility. We urge the United Nations to take a more aggressive role in the development of international arbitration of disputes and actual conflicts among nations by developing binding third-party arbitration. Bilateral or multilateral efforts outside of the United Nations should work in concert with, and not contrary to, its purposes.[14]

The United Nations, argues the UMC, is unique in its capacity to work toward global unity. It is "that singular international intergovernmental body that provides platforms for peoples and civil society, and nations and states, to come together to jointly seek and pursue peace and security, economic and social development, human rights, humanitarian assistance, and develop and enhance international law."[15] The UMC observes one Sunday each year as "United Nations Sunday," in recognition of the anniversary of the founding of the organization and its continued importance in world affairs.

Most other Mainline Protestant denominations have similarly positive views of international community and particularly of the United Nations. The Evangelical Lutheran Church in America, in its 1995 document, *For Peace in God's World*, advocated heightened levels of international cooperation. Specifically, the ELCA called for "increased respect for and adherence to international law," "efforts to strengthen the United Nations as a forum for international cooperation and peace," and "creation of an International Criminal Court."[16] In a 1999 document, "Pillars of Peace for the 21st Century," the National Council of Churches "reaffirm[ed] its support for the United Nations and call[ed] upon the United States government fully to support the United Nations in the fulfillment of its charter and in its highest calling to work for peace and justice for all the world's people." The NCC stated that "peace rooted in justice requires increased political collaboration and accountability within the United Nations system, among regional bodies, governments, local authorities, peoples' organizations, and global economic structures to seek the common good and equality for all."[17] The NCC and its member organizations publicly supported the formation of the International Criminal Court (ICC) and urged, unsuccessfully, the U.S. government to sign and ratify the Rome Treaty establishing it.[18]

Reflecting the importance they attach to the United Nations, many mainline churches, including the UMC, have formal, institutional links to that organization, which they lobby in support of causes they favor. The UMC's Church Center for the United Nations represents the denomination at the U.N., focusing on economic and social development, human rights, humanitarian affairs, international law, and peace and security.[19] The Presbyterian United Nations Office performs the same function, bearing "witness to Jesus Christ by advocating the concerns" of the church to the United Nations.[20] These concerns have included HIV/AIDS, Children's Rights, Global Racism, Human Trafficking, the ICC, the humanitarian situation in Iraq following the 2003 U.S. invasion of that country, Israel/Palestine, Sustainable Development, Terrorism, and Women's Rights.[21] The Evangelical Lutheran Church in America is represented at the United Nations by the Lutheran Office for World Community.[22] Since 1991, the Episcopal Church, together with other members of the worldwide Anglican Communion, has been represented by the Office of the Anglican Observer at the United Nations. The Office has concentrated on a list of issues very similar to those of the UMC and the PCUSA: women's rights, environment and sustainable development, children's rights, indigenous peoples, human rights, and economic and global security. It has

> advocated for peace in numerous areas around the world: in the Middle East; Africa; and in the Pacific. Under the aegis of the Anglican Observer's ministry, roundtable discussions in several regions of the United States and England are

being established with lay Muslims to explore the problems of civil society in addressing the growth of democracy, the rule of law, and human rights.[23]

According to the Observer's Office, this work is accomplished "through strategic discussions with personnel from the U.N. Department of Political Affairs, members of the Security Council, ambassadors and permanent mission staff, through news releases and news conference statements, and panel discussions involving government, UN and NGO [nongovernmental organization] personnel."[24] Most of the Mainline Protestant organizations listed above are accredited as NGOs by the United Nations and possess official consultative status with the U.N. Economic and Social Council (UNESCO) under the terms of Article 71 of the U.N. Charter, which authorizes UNESCO to make "suitable arrangements for consultation with non-governmental organizations which are concerned with matters within its competence."[25] They do not, in contrast to the Holy See, which represents the Roman Catholic Church (see below), participate in the General Assembly, nor do they play any role in the Security Council.

While they hold it in high regard and participate in its activities to the extent permitted, mainline denominations do not suggest that the United Nations is an ideal institution. The United Church of Christ (UCC), for example, has advocated reforming several of the U.N.'s key organs, including the Security Council, where membership and voting arrangements—especially the veto power of the five permanent members—have been under critical scrutiny since the end of the Cold War. Still, support for the organization itself remains strong. The UCC General Synod has called on the U.S. government "to increase U.S. contributions and commitments to U.N. projects." It expressed dismay at the Bush administration's "increasingly inflexible" policy on U.N. reform, which threatened withdrawal of political and financial support from the United Nations if changes satisfactory to Washington were not enacted.[26]

Mainline churches have in fact consistently pushed the U.S. government to support the United Nations in spite of its defects. In the late 1990s, when the United States was more than $1.5 billion in arrears in its financial obligations to the U.N., the National Council of Churches decided to make the issue of U.N. funding one of its "key legislative priorities."[27] Lobbying by the NCC may have contributed to the so-called Helms-Biden legislation, passed by Congress and signed by President Clinton in 1999, which authorized the payment of roughly three-quarters of the monies owed. The law, however, tied U.S. contributions to the United Nations to a series of U.N. reforms, some of which the United Nations was unwilling or unable to achieve. Thus, nearly a decade later, in 2008, the NCC dispatched a letter to members of Congress again "highlighting the status of unpaid U.S. obligations to the U.N." and "urging the U.S. debt be paid." The letter was signed by representatives of many of the major mainline denominations: the Evangelical Lutheran Church in America, the United Church of Christ, the United Methodist Church, the American Friends Service Committee, and the Presbyterian Church (USA).[28]

Perhaps the majority position of Mainline Protestants with respect to the United Nations is best summarized by the United Methodist Church's resolution, "In Support of the United Nations": "The world needs a new vision, a vision of peace rooted in justice, a vision of a world bound together in intentional community dedicated to the well-being of all people and all creation. The United Nations, however limited, represents the best efforts made so far by governments and peoples of the world toward such a vision."[29]

Roman Catholics

In December 1939, Pope Pius XII delivered a Christmas message outlining a plan for ending World War II and preserving the peace thereafter. The pope's "Five Point Peace Program" articulated the rights of all states to exist and be independent, and it emphasized the need for disarmament. More importantly, from the standpoint of this chapter, it envisioned the postwar establishment of an effective international organization that, unlike the failed League of Nations, would possess the capacity to make decisions and enforce them. During the late 1930s and early 1940s, the U.S. Catholic hierarchy had been largely isolationist, in part because its mainly Irish–American leadership found the idea of making common cause with Britain repulsive. As Joseph Rossi writes, the Five Point Program "committed the once isolationist American Catholic Church to the notion of participation in world organization with the United States as an undoubted principal."[30]

In principle, the Roman Catholic bishops in the United States, represented by the National Catholic Welfare Conference (NCWC) were, like most of their Mainline Protestant counterparts, in favor of a postwar international organization. The NCWC's 1944 "Statement on International Order" articulated the essential elements of such an institution:

> The international institution must be universal. It must seek to include, with due regard to basic equality of rights, all the nations, large and small, strong and weak. Its constitution must be democratic. While it is reasonable to set up a Security Council with limited membership, the Council must not be an instrument for imperialistic domination by a few powerful nations. Before it every nation must stand on its rights and not on its power. It must not allow any nation to sit in judgment in its own case.[31]

The NCWC argued for the creation of a world court, the codification of international law, and compulsory arbitration of disputes. Although the international institution, it declared, must never violate a state's sovereignty, this "did not absolve a nation from its obligations to the international community" and to the rights and welfare of its inhabitants. Sovereignty was, in short, less than absolute.[32]

From the perspective of the Catholic bishops, the plans for a United Nations organization that began to take shape at the Dumbarton Oaks Conference fell far short of fulfilling the criteria elaborated in their statement. Particularly objectionable were the veto power of the five permanent members of the Security Council and the compromises made by the Roosevelt administration on the human rights principles of the Atlantic Charter in an effort to placate the Soviet Union. The resistance of the U.S. government to membership for Franco's Spain (with its Catholic population) was another point of contention, as was Washington's refusal to push for the inclusion of the (Catholic) Polish government-in-exile. Although the Catholic Association for International Peace (CAIP) supported the Dumbarton Oaks proposals despite their perceived flaws, the NCWC, to which the CAIP was in theory subordinate, was more hostile. As late as early 1945, "owing to its size and international makeup, the Catholic Church in the United States, represented by the NCWC, posed the most significant sectarian threat to the Dumbarton proposals."[33]

Fortunately for the Truman administration, by the time the UNCIO opened in April, the Administrative Board of the NCWC had been persuaded by the CAIP that its efforts would be better directed toward modifying the Dumbarton Oaks proposals rather than attempting to scuttle them altogether. But these efforts were largely unsuccessful. Like the Mainline Protestant organizations, the U.S. Catholic hierarchy was represented at the San Francisco Conference by consultants to the U.S. delegation. Unlike their Protestant counterparts, the Catholic representatives frequently found themselves at loggerheads with the U.S. State Department, which was determined to secure Soviet cooperation and to maintain the dominance of the United States and its allies into the postwar era. At the end of World War II, the U.S. Catholic position regarding the United Nations was what one historian has described as "benign sufferance."[34] By 1946, however, as events in Eastern and Central Europe caused the collapse of U.S.-Soviet collaboration and the Truman administration moved in the direction of a more aggressive containment policy, the NCWC decided "on a course of maximum UN participation as the primary vehicle for a policy to forestall the spread of Soviet totalitarianism."[35]

Beginning in 1946, the American branch of the Roman Catholic Church was represented at the United Nations by the NCWC's Office for United Nations Affairs. This office served as the Division for U.N. Affairs of the National Conference of Catholic Bishops (NCCB) and the United States Catholic Conference (USCC). Led throughout its existence by Catherine Schaefer, a CAIP consultant to the U.S. delegation at the San Francisco Conference, the Office of U.N. Affairs was disbanded by the USCC/NCCB in 1972, ostensibly because its original *raison d'etre*, to represent the Church in the absence of an official Vatican presence, no longer existed since the appointment of a Vatican Observer in 1964. It seems clear in retrospect that financial and other considerations also played a role in the decision, which was opposed by other international Catholic organizations and by officials in Rome.[36]

The Second Vatican Council (commonly known as Vatican II) and especially the issuing by Pope John XXIII of his landmark encyclical, *Pacem in Terris*, marked a significant shift in Catholic thinking concerning international organization. As George Weigel has noted, *Pacem in Terris* articulated the notion that there existed "a universal common good" that could not be achieved by the existing system of independent nation-states. A "universal public authority" had to be created, with "the protection and promotion of human rights" as its "fundamental objectives." The document also envisioned cautious cooperation with totalitarian governments and called for general and complete disarmament. Underlying the encyclical was an optimism, which critics saw as naïve utopianism, regarding the possibility of achieving significant levels of international cooperation in a world of self-interested individuals and states.[37] In many respects, *Pacem in Terris*, as Paul Ramsey observed, was almost indistinguishable from Mainline Protestant documents addressing the same issues:

> The highest tribute to be paid the encyclical is that—both in tone and substance— the pontiff sounds so much like a liberal Protestant parson. This is also a way to express succinctly the chief criticism to be made: the encyclical sounds too much like liberal Protestant statements which, while rightly stressing what positively needs to be done for the attainment of the universal common good, fail to grapple with the problem of power except in *those* terms.[38]

The Roman Catholic Church does not merely support the United Nations. It is, for all intents and purposes, a member of the organization. It enjoys this privilege because, unique among Christian denominations—among the world's religions, in fact—it controls a state: Vatican City. This state is governed by the Holy See (or Apostolic See), technically the ecclesial jurisdiction and associated bureaucratic apparatus of the Bishop of Rome (the pope) and effectively the central government of the Church. The Holy See has been involved in international diplomacy since the fourth century, well before the formation of the no-longer-existing Papal States and the establishment of Vatican City under the terms of the Lateran Treaty in 1929. Internationally, the Holy See represents Vatican City and enters into agreements on its behalf. It currently enjoys normal diplomatic relations with 174 of the 192 member states of the United Nations.[39]

The Holy See holds Non-Member State Permanent Observer status at the United Nations. It is the only entity to have this status; the Palestinian Authority also maintains a permanent observer mission, but it is not a state. Although the Holy See does not possess the right to vote on General Assembly resolutions, it does enjoy many of the rights of member states, including "the right to participate in the general debate of the General Assembly; the right of reply; the right to have its communications issued and circulated directly as official documents of the Assembly; and the right to co-sponsor draft resolutions and decisions that make reference to the Holy See."[40] As a state recognized by the United Nations, the Holy See is entitled to full membership but has not sought to attain it, officially because of its desire to maintain a neutral stance on "specific political problems."[41] (For much the same reason, Switzerland was a longtime Non-Member State Permanent Observer, becoming a full member only in 2002.) It should be noted, however, that the permanent observer status of the

Holy See has not been without controversy; the Holy See is not itself a state (though Vatican City is), and it has often been argued that the granting of permanent observer status to the Holy See gives rights of statehood to what is fundamentally a religious organization, rights that are possessed by no other religious entity. In 1999, Catholics for Choice, a group that opposes the Church's staunch antiabortion position, initiated a "See Change" campaign in an attempt to convince the United Nations to review the permanent observer status of the Holy See and to revoke it, contending that, like other religious organizations, including Mainline Protestant ones, the Holy See should be treated by the United Nations as a nongovernmental organization.[42] The effort was eventually joined by more than 400 other organizations. Confronted with a countercampaign mounted by pro-life groups, including U.S. evangelical organizations such as James Dobson's Focus on the Family, Chuck Colson's Prison Fellowship, and the National Association of Evangelicals, See Change never came close to success.[43] Still, a request by the Holy See for full membership in the United Nations could easily provoke a political free-for-all, and an anti-Catholic backlash, which the Church would surely prefer to avoid.

As a quasi-member of the United Nations, the Roman Catholic Church participates actively in the organization. The Permanent Observer of the Holy See has made numerous statements in General Assembly discussions and at sessions of other U.N. organs, including the Security Council, the Disarmament Commission, the Commission on Sustainable Development, and a wide variety of committees.[44] The Holy See's Mission has organized a variety of events in association with the United Nations, including a "Peace on Earth" symposium commemorating the fortieth anniversary of the issuing of the papal encyclical, *Pacem in Terris*, in 2003.[45] Popes have addressed the U.N. General Assembly on three occasions, most recently in April 2008, when Benedict XVI told the delegations gathered in New York that

> Through the United Nations, States have established universal objectives which, even if they do not coincide with the total common good of the human family, undoubtedly represent a fundamental part of that good. The founding principles of the Organization—the desire for peace, the quest for justice, respect for the dignity of the person, humanitarian cooperation and assistance—express the just aspirations of the human spirit, and constitute the ideals which should underpin international relations.[46]

He continued, "My presence at this Assembly is a sign of esteem for the United Nations, and it is intended to express the hope that the Organization will increasingly serve as a sign of unity between States and an instrument of service to the entire human family."[47]

In part because of its belief that only the United Nations could legitimately authorize a war against Iraq, the Roman Catholic Church opposed the invasion planned and carried out by the United States in the spring of 2003. Asked in September 2002, whether U.S. military action in Iraq would be justified, Cardinal Joseph Ratzinger, head of the Church's Congregation for the Doctrine of the Faith and the man who would later become Pope Benedict XVI, replied that it would not. "The United Nations," stated Ratzinger, "exists. It must make the decisive choice."[48]

In the United States, the United States Conference of Catholic Bishops consistently pushed the Bush administration to work through the United Nations rather than to act unilaterally. In June 2004, more than a year after the invasion, the bishops stated that

A new Iraq cannot be imposed by the United States or any other occupying power. As the Holy Father said in his recent meeting with President George W. Bush, "It is the evident desire of everyone that this situation now be normalized as quickly as possible with the active participation of the international community and, in particular, the United Nations Organization, in order to ensure a speedy return of Iraq's sovereignty, in conditions of security for all its people." We are encouraged by the new efforts of the United States to work with the United Nations to ensure that Iraqis have the means and a clear plan for reassuming their sovereign responsibilities. Continued support for an active UN role seems critical to ensuring the success of this process.[49]

More generally, the bishops wrote,

The war and occupation in Iraq have raised fundamental questions about the U.S. role in the world. These include the need to find ways other than preventive war to deal with challenges posed by the proliferation of weapons of mass destruction and terrorism; to abide by strict limits on the use of military force; and to strengthen the United Nations and respect international law, including the Geneva Conventions. Our nation cannot accept a permissive interpretation of international law, the inevitability of civilian casualties or the abuse of human rights, or an over-reliance on military responses to the problem of global terrorism. The United States would contribute to an improvement in the international situation if it adopted a collaborative approach based on respectful consideration of the viewpoints of others, as part of a broader effort to develop a global system of cooperative security.[50]

The U.S. bishops have emphasized international cooperation and collaboration with the United Nations by the U.S. government on issues besides Iraq. In September 2006, for example, Bishop Thomas Wenski, head of the USCCB's Committee on International Policy, issued a statement urging the administration and congressional leaders to work toward peace in Darfur and welcoming their support of a U.N. Security Council resolution authorizing the United Nations to take over peacekeeping operations in Southern Sudan.[51] Although it has consistently advocated against U.S. funding for U.N. programs that promote family planning and abortion, the USCCB has otherwise called on the U.S. government to fulfill its financial obligations to the United Nations. Like the mainline churches, it has opposed administration and Congressional efforts to withhold fiscal contributions as a signal of displeasure with certain U.N. policies and/or as stimulus to U.N. reform. A July 2001, letter from the chair of the USCCB's Committee on International Policy to members of the Senate Foreign Relations Committee is representative of these efforts. The letter noted that although the recent loss of the U.S. seat on the U.N. Human Rights Commission was a "serious matter," it did "not justify a delay in payment of our agreed outstanding debts. Given the global importance of the UN and U.S. leadership there and in the world, we urge you to support payment of our dues and to fund fully the agreed current dues assessment, including peacekeeping operations."[52]

Evangelical Protestants

Evangelical Protestant skepticism regarding the possibility of world community and opposition to U.S. participation in efforts aimed at international cooperation were evident in the early years of the twentieth century, when conservative evangelicals fought the formation of the League of Nations.[53] During World War II, the National Association of Evangelicals was formed in part to counter the internationalist postwar agenda of the Federal Council of Churches, which included the future United Nations. As Inboden notes, "The NAE did not share any of the American mainline's enthusiasm for the UN." Doubtful that communist states and their peoples would abide by international legal strictures, the NAE recommended that instead of trying to achieve the codification of international law the United States should work to boost the efforts of Christian missionaries, so that the sense of "moral responsibility" of peoples around the world would be enhanced. In 1950, the NAE declared its opposition to "vague proposals for world federation and world government," complaining that they were "invitations to disaster for our national sovereignty" and would open the door to "world socialism and world dictatorship." It demanded changes to the Universal Declaration of Human Rights on the grounds that the document suggested that human rights were "man's due reward for his goodness" rather than "bounties from God to His creatures."[54]

Evangelical Protestants today remain less enthusiastic about global unity and efforts to achieve it than their Mainline Protestant and Roman Catholic counterparts. They also tend to be more negative in their views of international law and organizations, and particularly the United Nations. It would be an exaggeration, and a gross oversimplification, to state, as one analyst has done, that "Evangelical Christians regard the United Nations' blue helmets with about as much enthusiasm as Satan's red horns."[55] Still, there are discernible differences among the three groups, even at the rank-and-file level. A 2006 analysis of polling data by World Public Opinion found that 61 percent of all Americans agreed that the United States should be willing to make decisions within the United Nations "even if this means that the United States will sometimes have to go along with a policy that is not its first choice."

Among evangelicals, 48 percent agreed, while 46 percent did not.[56] Other surveys show similar results. A September 2008 survey conducted for *Religion and Ethics Newsweekly* and the United Nations Foundation found that 42 percent of white evangelicals considered strengthening the United Nations to be "important" or "very important" as compared to 52 percent of Mainline Protestants and 44 percent of Roman Catholic respondents.[57] Although it did not report results for Mainline Protestants or Roman Catholics, a 2007 Fox News poll found roughly two-thirds of evangelicals held negative views of the United Nations.[58]

Beginning in the 1990s, a small number of evangelical organizations—Concerned Women for America (CWA), the Family Research Council, and Focus on the Family—"sought and acquired consultative status at the United Nations" in an effort "to challenge what they perceived as a liberal bias that sought to introduce legislation into America via the circuitous route of the UN in New York."[59] As the names of these organizations suggest, their primary concern has been what might be labeled "family issues"—defining marriage as a union of man and woman, maintaining traditional gender roles, and preventing abortion, among others. The activities of these groups, however, do not signal approval of the United Nations so much as recognition that it is a forum in which policy battles may need to be fought and conservative values may sometimes be advanced.

For the most part, Evangelical Protestant churches and other organizations do not hold NGO status at the United Nations. They do not have offices specifically devoted to lobbying or working with members of that organization. They do not observe "United Nations Sunday" or otherwise celebrate the formation, existence, and activities of the United Nations. With some exceptions (see below), few of the official documents produced by major evangelical organizations mention the United Nations explicitly or express a view regarding it. While many evangelicals do not object to the United States working through the United Nations, they do not believe that the will of the international community as expressed through the United Nations should constrain U.S. foreign policy. The National Association of Evangelicals in 1962 adopted a resolution on "International Relations" that read, in part, "The growing influence of the United Nations in our national affairs, affecting our sovereign rights as a great nation, is a cause of mounting concern to many of our citizens and to many of our evangelical missionary agencies which are being hampered by some of the programs and policies of this world organization."[60] Richard Land, leader of the Southern Baptist Convention's Ethics and Religious Liberty Commission, supported the Bush administration's efforts to obtain U.N. Security Council approval for the 2003 invasion of Iraq, but he did not consider the Council's imprimatur to be necessary, and he, like the SBC as a whole, supported the war when U.N. authorization could not be obtained.

Over time, it must be noted, the attitude of the NAE toward the United Nations has become more favorable. In 2005, Richard Cizik, the NAE's vice president for governmental affairs, speaking at the Church Center at the United Nations, expressed support for the U.N.'s Millennium Development Goals.[61] These eight goals, which were adopted by the United Nations in 2000 and are to be accomplished by 2015, are as follows: (1) eradicate extreme poverty and hunger, (2) achieve universal primary education, (3) promote gender equality and empower women, (4) reduce child mortality, (5) improve maternal health, (6) combat HIV/AIDS, malaria and other diseases, (7) ensure environmental sustainability, and (8) develop a global partnership for development.[62] In October 2007, Cizik and other NAE leaders invited the secretary-general of the United Nations, Ban Ki-moon of South Korea, to be the keynote speaker at an NAE dinner in suburban Washington, DC.[63] Prior to Ban's arrival, Cizik addressed the potentially controversial nature of the invitation within the evangelical community, joking that "some people will say the evangelical Christians have invited the Antichrist to the Last Supper."[64] The NAE's president, Leith Anderson, felt compelled to distance the organization from the United Nations, telling the guests that "We're not here for the secretary-general—we're here for the people who are poor and hurting and war-torn."[65] Still, the event would have been unimaginable only a few years before.

The evolving position of the NAE with respect to the United Nations, together with the public opinion survey data reported above, reveals a growing split within the evangelical community. The NAE and those evangelicals who fall into the "freestyle" category are coming more and more to support the United Nations (and to favor international cooperation generally) because they see it as part of the solution to problems with which they are becoming increasingly concerned. These include climate change, human rights, HIV/AIDS, and global poverty. On the other hand, more conservative or fundamentalist evangelicals continue to cling to largely negative views.

Hal Lindsey, author of *The Late Great Planet Earth*, in a 2005 essay, "The Incredibly Irrelevant United Nations," wrote that the U.N. has become "a malevolent, global facilitator of evil in dark places around the globe. The only thing more frightening to contemplate," he continued, is "what will arise to replace the United Nations when it finally arrives on the ash heap of history. Bible prophecy gives us the answer. There is a one-world government waiting in the wings. It only awaits the unveiling of its ultimate 'leader'—the Antichrist."[66] In the extraordinarily popular *Left Behind* series, authored by evangelicals Tim LaHaye and Jerry Jenkins, the secretary-general of the United Nations *is* the Anti-Christ.[67] Jerry Falwell, in a sermon to his congregation at Thomas Road Baptist Church in Lynchburg, Virginia, called the United Nations "a useless bunch" and stated that the U.N. would be the "infrastructure, the stage on which the Antichrist will build his one-world government."[68] Landmark Baptist Bible Net, produced in Thailand by a mission of Emmanuel Baptist Church in Irving, Texas, has asked its readers to help "patriotic Americans to get our country out of the United Nations and the United Nations out of our country."[69]

Explaining the Differences

Why do Evangelical Protestants, especially fundamentalists, hold more negative views of international law and institutions, and particularly the United Nations, than their Mainline Protestant and Roman Catholic brothers and sisters? One reason is that they object more frequently to the substance of the policies advocated and pursued by these organizations, particularly in such realms as family planning (abortion), environmental protection, and regulation of the international (and domestic) economy. Another is the greater emphasis they place on the exceptional nature of the United States as a country uniquely blessed by Providence, as well as the hostile position they tend to adopt with respect to other world religions. (See Chapter 3.) A third reason is that some evangelicals do not believe that peace, the primary goal of many international organizations, including the United Nations, can be achieved by human beings whose nature is greedy and belligerent. Peace, they argue, will arrive only with the Second Coming of Jesus and the defeat of Satan. Until that time, the efforts of international organizations are destined to fail. Pat Robertson has written, for example, that when the millennial

> prophecy is fulfilled, when Satan's final rebellion is crushed, there will be permanent peace. God will put away, out of his kingdom forever, everything that offends. He will take Satan and his followers and put them permanently into a place of captivity. From that time forward, there will never again be war. Until the earthly reign of Jesus comes, however, men will continue to fight one another.[70]

Thus, he states,

> There is no way that a United Nations, a League of Nations, peace treaties, disarmament treaties, or any other human instrument can bring about peace. Such things mean nothing when one nation desires the land and resources of another. A lasting peace will never be built upon man's efforts, because man is sinful, vicious, and wicked. Until men are changed and Satan's power is removed, there will not be peace on earth.[71]

Astute readers will notice that Robertson's position is not very different from that of certain realist scholars of international relations who believe that a permanent peace among states is impossible and a temporary peace is attainable only through the maintenance of a balance of power. Indeed, classical realism, as reflected in the works of Hans Morgenthau, for example, comes out of a conservative philosophical tradition that regards human nature as being essentially evil.[72]

A fourth important reason for the generally dim view of international organizations, and especially the United Nations, among certain evangelicals has to do with the role of the organizations in the so-called New Age Movement or New Age Globalism. The New Age Movement, as described in fundamentalist evangelical literature, has its origins in the late nineteenth century in the writings of Helena Petrovna Blatavsky, and in the 1920s, with the teachings of Alice Ann Bailey. Although it appears to be "a loose knit group of innocent organizations with ambiguous goals or leadership," there exists, below the surface, "a definite, organized, secret leadership and strategy which guides the vast movement."[73] The New Age Movement is characterized by its promotion of the unity of the world's religions, its emphasis on mysticism, meditation, and the occult, and its humanism. According to the NAE,

> The New Age Movement denies the Judeo-Christian belief in a personal, righteous God. It obliterates distinctions between the spiritual and the material, claiming that there is a universal and pervasive spirituality which, as a vast, interconnected web of higher consciousness, binds everything and everyone together. . . . The New Age Movement uses religious language and a selective collection of borrowed spiritual concepts as it contends for its own utopian world vision. This makes it attractive to a largely materialistic society that is abandoning traditional Judeo-Christian beliefs, yet has failed to provide a replacement to meet the spiritual hunger of humanity. For this reason, the New Age Movement is dangerous.[74]

In 1998, the Southern Baptist Convention adopted a "Resolution on the New Age Movement," which stated that the movement

> gives people false hope by its beliefs (1) in reincarnation, (2) in endeavoring to reveal a person's future through astrology, fortune telling, and palm reading, (3) in Universalism, the belief that there are many ways to eternal life, and that all will be saved, (4) by secular humanism, which testifies by its own manifesto, no deity will save us, we must save ourselves.[75]

The resolution urged the denomination's agencies, pastors, and church staffs to "warn and educate our Baptist constituency of the deception and critical dangers of this movement."[76] Two years later, continuing this theme, the SBC adopted a second resolution, "On the Threat of New Age Globalism." The resolution warned that "The New Age globalism movement advocates a one-world government, a one-world religion, and a one-world economy," and that its success "would mean the destruction of the sovereignty of nations." It stated that "New Age globalism also poses a threat to the traditional family, proposing recognition of five genders (male, female, homosexual, bisexual, transsexual), wholesale abortion as a means of population control, and the elevation of the rights of children above parents, asserting that the state has the primary responsibility for the upbringing of children." Wrote the SBC, "A key principle behind globalism is the philosophy of secular humanism, a foundational component of which is the belief that no religion can or does possess objective truth and that all religions are of equal worth."[77]

What do concerns about the New Age Movement and New Age Globalism among conservative evangelicals have to do with their views concerning the United Nations and other manifestations of international cooperation? First, international institutions are regarded as evidence of the spread of New Age ideas. Second, they are regarded as promoters of them. The SBC has identified the United Nations, and international organizations more generally, as major contributors to the menace posed by "New

Age-ism." In "On the Threat of New Age Globalism," the SBC urged "Congress, the President, and other national leaders to guard our national sovereignty, to prevent the placement of American troops under foreign military command or direction, to scrutinize and reverse the trend toward globalism, and to resist its encroachments by certain elements within our own government, the United Nations, and other organizations."[78]

The depth of fundamentalist evangelical objections to the United Nations and other international institutions cannot be understood without reference to eschatology. Many fundamentalists consider the United Nations, either alone or as part of a network of international organizations, to be the one-world government that the New Age Movement and New Age Globalism seek to establish. And the one-world government is either the Anti-Christ or is led by him. It might be supposed that the formation of this government and the arrival of the Anti-Christ would be welcomed by fundamentalists since they would represent the fulfillment of biblical prophecy and herald the Second Coming of Jesus. But the Anti-Christ is evil and will seek to deceive Christians into abandoning God and forsaking the salvation that they would otherwise attain. For this reason, most fundamentalists believe that he must be opposed.

As noted in Chapter 5, the Christian Bible, primarily in the Old Testament book of Daniel and the New Testament book of Revelation, contains prophecies regarding the end of human history. The most important of the prophecies, for the purposes of this chapter, is found in Rev. 13.1–8, in which John writes,

> Then I stood on the sand of the sea. I saw a beast coming up out of the sea, having ten horns and seven heads. On his horns were ten crowns, and on his heads, blasphemous names. The beast which I saw was like a leopard, and his feet were like those of a bear, and his mouth like the mouth of a lion. The dragon gave him his power, his throne, and great authority. One of his heads looked like it had been wounded fatally. His fatal wound was healed, and the whole earth marveled at the beast. They worshiped the dragon, because he gave his authority to the beast, and they worshiped the beast, saying, "Who is like the beast? Who is able to make war with him?" A mouth speaking great things and blasphemy was given to him. Authority to make war for forty-two months was given to him. He opened his mouth for blasphemy against God, to blaspheme his name, and his dwelling, those who dwell in heaven. It was given to him to make war with the saints, and to overcome them. Authority over every tribe, people, language, and nation was given to him. All who dwell on the earth will worship him, everyone whose name has not been written from the foundation of the world in the book of life of the Lamb who has been killed.

It is these passages, some fundamentalist Christians believe, that foretell the emergence of the one-world government and of the Anti-Christ. Biblical literalists see signs of the fulfillment of biblical prophecy all around them. Some believe components of the Anti-Christ's plan include the European Union and the Roman Catholic Church. Attempts to increase solidarity among the various Christian denominations and, more importantly, to increase dialogue among Christians, Jews, Muslims, Hindus, and people of other faiths are also sometimes regarded as the work of the Anti-Christ. Indeed, almost any effort at international cooperation can be viewed in this way. Many fundamentalists see evidence of the formation of a one-world government in the proliferation of international organizations, agreements, and other forms of international cooperation during the past half century. Terry J. Malone, author of *Revelation Revealed* and *The Calvary Prophecy Report*, writes,

> We are, without even knowing it, in the middle of the formation of a one world government that will set the stage for the tribulation period and the ushering in of the antichrist as world leader.
>
> Unfortunately, there is a force at work throughout the world that aims to unite people, nations, communities and other groups into larger units. Centralization, you might call it. It's still theory and conjecture, but, in my opinion, here's how the grand plan will begin to unfold: The insiders who meet under the auspices of the Trilateral Commission, Council on Foreign Affairs, the Bilderberg Group, etc., intend to use the United Nations and the European Community as the models for other regional groups of nations. Already the Islamic nations of the world have formed a coalition. Latin American nations have grouped together through an "integration association." The nations of Southeast Asia have there [sic] own association. West African states have their own economic community. And, of course, the U.S. Canada and Mexico formed the North America Free Trade Area in 1989, which resulted in a treaty ratified by the U.S. Congress in October, 1993 (NAFTA).
>
> But these international groupings are merely an interim step toward total world unification. And in the 1990s, the world seems to be on a fast track toward global government. Its [sic] never been so clear before.[79]

These sentiments are echoed by Contender Ministries, which lists "plans for the one world government" among the "eleven fulfillments of Bible prophecy required for the end of the age." According to the organization,

> The United Nations, World Trade Organization, International Criminal Court, UN peacekeeping/police force, numerous UN NGO's, and other agencies are preliminary steps to the formation of a one world government. We now have the communications technology, transportation, and the pro-globalization media necessary to usher in the one world government headed by the antichrist. The increasing terrorist threat and the middle east conflict will only speed up the formation of this governing body as fear and promises of better security make more people willing to give up their national sovereignty for global governance.[80]

The sense among fundamentalist evangelicals that the emergence of the one-world government and appearance of the Anti-Christ are close at hand was strengthened in the late 1980s and 1990s by the end of the Cold War and the idea of a "new world order" articulated by then U.S. president George H. W. Bush. In a speech to the American people announcing the opening of the Persian Gulf War, Bush stated:

> This is an historic moment. We have in this past year made great progress in ending the long era of conflict and cold war. We have before us the opportunity to forge for ourselves and for future generations a new world order—a world where the rule of law, not the law of the jungle, governs the conduct of nations. When we are successful—and we will be—we have a real chance at this new world order, an order in which a credible United Nations can use its peacekeeping role to fulfill the promise and vision of the U.N.'s founders.[81]

At the conclusion of the conflict, in an address to Congress, the president repeated the theme, saying,

> Now, we can see a new world coming into view. A world in which there is the very real prospect of a new world order. In the words of Winston Churchill, a world order in which "the principles of justice and fair play protect the weak against the strong. . . ." A world where the United Nations, freed from cold war stalemate, is poised to fulfill the historic vision of its founders. A world in which freedom and respect for human rights find a home among all nations. The Gulf war put this new world to its first test. And my fellow Americans, we passed that test.[82]

The term "new world order" was adopted by pundits, political commentators, and scholars, and pervaded popular and academic discourse for much of the decade.

According to some fundamentalists, the "New World Order is World Government."[83] And, as Bush himself did, many have placed the United Nations at its center. The views of Lindsey, LaHaye, and Falwell are recorded above. But they are only the best known of the fundamentalist evangelicals to take such a position. Others have done so, too. Landmark Bible Baptist reports that "the governmental arm of the New World Order is shaping up to be the United Nations. This corrupt, unjust and occult organization is antichrist to it's [sic] roots."[84] Endtime Ministries writes that

> Since its formation in 1945, The United Nations has exercised increasing control over world politics. Furthermore, it has repeatedly made decisions favoring the communist world, and has voted and spoken regularly against capitalism and democracy. The United Nations has been instrumental in establishing and increasing the powers of the World Court. Furthermore, the Commission on Global Governance has called for a global tax as well as a standing UN army.

Clearly, the fulfillment of Revelation 13: 1–2 is upon us and is being fulfilled through the United Nations and the New World Order![85]

Contender Ministries, which maintains a "United Nations Watch," sums up the view of the United Nations held especially by more fundamentalist evangelicals:

The United Nations has been working diligently for decades to implement the one world government and one world religion as prophesied in the Bible. Hiding behind words such as: sustainable development, global warming, global consciousness, and civil liberties, they are busy implementing the plans laid out in the UN Charter, the Earth Charter, and many other UN resolutions. . . . It is important for Christians to be aware of these subtle changes in our policies and government. If we are caught off guard along with the rest of the world, who will be left to share the truth with those who would be lured into the false religion of the Anti-Christ?[86]

Mainline Protestants and Roman Catholics, who tend to read the Bible figuratively, do not generally believe that the fulfillment of biblical prophecies can be discerned in past and contemporary political, social, and economic events, and they do not believe that such events can be used to calculate the time of Jesus' return to Earth. In "The Year of Our Lord 2000," the Conference of Bishops of the Evangelical Lutheran Church in America wrote: "To all who would fix a date for his coming, however, our Lord says, 'About that day and hour no one knows, neither the angels of heaven, nor the Son, but only the Father' (Mark 13:32). And in another passage, 'It is not for you to know the times and the period that the Father has set by his own authority' (Acts 1:7)."[87] In the same way that many Mainline Protestants and Catholics do not believe in the personhood of Satan, they do not believe in the literal reality of an Anti-Christ.

Although Mainline Protestants and Roman Catholics tend to subscribe to the traditional Christian view of human beings as sinful and in need of redemption, they are not as pessimistic about the possibilities of improving the world as their fundamentalist evangelical counterparts. In part because they tend to be amillennialists rather than premillennialists—believing that the kingdom of God was established on Earth with Jesus' resurrection and ascension into heaven—Mainline Protestants and Roman Catholics typically regard attempts at international cooperation as furthering the kingdom and doing God's will.[88] They have no theological reason to be suspicious of international cooperation in general or the United Nations in particular. In fact, quite the opposite is true.

Beyond this, Mainline Protestants and Roman Catholics, to a greater extent than their evangelical counterparts, tend to support the substantive policies embodied in international law and pursued by international institutions such as the United Nations. As noted in other chapters, Mainline Protestant denominations and the Roman Catholic Church typically favor efforts to maintain international peace, protect the environment, and enhance a wide range of human rights.

Summary

Mainline Protestant churches and the Roman Catholic Church are strongly support-ive of international cooperation and its institutional manifestations. Members of these denominations also tend to have positive attitudes toward international law and institutions. Evangelical Protestants do not view international cooperation as favorably, although less conservative evangelicals are becoming more accepting of the United Nations than are fundamentalists. These differences, and the reasons for them, are shown in Table 6.1.

The opposition to international law and organization, and especially to the United Nations, among conservative evangelicals has its roots in fundamentalist eschatology. Many fundamentalists regard the United Nations, along with other international institutions, as being, or as being the framework for, the one-world government that they believe will be headed by the Anti-Christ. The alleged involve-ment of the United Nations in the so-called New Age Movement and in New Age Globalism is related to this objection. Conservative evangelicals also oppose interna-tional cooperation for other reasons: (1) they object to the substance of the policies pursued by these organizations, (2) they view these organizations as infringing upon the sovereignty of the United States, which they regard as having a special mission from God, and (3) they do not believe these organizations can secure world peace in advance of the Second Coming of Jesus and are therefore doomed to failure.

Mainline Protestants and Roman Catholics, who do not subscribe to fundamen-talist eschatology, see the United Nations and other international organizations as doing God's work, not Satan's. More accepting of other religious traditions and less inclined to see the United States as being uniquely blessed by God, they are less concerned about U.S. sovereignty. Although Roman Catholics sometimes object to policies pursued by international organizations, especially in the realm of family planning (abortion), they and Mainline Protestants typically favor the substance of such policies. Finally, adhering to an amillennialist eschatology, these groups believe that the kingdom of God on Earth was established with the First Coming of Jesus, and they are therefore much more optimistic about the prospects for successful international cooperation, including the attainment of world peace.

Mainline Protestant leaders and organizations played a crucial role in creating popular support for the United Nations during the mid-1940s. They helped shape the U.N. Charter and played a significant role in the establishment of the U.N. Commission on Human Rights and in the Universal Declaration of Human Rights. Although mainline churches have been active in the United Nations since that time, and have pressured the U.S. government to support the organization, they have clearly been less influential over the past half century or so. They may have been partly responsible for the payment of arrears owed to the United Nations during the 1990s, but it is difficult to establish conclusively that they have affected U.S. policy toward the organization in other ways.

The Roman Catholic Church and especially Evangelical Protestant organizations have, as noted in Chapter 4, influenced U.S. policy toward the United Nations on

Table 6.1: Views of U.S. Christians Regarding International Law and Institutions/United Nations

	Mainline Protestants	Evangelical Protestants	Roman Catholics
International Institutions/United Nations	Strongly supportive, especially at the organizational level	Range from modestly supportive to indifferent to hostile	Strongly supportive, especially at the institutional level
Eschatology	Mostly amillennialist; do not see international institutions as fulfillment of biblical prophecy concerning one-world government or the Anti-Christ	Frequently dispensationalist and premillennialist; fundamentalists often see the United Nations and other institutions as part of one-world government to be headed by the Anti-Christ	Officially amillennialist; do not see international institutions as fulfillment of biblical prophecy concerning one-world government or the Anti-Christ
View of Possibility of World Peace	Regarded as possible; can be achieved with help of organizations doing God's work	Regarded, especially by fundamentalists, as difficult or impossible because human beings are evil and incapable of living in peace with one another until the Second Coming of Jesus	Regarded as possible; can be achieved with help of organizations doing God's work
View of Substance of Policies Pursued by the United Nations and other Organizations	Generally strongly supportive, favoring protection of the environment, regulation of the international economy, population control and family planning, and so forth	Less supportive, although freestyle evangelicals and the NAE are becoming more supportive	Generally strongly supportive, with the exception of family planning policies
Relationship between God and the United States, Importance of U.S. Sovereignty	Tend to regard the United States as not specially favored; hence not strongly protective of U.S. sovereignty	Tend to regard the United States as specially favored by God; hence highly protective of U.S. sovereignty	Tend to regard the United States as not specially favored; hence not strongly protective of U.S. sovereignty

abortion-related human rights issues, helping to persuade Republican administrations to withhold U.S. contributions to the United Nations Population Fund. The opposition to the United Nations among fundamentalist evangelicals has not, however, been sufficient to cause the U.S. government to question in any real way its commitment to the organization. This is most likely a consequence of the benefits—diplomatic, political, economic, and other—that the U.S. government sees deriving from the United Nations and from U.S. membership therein, but the support for the United Nations consistently and vigorously expressed by Roman Catholics and Mainline Protestants may be a contributing factor.

Notes

1. George Washington, "Washington's Farewell Address to the People of the United States," U.S. Senate, 106th Cong., 2nd sess., Senate Document No. 106–21 (Washington, DC: USGPO, 2000), 26, www.access.gpo.gov/congress/senate/farewell/sd106-21.pdf.
2. Washington, "Washington's Farewell Address," 27.
3. Washington, "Washington's Farewell Address," 26.
4. Patrick Garrity, "Warnings of a Parting Friend (US Foreign Policy Envisioned by George Washington in his Farewell Address)," *The National Interest*, no. 45 (Fall 1996), www.mtholyoke.edu/acad/intrel/garrity.htm.
5. Quoted in Garrity, "Warnings of a Parting Friend."
6. Quoted in Canon John Nurser (John S. Nurser), "The 'Ecumenical Movement' Churches, 'Global Order,' and Human Rights: 1938–1948," *Human Rights Quarterly*, 25, no. 4 (November 2003): 856, www.jstor.org/stable/20069697.
7. Heather A. Warren, *Theologians of a New World Order: Reinhold Niebuhr and the Christian Realists, 1920–1948* (New York: Oxford University Press, 1997), 103.
8. Inboden, *Religion and American Foreign Policy*, 30; see also, Warren, *Theologians of a New World Order*, 103–104.
9. Inboden, *Religion and American Foreign Policy*, 30.
10. For an excellent analysis of the role of the churches in influencing the U.N. Charter, especially with regard to human rights, see John S. Nurser, *For All Peoples and All Nations: The Ecumenical Church and Human Rights* (Washington, DC: Georgetown University Press, 2005).
11. Warren, *Theologians of a New World Order*, 105–106.
12. Inboden, *Religion and American Foreign Policy*, 30–31.
13. UMC, "The World Community," *Social Principles*, ¶165, www.umc-gbcs.org/site/c.frLJK2PKLqF/b.3713161/k.1F25/182165_The_World_Community/apps/nl/newsletter.asp.
14. UMC, "The World Community."
15. UMC, General Board of Church and Society, "United Nations and International Affairs," www.umc-gbcs.org/site/c.frLJK2PKLqF/b.2809019/.
16. ELCA, *For Peace in God's World*.
17. NCC, "Pillars of Peace for the 21st Century," www.ncccusa.org/about/pillars.html.
18. NCC, "Resolution on the International Criminal Court," www.ncccusa.org/about/icc.html.

19. UMC, General Board of Church and Society, "United Nations and International Affairs."
20. PCUSA, United Nations Office, "The Presbyterian United Nations Office," www.pcusa.org/peacemaking/un/index.htm.
21. PCUSA, United Nations Office, "Global Issues," www.pcusa.org/peacemaking/un/issues.htm.
22. ELCA, "About the Lutheran Office for World Community," http://archive.elca.org/advocacy/international/.
23. Office of the Anglican Observer at the United Nations, "Voice of a Global Community," www.anglicancommunion.org/un/resources/AUN_brochure.pdf.
24. Office of the Anglican Observer, "Voice of a Global Community."
25. There are currently more than 2,700 NGOs accredited by the United Nations and possessing consultative status. A full list can be found at Global Policy Forum, "Basic Information on NGOs and the UN," www.globalpolicy.org/ngos/ngo-un/infoindex.htm.
26. UCC, "United Nations," www.ucc.org/justice/united-nations/.
27. Mary Gray Davidson, "Faith in the United Nations," *Courier Online* (Summer 1998), www.stanleyfoundation.org/courier/1998summer3.html.
28. NCC, "Recent NCC Statements on Issues in the Public Square," www.ncccusa.org/about/justicestatements.html.
29. UMC, "In Support of the United Nations," *Book of Resolutions–2004*, http://archives.umc.org/interior.asp?ptid=4&mid=1045.
30. Joseph S. Rossi, *American Catholics and the Formation of the United Nations*, Melville Studies in Church History, vol. IV (Lanham, MD: University Press of America, 1993), 1–9.
31. Quoted in Weigel, Tranquillitas Ordinis, 61.
32. Weigel, Tranquillitas Ordinis, 61.
33. Rossi, *American Catholics and the Formation of the United Nations*, 276.
34. Rossi, *American Catholics and the Formation of the United Nations*, 287.
35. Rossi, *American Catholics and the Formation of the United Nations*, 291.
36. An excellent history of the formation, activities, and demise of the Office of U.N. Affairs is Joseph S. Rossi, S. J., *Uncharted Territory: The American Catholic Church at the United Nations, 1946–1972* (Washington, DC: Catholic University of America Press, 2006).
37. Weigel, Tranquillitas Ordinis, 78–82.
38. Quoted in Weigel, Tranquillitas Ordinis, 90.
39. Holy See, "A Short History of the Holy See's Diplomacy," www.holyseemission.org/short_history.html.
40. Holy See, "Welcome to the Permanent Observer Mission of the Holy See to the United Nations," http://holyseemission.org/index2.html.
41. Holy See, "A Short History of the Holy See's Diplomacy."
42. See the website of Catholics for Choice, www.seechange.org/.
43. "Religious Right Backs Special Role At UN for Catholic Church," *Church and State*, May 1, 2000, www.thefreelibrary.com/Religious+Right+Backs+Special+Role+At+UN+For+Catholic+Church-a062402432.
44. For an annual listing of the statements of the Holy See's Observer at the United Nations see Holy See, "Interventions," www.holyseemission.org/interventions.html.

45. Holy See, "Events Organized by the Holy See Mission," www.holyseemission.org/events.html. See also Holy See, "*Pacem in Terris* Symposium," www.holyseemission.org/Pacem%20en%20Terris.htm.
46. Pope Benedict XVI, "Address to the United Nations General Assembly," April 18, 2008, http://ewtn.org/USPapalVisit08/words/unitednations.asp.
47. Pope Benedict XVI, "Address to the United Nations General Assembly."
48. Cindy Wooden, "Cardinal Ratzinger Says U.S. Attack on Iraq Not Morally Justifiable," *Catholic News Service*, September 25, 2002, www.usccb.org/sdwp/international/cns-1-ra.shtml.
49. USCCB, "Bishop Gregory Cites 'Grave Moral Responsibilities' of United States in Iraq," June 22, 2004, www.usccb.org/comm/archives/2004/04-119.shtml.
50. USCCB, "Bishop Gregory Cites 'Grave Moral Responsibilities' of United States in Iraq."
51. USCCB, "U.S. Bishops Urge Leaders to Work Harder for a Lasting Peace in Darfur, Support Resolution for United Nations Mission," September 15, 2006, www.usccb.org/comm/archives/2006/06-173.shtml.
52. USCCB, "Letter to the Senate Foreign Relations Committee," July 31, 2001, www.usccb.org/sdwp/international/dearsen.shtml.
53. Markku Ruotsila, *The Origins of Christian Anti-Internationalism: Conservative Evangelicals and the League of Nations* (Washington, DC: Georgetown University Press, 2008).
54. Inboden, *Religion and American Foreign Policy*, 57–58.
55. Dana Millbank, "Guess Who Came to the Evangelicals' Dinner," *Washington Post*, October 12, 2007, www.washingtonpost.com/wp-dyn/content/article/2007/10/11/AR2007101102537.html.
56. "WPO Poll Analysis: American Evangelicals are Divided on International Policy," October 2, 2006, www.worldpublicopinion.org/pipa/articles/brunitedstatescanadara/270.php?lb=brusc&pnt=270&nid=&id=.
57. "Religion and Ethics Newsweekly/UN Foundation Survey Explores Religion and America's Role in the World," *Religion and Ethics Newsweekly*, October 22, 2008, www.pbs.org/wnet/religionandethics/episodes/by-topic/civil-society/religion-ethics-newsweeklyun-foundation-survey-explores-religion-and-americas-role-in-the-world/1190/. The entire report may be downloaded in pdf format from this webpage.
58. Mike McManus, "Evangelicals Embrace Global Millennial Goals," *VirtueOnline*, October 18, 2007, www.virtueonline.org/portal/modules/news/article.php?storyid=6915. A different source reported the poll results somewhat differently: "Republicans (including the vast majority of evangelicals) took a dim view of the United Nations by 2 to 1." See Millbank, "Guess Who Came to the Evangelicals' Dinner."
59. Lee Marsden, *For God's Sake: The Christian Right and US Foreign Policy* (London and New York: Zed Books, 2009), 137–39.
60. NAE, "International Relations, 1962," www.nae.net/resolutions/233-international-relations-1962.
61. Cizik, "The United Nations' MDG Campaign for a Better World," June 8, 2005, www.globalinterfaithed.org/cizik.htm.
62. United Nations Development Programme, "About the MDG's: Basics," www.undp.org/mdg/basics.shtml.
63. For an account of the event, see Millbank, "Guess Who Came to the Evangelicals' Dinner."
64. Quoted in Millbank, "Guess Who Came to the Evangelicals' Dinner."

65. Quoted in Millbank, "Guess Who Came to the Evangelicals' Dinner."
66. Hal Lindsey, "The Incredibly Irrelevant United Nations," *WorldNetDaily*, February 3, 2005, www.wnd.com/news/article.asp?ARTICLE_ID=42684.
67. See Chapter 5.
68. "Falwell, '[C]ashless Society,' 'One-World Government' will Happen Near Rapture," MediaMatters For America, August 28, 2006, http://mediamatters.org/mmtv/200608280008.
69. "Landmark Bible Baptist News: The New World Order," http://landmarkbiblebaptist.net/news.html.
70. Robertson, "Where are We Going?—200 Questions," www.cbn.com/spirituallife/200questions/article_4.aspx?#39.
71. Robertson, "Where are We Going?—200 Questions."
72. For an excellent discussion of the philosophical foundations of theories of war, see Keith L. Nelson and Spencer C. Olin, Jr., *Why War? Ideology, Theory, and History* (Berkeley, CA: University of California Press, 1979).
73. A representative account is Dale A. Robbins, "The New Age Movement: What Christians Should Know," www.victorious.org/newage.htm.
74. NAE, "The New Age Movement," www.nae.net/resolutions/319-the-new-age-movement-1990-.
75. SBC, "Resolution on the New Age Movement," June 1988, www.sbc.net/resolutions/amResolution.asp?ID=785.
76. SBC, "Resolution on the New Age Movement."
77. SBC, "On the Threat of New Age Globalism," June 2000, www.sbc.net/resolutions/amResolution.asp?ID=786.
78. SBC, "On the Threat of New Age Globalism."
79. "One World Government," www.calvaryprophecy.com/oneworld.html.
80. Jennifer Rast, "Prophetic Signs that We are in the End Times," http://contenderministries.org/prophecy/endtimes.php.
81. Bush, "Address to the Nation Announcing Allied Military Action in the Persian Gulf," http://bushlibrary.tamu.edu/research/public_papers.php?id=2625&year=1991&month=01.
82. Bush, "Address Before a Joint Session of the Congress on the Cessation of the Persian Gulf Conflict," March 6, 1991, www.c-span.org/executive/transcript.asp?cat=current_event&code=bush_admin&year=0391.
83. Endtime Ministries, "New World Order is World Government," www.endtime.com/ProphecyTopic.aspx?id=2.
84. "The New World Order," *Landmark Bible Baptist News*, http://landmarkbiblebaptist.net/news.html.
85. Endtime Ministries, "New World Order is World Government."
86. Contender Ministries, "United Nations Watch," www.contenderministries.org/UN/unwatch.php.
87. ELCA, "In the Year of Our Lord 2000," www2.elca.org/synods/bishopsmillennium.html.
88. See Chapter 5.

CHAPTER 7

Protection of the International Environment

In 1962, Rachel Carson published *Silent Spring.*[1] The biologist and best-selling nature writer opened her book with a "Fable for Tomorrow," a sobering account of a U.S. town, once teeming with plant and animal life, but now quiet and barren. Behind the nightmare, according to Carson, was the indiscriminate use of pesticides, especially dichloro-diphenyl-trichloroethane, better known as DDT. Carson's carefully crafted case convinced many scientists and government officials, though not U.S. chemical manufacturers, that an ecological catastrophe was in the making. Today, the appearance of *Silent Spring* is widely regarded as marking the beginning of the environmental movement in the United States and around the world.

Since the 1960s, scientists and other observers have identified a variety of other environmental problems. Global climate change (often referred to as global warming), ozone depletion, acid precipitation, other forms of air and water pollution, degradation of arable land, deforestation, desertification, and loss of biodiversity are just some of the major ones. Although environmental problems are sometimes contained largely within a single country, they are often transnational in scope. Agricultural and industrial practices in one state frequently affect the quality of the environment in others. As importantly, certain forms of environmental degradation—climate change and ozone depletion are two examples—are not merely caused by the activities of multiple countries, but their effects are truly global. For this reason, they can only be addressed effectively via international cooperation.

The United States has compiled a mixed record with respect to protection of the international environment. In 1974, it became the first country to ratify the Convention on International Trade in Endangered Species of Wild Fauna and Flora (CITES). That treaty, which entered into force the following year, seeks to prevent trade in certain plant and animal species from threatening their survival.[2] In 1986, the United States became a party to the 1971 Convention on Wetlands (Ramsar Convention), under which member states agree to "work towards the wise use of all their wetlands through national land-use planning, appropriate policies and legislation, management actions, and public education; designate suitable wetlands for the List of Wetlands of International Importance ('Ramsar List') and ensure their effective management; and cooperate internationally concerning transboundary wetlands, shared wetland systems, shared species, and development projects that may affect wetlands."[3] In 2000, the U.S. government ratified the 1994 United Nations Convention to Combat Desertification (UNCCD), by which it committed itself, along with the governments of other developed countries, to assist developing countries, particularly those in Africa, in fighting desertification by providing financial resources, technology, and knowledge.[4]

The U.S. government played a leading role in negotiating the 1987 Montreal Protocol, an agreement aimed at halting and then reversing the damage being done to Earth's stratospheric ozone by the use of chlorofluorocarbons (CFCs) as refrigerants, aerosol propellants, and in other capacities. The Montreal Protocol called for CFC production to be cut by 50 percent from 1986 levels; in 1990, it was amended to require the cessation of CFC production altogether.[5] In part because of this agreement, depletion of the ozone layer—which protects Earth, including plant and animal life, from excessive ultraviolet radiation—has been brought under control, and scientists expect that in time it will regain its former robustness.[6]

By contrast, the United States has failed to exercise leadership, or even to participate, in other international efforts at environmental protection. The position of the U.S. government on global climate change was initially encouraging to environmentalists. Under President George H. W. Bush, the United States signed and ratified the United Nations Framework Convention on Climate Change (UNFCCC) in 1992. This treaty encouraged, but did not require, states to cut the emission of greenhouse gases (mainly carbon dioxide and methane) from the burning of fossil fuels. Partly for this reason, Democratic presidential candidate Bill Clinton made addressing global warming a major issue in his successful 1992 campaign against Bush. Early in his presidency, Clinton and his advisors sought to negotiate an agreement that would set mandatory limits on greenhouse gas emissions. The Kyoto Protocol, which was concluded in 1997, called for significant reductions in such emissions from 1990 levels. The United States signed the treaty, but the accord was never submitted to the Senate for ratification because the Clinton administration recognized that Senate approval could not be obtained. Much of the Congressional opposition stemmed from the fact that, under the terms of the agreement, the United States was required to reduce its emissions of greenhouse gases to below 1990 levels, while developing countries, including major polluters such as China, assumed no similar obligations. Many members of Congress, supported by industry groups and organized labor, argued that the United States would suffer economically from having to make the reductions, while at the same time there would be no lessening of greenhouse gas emissions on the global level and, hence, no environmental benefit. George W. Bush, Clinton's successor, opposed the Kyoto Protocol for these reasons and decided to abandon it.[7] When the treaty entered into effect, in 2005, with the participation of the vast majority of the world's countries, the United States was not among them. As of this writing, the Kyoto Protocol has been ratified by 183 states.[8] The United States is still not a party to the agreement and is unlikely to become one, although the Obama administration is interested in negotiating and signing a successor accord.

The position of the U.S. government with respect to the preservation of global biodiversity has mirrored, to a considerable extent, that regarding climate change. The Clinton administration signed the 1992 Convention on Biological Diversity

(CBD) and submitted it to the Senate for ratification. However, although the Senate Foreign Relations Committee voted legislation to ratify the agreement out of committee by a margin of 16–3, a floor vote was never held because a group of Republican senators sufficiently large to prevent the bill's passage had declared their opposition to it. Objections to the CBD were varied and ranged from complaints that the treaty would infringe on Congressional prerogatives to concerns that it might impose excessive financial obligations on the United States. According to one scholar, the primary reason for Republican opposition was partisan politics and the desire to deal President Clinton a political defeat.[9] When Republicans gained control of the Senate in the 1994 midterm election, it was clear to the Clinton administration that ratification was impossible. Today the United States is one of five countries—the others are Andorra, the Holy See, Iraq, and Somalia—that are not party to the CBD.[10]

Mainline Protestants

There is little or no public opinion survey data regarding the attitudes of different religious groups toward international efforts to protect the environment, or toward specific treaties and other agreements. On the other hand, there do exist data concerning the views of these groups regarding the seriousness of environmental and ecological problems and the desirability of governmental action to address them. These data suggest that Mainline Protestants are the U.S. Christian group most concerned about the degradation of Earth's environment and most favorably disposed toward more rigorous environmental regulation. A 2007 Barna Group poll found that 59 percent of Mainline Protestants regarded global warming as a "major" problem, the same percentage as Roman Catholics. By contrast, only 33 percent of evangelicals considered global warming to be a major problem.[11] The same general pattern appears in other studies. According to the Pew Forum's survey on the U.S. religious landscape, 64 percent of Mainline Protestants believed that stricter environmental laws and regulations were worth the cost in lost jobs and harm to the economy, as compared to 60 percent of Catholics, and 54 percent of evangelicals.[12] The 2006 Baylor Religion Survey found that Mainline Protestants were more likely than either Roman Catholics or Evangelical Protestants to favor additional measures to protect the environment.[13]

   Mainline Protestant organizations have had a longstanding commitment to protection of the international environment.[14] Since 1983, the Eco-Justice Working Group of the National Council of Churches has provided a forum for cooperation among Mainline Protestant (and Orthodox) denominations on a range of environmental issues, including climate and global warming, water, energy, biodiversity, and land.[15] Each year, the NCC designates one Sunday as "Earth Day Sunday," and provides assistance in celebrating it to the congregations of member denominations. The NCC has consistently supported international efforts to protect the environment and has pushed the U.S. government to participate in them. In 1998, the NCC embarked on a concerted campaign to "provide a new level of determination and concrete plans to see the Kyoto Protocol submitted by the President and ratified by the Senate."[16] The campaign included a letter to President Clinton, letters to U.S. senators, the sending of strategy packets to 540 environmental justice coordinators in NCC member denominations across the United States, and the holding of a Midwest Interfaith Climate Change conference in Columbus, Ohio. That conference provided the foundation for the NCC's Midwest Interfaith Global Warming Campaign, which by 2001 had been extended to 18 states.[17] While the Bush administration's renunciation of the Kyoto Protocol rendered moot further advocacy of the treaty for a period of 8 years, the inauguration of President Barack Obama in January 2009, represented an opportunity to call for renewed efforts to protect the environment. Even before Obama had been elected, the NCC addressed him in an open letter, writing that

> Already, global warming has damaged the precious balance of God's creation causing long-term drought in Africa, increased disease in many of the world's poorest countries, and an increase in natural disasters that are destroying homes and lives. Any steps we take to address climate change must follow scientific recommendations and focus on the short-term goal of reducing U.S. carbon emissions by 15–20 percent reduction by 2020 with a long-term vision to achieve carbon emissions reductions of 80 percent by 2050.[18]

On January 27, 2009, when President Obama signed an executive order to allow states to establish more stringent emissions standards for automobiles, Cassandra Carmichael, the director of the NCC's Eco-Justice Programs, was invited to the White House to witness the event.[19]

Mainline Protestant denominations have repeatedly articulated their concern for the environment and their support for international (and domestic) initiatives intended to protect it. In 1993, the Evangelical Lutheran Church in America issued a social statement, *Caring for Creation: Vision, Hope, and Justice*, which expressed the conviction that Earth was already experiencing an ecological crisis. Among the damages being done to the environment, according to the ELCA, were "depletion of non-renewable resources, especially oil; loss of the variety of life through rapid destruction of habitats; erosion of topsoil through unsustainable agriculture and forestry practices; pollution of air by toxic emissions from industries and vehicles, and pollution of water by wastes; increasing volume of wastes; and prevalence of acid rain, which damages forests, lakes, and streams." Two problems were regarded by the denomination as being most severe: the depletion of the protective ozone layer, resulting from the use of volatile compounds containing chlorine and bromine; and dangerous global warming, caused by the buildup of greenhouse gases, especially carbon dioxide.[20]

Although the ELCA did not specifically endorse the Montreal Protocol, the Kyoto Protocol, or other pieces of international environmental legislation, other mainline denominations did so. The General Synod of the United Church of Christ, in 1999, citing the conclusion of the United Nations Intergovernmental Panel on Climate Change (IPCC) that global warming was being caused by human-made greenhouse gases and noting that the continued release of such gases would "cause devastating effects on agriculture and natural ecosystems, the flooding of coastal regions and island nations, increased volatility of weather patterns with severe heat waves and storms, migration of tropical insects, diseases, deforestation, desertification and displacement of human populations," voted to encourage its "local churches, Conferences, and national agencies to educate and advocate for ratification of the Kyoto Climate Change Treaty." It also urged UCC members to "contact their U.S. Senators affirming the need to ratify this treaty as a first step in meeting the threat of global warming."[21]

Similarly, the Presbyterian Church (USA) in both 1998 and 1999 adopted resolutions calling on the United States to ratify the Kyoto Protocol. When the chair of the Senate Energy and Natural Resources Committee, Frank Murkowski, declared the treaty dead, the Washington Office of the PCUSA issued an action alert, stating that "only a groundswell of public pressure early in the 106th Congress offers hope of reversing this attitude," and calling on Presbyterians to contact their senators and press them to work for ratification.[22] The PCUSA, it should be noted, considered that the agreement did not go nearly far enough in addressing the problem of global climate change. In its 1999 resolution urging ratification, the denomination's General Assembly asked "the U.S. Administration and Congress to devise, fund, and implement plans that aim well beyond the still very inadequate targets of the Kyoto Protocol."[23]

The United Methodist Church has an especially well developed and thoroughly articulated set of positions and policy recommendations regarding the environment.[24] In its resolution, "Environmental Justice and a Sustainable Future," adopted in 1992 and amended and readopted in 2004, the UMC expressed support for the Montreal Protocol, calling on the United States and other countries to "enforce agreements banning the use of chlorofluorocarbons (CFCs) to stop the depletion of the ozone layer." It advocated "measures calling for the reduction of carbon dioxide, methane, nitrogen oxides, and sulfur dioxide, which contribute to acid rain and global climate change." And it specifically called for the "ratification and enforcement of international frameworks, such as [the] Kyoto Protocol, that seek to reduce global greenhouse gas emissions."[25]

When U.S. support for international treaties concerning the environment has seemed out of reach politically, Mainline Protestant denominations have focused their advocacy efforts on domestic measures. In 2007, for example, U.S. senators Joseph Lieberman and John Warner, along with ten other cosponsors, introduced bipartisan legislation aimed at reducing emissions of greenhouse gases. The Climate Security Act would have created a "cap and trade" system in which corporations that were unable to meet their emission targets on schedule could have purchased extra carbon credits from companies that did not need them because their production processes were more environmentally friendly.[26] The bill, which was never voted upon, was reintroduced in 2008 by Senator Barbara Boxer.[27] Although the legislation again failed to reach a vote on the Senate floor, a variety of religious organizations joined together in a letter to the Senate supporting the legislation. Most of the major Mainline Protestant churches were among them, including the Episcopal Church, the ELCA, the Friends Committee on National Legislation, the PCUSA, the UCC, and the UMC.[28]

It is difficult, as Michael Moody has observed, to assess the impact of the activities of Mainline Protestant organizations on U.S. environmental policy, both domestically and internationally. In 1995, mainline denominations, acting largely through the National Religious Partnership for the Environment (NRPE), joined with the Evangelical Environmental Network (EEN, see below) in an effort to block revisions to the Endangered Species Act (ESA) proposed by the new Republican majority in Congress. Their lobbying, public education, and letter-writing campaign succeeded, and the attempt to weaken the ESA was shelved. Environmental advocates and even some Republican supporters of changes to the ESA credited the Christian groups with turning the tide.[29] But this episode seems to have been the exception rather than the rule. More often, Mainline Protestant organizations, concludes Moody, have been "quietly influential," exercising a "moderate and incremental influence on environmental legislation and other forms of policymaking."[30]

Roman Catholics

Like most Mainline Protestant denominations, the Roman Catholic Church has been a long-time advocate of protecting the global environment. On January 1, 1990, Pope John Paul II expressed the Church's concern with what he termed "the ecological crisis," and he urged action both internationally and domestically to address it. Said the pope:

> The gradual depletion of the ozone layer and the related "greenhouse effect" has now reached crisis proportions as a consequence of industrial growth, massive urban concentrations and vastly increased energy needs. Industrial waste, the burning of fossil fuels, unrestricted deforestation, the use of certain types of herbicides, coolants and propellants: all of these are known to harm the atmosphere and environment. The resulting meteorological and atmospheric changes range from damage to health to the possible future submersion of low-lying lands.
>
> While in some cases the damage already done may well be irreversible, in many other cases it can still be halted. It is necessary, however, that the entire human community—individuals, States and international bodies—take seriously the responsibility that is theirs.[31]

The United States Catholic Conference, following the lead of the pope, issued a pastoral statement on the environment in November 1991. Entitled *Renewing the*

Earth, the document cited a long list of ecological problems: acid rain, air and water pollution, loss of farmlands and wetlands, ozone depletion, deforestation, extinction of plants and animals, and global warming. Wrote the bishops,

> Our mistreatment of the natural world diminishes our own dignity and sacredness, not only because we are destroying resources that future generations of humans need, but because we are engaging in actions that contradict what it means to be human. Our tradition calls us to protect the life and dignity of the human person, and it is increasingly clear that this task cannot be separated from the care and defense of all of creation.[32]

In 1998, the Domestic and International Policy Committees of the USCC began studying the issue of global climate change, meeting with scientists and policy experts. Three years later, the USCC, together with the NCCB, issued the product of this study, *Global Climate Change: A Plea for Dialogue, Prudence, and the Common Good.* The bishops' statement accepted the conclusion of the IPCC that there was a sound scientific basis for the belief that global warming was being caused by human activity, and particularly by the emission of greenhouse gases from the combustion of fossil fuels. The NCCB/USCC also accepted the IPCC's portrayal of the long-term consequences that might ensue, noting that these consequences were likely to fall most heavily on "the poor, the vulnerable, and generations yet unborn." Although they declined to endorse the specifics of either the UNFCCC or the Kyoto Protocol, they wrote that "we Catholic bishops acknowledge the development of these international negotiations and hope they and other future efforts can lead to just and effective progress."[33]

The USCCB encouraged members of the U.S. Congress to amend the Energy Policy Act of 2005 in ways that would "genuinely help mitigate the adverse effects of climate change."[34] The bishops worked to ensure that the Climate Stewardship and Innovation Act of 2005 would address the needs of the poor both in the United States and elsewhere.[35] Shortly before a Group of 8 (G-8) summit meeting in July 2005, the USCCB wrote to President Bush, urging him to work with other global leaders toward meaningful action on climate change:

> The Summit agenda includes global climate change, an issue of particular concern to us. Because of where they live and their limited resources, the poor will experience most directly the possible harmful effects of climate change and any measures to address it, including potential escalating energy costs, work displacement and health problems. This is true here in the United States as well as abroad. While there are many technical aspects that need to be considered in addressing global climate change, we recognize our moral responsibility of stewardship. Our actions and decisions, particularly those regarding our use of energy resources, have a profound effect today and for future generations. While there may not be full scientific consensus or complete certainty as to the

consequences of climate change, there seems to be a sufficient scientific consensus that prudence would dictate taking preventive and mitigating action now.

When you and your G8 colleagues take up climate change at the Summit, we urge that you give priority to further research on the possible impact of climate change on the poor, and the need for programs to help the poor adapt and mitigate the worst effects. An agreement on even modest efforts could help send a signal that the time has come to move forward.[36]

Since 2005, the USCCB has written letters to Congressional leaders regarding the Church's position on global climate change. Their messages have expressed the need for "serious and urgent action to address the potential consequences of climate change." While declining to take a position on the specific provisions of particular pieces of legislation, the bishops have set forth three principles that they believe any legislation should embody: (1) prudence, taking action now to address problems that are likely to get worse over time, (2) pursuit of the common good rather than of parochial interests, and (3) priority for the needs of the poor.[37] John L. Carr, secretary of the USCCB's Department of Social Development and World Peace, articulated these principles in his 2007 testimony before the Senate Committee on Environment and Public Works.[38] In 2008, the USCCB issued two action alerts concerning the Climate Security Act, calling on Catholics to contact their senators and "urge them to support climate change legislation that reflects the demands of prudent action, promotes the common good and protects the poor."[39] When the bill failed to reach the floor of the Senate, the bishops wrote that "this non-victory is worth celebrating as it laid significant groundwork for next year."[40]

Evangelical Protestants

Evangelical Protestants have traditionally evinced less concern about protecting the environment than either Mainline Protestants or Roman Catholics. At the rank-and-file level, this is revealed in public opinion surveys, as noted above. By and large, the same has been true of evangelical denominations and other organizations. In 1971, the National Association of Evangelicals issued a brief statement on "Environment and Ecology" in which it identified a range of environmental issues and pledged its "cooperation to any responsible effort to solve critical environmental problems, and our willingness to support all proven solutions developed by competent authorities."[41] The language of this document—"responsible effort," "proven solutions," "competent authorities"—suggested only limited enthusiasm by the organization for policies aimed at environmental protection. Similarly, the Southern Baptist Convention in 1990 adopted a brief "Resolution on Environmental Stewardship," but the organization has not developed any set of detailed analyses or policy recommendations regarding the environment; neither has it established an organizational framework through which to advocate on environmental issues.[42]

The last decade of the twentieth century and the first decade of the twenty-first witnessed a potentially important shift in evangelical views regarding the global environment and efforts to protect it. Many evangelicals began to take a serious interest in environmental protection—often referred to in evangelical circles as "Creation Care."[43] In 1993, a group of progressive evangelicals formed the Evangelical Environmental Network (EEN). The organization "seeks to educate, inspire, and mobilize Christians in their effort to care for God's creation, to be faithful stewards of God's provision, and to advocate for actions and policies that honor God and protect the environment."[44] As noted above, one of the first efforts of the EEN, undertaken in the mid-1990s, was "to support the Endangered Species Act and prevent changes it feared would weaken the law."[45] In 2002, the EEN embarked upon a campaign, "What Would Jesus Drive?" aimed at reducing the usage of sport utility vehicles and other gasoline-guzzling cars and trucks.[46] "On the Care of Creation," authored by the EEN, reads very much like the statements of Mainline Protestant organizations and the Roman Catholic Church in its cataloging of environmental problems: land degradation, deforestation, species extinction, water degradation, global toxification, the alteration of atmosphere, human and cultural degradation.[47] Fact sheets produced by the EEN regarding these issues are virtually indistinguishable from those distributed by other Christian organizations in terms of the data they contain and their efforts to convey the severity of environmental problems.[48] What distinguishes the EEN from these other groups is primarily its emphasis on individual responsibility. Although it encourages Christians to make their voices heard by governmental officials, the EEN stresses actions to protect the environment that people can take in their own lives—from purchasing organic produce to recycling to driving less.[49] Much less attention is paid to regulation at either the national or international level.

The movement started by the EEN in the early 1990s subsequently spread to other, larger, and generally more conservative evangelical organizations. In October 2004, the National Association of Evangelicals adopted a statement, *For the Health of the Nation: An Evangelical Call for Civic Responsibility*, which read, in part: "We urge Christians to shape their personal lives in creation-friendly ways: practicing effective recycling, conserving resources, and experiencing the joy of contact with nature. We urge government to encourage fuel efficiency, reduce pollution, encourage sustainable use of natural resources, and provide for the proper care of wildlife and their natural habitats."[50] In March 2005, officials of the NAE held 2 days of meetings with members of Congress and the Bush administration to discuss how the problem of global warming might be addressed.[51] Said Richard Cizik, the NAE's vice president of governmental affairs, on Judgment Day, "I don't think God is going to ask us how he created the earth, but he will ask us what we did with what he created."[52] The president of the NAE, Ted Haggard, stated that "he had become passionate about global warming because of his experience scuba diving and observing the effects of rising ocean temperatures and pollution on coral reefs."[53]

Although environmentalism has gained considerable traction within the Evangelical Protestant community, it has not become dominant. Indeed, the evangelical environmental movement has sparked a countermovement, and, at this writing, evangelicals are sharply divided. Responding to the formation of the Evangelical Environmental Network and its activities, a group of more conservative evangelicals established the Cornwall Alliance for the Stewardship of Creation.[54] In 2000, it issued the "Cornwall Declaration on Environmental Stewardship," and, subsequently, "The Cornwall Stewardship Agenda."[55] Writing that "much environmental advocacy and activism contradict sound theology and sound science," the authors argued that "scripturally sound stewardship honors God's emphasis on meeting human needs (particularly those of the poor), cultivating human creativity and helping people flourish. Therefore, environmental policies should harness human creative potential by expanding political and economic freedom, instead of imposing draconian restrictions or seeking to reduce the 'human burden' on the natural world."[56] The Cornwall Alliance "opposes attempts under the Kyoto Protocol and other international agreements or domestic laws to curtail the use of fossil fuels, or to subsidize the production or use of alternative energy sources."[57]

The simmering tensions among evangelicals over the protection of the global environment, and especially over addressing climate change, came to a boil in 2006. In February of that year, the Evangelical Climate Initiative (ECI) issued "Climate Change: An Evangelical Call to Action."[58] The 86 signers included Rick Warren, pastor of the Saddleback Community Church and author of the best-seller, *The Purpose Driven Life*, who later delivered the invocation at the inauguration of President Barack Obama; David Neff, editor of the leading evangelical journal, *Christianity Today*; and Leith Anderson, a future president of the National Association of Evangelicals; as well as presidents of 39 evangelical colleges and universities.[59] They acknowledged that "for most of us, until recently this has not been treated as a pressing issue or major priority. Indeed, many of us have required considerable convincing before becoming persuaded that climate change is a real problem and that it ought to matter to us as Christians. But," they wrote, "now we have seen and heard enough to offer the following moral argument related to the matter of human-induced climate change." The document argued that human-induced climate change is real, that its consequences will be significant and most adversely affect the poor, that Christian moral convictions require a response, and that the need to act is urgent. It called on the U.S. government to promote reductions in carbon dioxide emissions through "cost-effective, market-based mechanisms" such as cap-and-trade.[60]

In response, 22 other evangelical leaders, among them James Dobson, founder of Focus on the Family, Chuck Colson, founder of Prison Fellowship Ministries, and Richard Land, president of the Ethics and Religious Liberty Commission of the Southern Baptist Convention, representing the newly formed Interfaith Stewardship Alliance (ISA), sent a letter to the NAE, asking that it not take a position on the matter of global warming because it was not "a consensus issue." NAE president Ted Haggard was forced to deny "reports that the NAE had circulated a draft paper calling for the Bush administration to support mandatory limits on carbon dioxide emissions."[61] Citing the "lack of consensus among the evangelical community on this issue," he assured the ISA that the NAE was "not considering a position on global warming."[62] Evangelical environmentalists were bitterly disappointed by what they saw as the NAE's retreat from its 2004 position, but members and supporters of the ISA were delighted.

A kind of civil war over global climate change continued among evangelicals after 2006. The Interfaith Stewardship Alliance targeted Richard Cizik, the NAE's vice president for governmental affairs, a founder of the Evangelical Climate Initiative and, as noted above, an increasingly outspoken advocate of environmental protection. In March 2007, the ISA called for Cizik to resign from his post because his "preoccupation" with climate concerns was taking attention away from "the great moral issues of our time" and because Cizik's views did not represent those of the broader evangelical community. Wrote the ISA, "If he cannot be trusted to articulate the views of American evangelicals on environmental issues, then we respectfully suggest that he be encouraged to resign his position with the NAE."[63] Cizik managed to retain his job until December 2008, when he was forced to resign after telling National Public Radio's Terry Gross that he supported civil unions for gays and that the issue of "health care is just as important to younger evangelicals as is abortion," positions that were anathema to conservative evangelicals.[64] In the wake of Cizik's resignation, NAE president Leith Anderson reiterated that that organization did not "have a specific position" on climate change and that Cizik had "spoken as an individual on that."[65] Calvin Beisner, a leading member of the Cornwall Alliance and its national spokesman, issued a statement suggesting that personal ambition had led Cizik astray, causing him to favor what the world wanted over what God wanted:

I'm grateful for the clear statement from National Association of Evangelicals president Leith Anderson. Richard Cizik unquestionably cultivated the appearance of official support for his personal global warming crusade, despite the NAE's acknowledgment of "the lack of consensus" in its constituency and despite the board's instructions "to stand by and not exceed in any fashion our approved and adopted statements" (which never even mention climate change).

The lesson is clear: When we uncritically adopt the world's agendas as our own, as Rev. Cizik did with global warming, it's easy to see how confusion in one area can lead to others. Long before he expressed support for civil unions, Cizik had already begun calling man-made climate change one of the greatest moral issues of our day and pronouncing God's judgment on those who disagreed.[66]

Beisner, Colson, Dobson, Land, and other conservative evangelical leaders formed WeGetIt.org, which claims to represent "mainstream evangelical opinion on global warming."[67] According to the organization, mainstream evangelical opinion holds that concern about climate change is largely a product of media hype and that climate change is cyclical and not primarily the result of human activity.[68] Among the national partners of WeGetIt.org is the Ethics and Religious Liberty Commission of the Southern Baptist Convention.

With the nation's largest Protestant denomination and many leading evangelicals still staunchly opposed to significant efforts to protect the global environment, the future evolution of evangelical thinking in this area is unclear. Jim Wallis, president of Sojourners and a founder of the Evangelical Climate Initiative, wrote in 2006 that a "sea change in evangelical Christian politics" was occurring and that the religious right has "lost control on the environmental issue—caring for God's creation is now a mainstream evangelical issue, especially for a new generation of evangelicals."[69] Three years later, however, Lee Marsden concluded that "the notion that there has been a significant cleavage within the Christian Right over environmental policy has been greatly exaggerated" and that "the overwhelming majority of conservative evangelical leaders have not altered their position."[70]

Explaining the Differences

Why do Mainline Protestants and Roman Catholics support international and other efforts to protect the global environment to a degree that Evangelical Protestants, especially fundamentalists, do not? One answer concerns the nature of the relationship of humankind to God's creation. In a famous 1967 essay, Lynn White suggested that the prevalence of what he termed the "dominion" view of this relationship was responsible, in part, for the growing ecological crisis.[71] In brief, the "dominion"—or "subjectionist"—view is that God created Earth for the benefit of human beings, who are thus entitled to use it and its resources as they desire. Conventional wisdom holds that the biblical foundation of the dominion view is contained primarily in the book of Genesis, which states:

> Then God said, "Let Us make man in Our image, according to Our likeness; let them have dominion over the fish of the sea, over the birds of the air, and over the cattle, over all the earth and over every creeping thing that creeps on the earth." So God created man in His own image; in the image of God He created him; male and female He created them. Then God blessed them, and God said to them, "Be fruitful and multiply; fill the earth and subdue it; have dominion over the fish of the sea, over the birds of the air, and over every living thing that moves on the earth."

The dominion perspective is nicely illustrated by remarks made by evangelical author Tim LaHaye in an interview with television journalist Larry King. When asked by King why evangelicals were not more outspoken on environmental issues,

LaHaye responded, "Because we believe that the environment was made for us. And not us for the environment. . . . [W]e Christians are not against clean air and water and preserving proper life. But we ought to have our values in priority. And we believe that human beings are more important than animals."[72] Ann Coulter, conservative Christian author and talk-show host, put it rather more provocatively when she told Fox News that "God gave us the earth. We have dominion over the plants, the animals, the trees. God said, 'Earth is yours. Take it. Rape it. It's yours.' "[73]

White regarded the dominion perspective as being characteristic of Western Judeo-Christian thought in general; he did not distinguish among Christians of different stripes. But as the remarks of Coulter and LaHaye suggest, within the U.S. Christian community subjectionism is "most strongly associated with fundamentalists and conservative evangelicals."[74] While the connection between subjectionism and unconcern with the environment is clear in the comments of these particular individuals, the social-scientific literature has had difficulty verifying this link among the broader population of fundamentalist and other evangelicals. One study of religious activists found that the absence of a strong environmental ethic was connected to certain evangelical (especially fundamentalist) beliefs, including a literal interpretation of the Bible—on which the dominion view would seem to rest—but it did not test the causal importance of the dominion view directly.[75] From their analysis of data from the 1993 General Social Survey, Eckberg and Blocker concluded that fundamentalism was associated with unconcern for the environment, but noted,

We cannot at this time nail down the source of the effect of fundamentalism. It could come about because of dominion statements in Genesis 1 (or other powerful religious concepts like end-times theology). It could also be that morality, biblical inerrancy, and "greenness" have all become politicized, serve as symbols of the two sides in the culture wars and *therefore* are statistically linked in survey research.[76]

Contrasted with the dominion view of the relationship between humans and the natural world is what is sometimes called the "stewardship" view.[77] This perspective is grounded in a number of biblical passages, including God's declaration, in Genesis, that his creation was "good," and David's statement in Ps. 24 that "the earth is the Lord's." Also relevant is the parable of the unjust steward recorded in the book of Luke, which ends with Jesus saying,

Whoever can be trusted with very little can also be trusted with much, and whoever is dishonest with very little will also be dishonest with much. So if you have not been trustworthy in handling worldly wealth, who will trust you with true riches? And if you have not been trustworthy with someone else's property, who will give you property of your own?

The *Book of Discipline* of the United Methodist Church conveys the essence of the stewardship view:

All creation is the Lord's, and we are responsible for the ways we use and abuse it. Water, air, soil, minerals, energy resources, plants, animal life, and space are to be valued and conserved because they are God's creation and not solely because they are useful to human beings. God has granted us stewardship of creation. We should meet these stewardship duties through acts of loving care and respect. Economic, political, social, and technological developments have increased our human numbers, and lengthened and enriched our lives. However, these developments have led to regional defoliation, dramatic extinction of species, massive human suffering, overpopulation, and misuse and overconsumption of natural and nonrenewable resources, particularly by industrialized societies. This continued course of action jeopardizes the natural heritage that God has entrusted to all generations. Therefore, let us recognize the responsibility of the church and its members to place a high priority on changes in economic, political, social, and technological lifestyles to support a more ecologically equitable and sustainable world leading to a higher quality of life for all of God's creation.[78]

The language of "stewardship" is so powerful that evangelical denominations and other organizations opposed to environmental protection—for example, the Interfaith Stewardship Alliance and the Cornwall Alliance for the Stewardship of Creation—have appropriated the term in a way that one author has called "deceptive."[79] Evangelical environmentalists, whose ranks have been growing (see above), invariably subscribe to a stewardship perspective. But this view is still most prominent within Mainline Protestant institutions and the Roman Catholic Church.

Beyond the dominion-stewardship divide, there is a second reason that Evangelical Protestants differ from Mainline Protestants and Roman Catholics on the need for protection of the international environment: the proximity, or lack thereof, of the end times and the Second Coming. Mainline Protestants and Catholics, for reasons discussed in previous chapters, do not generally believe humans can know when the world will come to an end. Because the end may be thousands, even millions of years away, it is incumbent upon Christians, they believe, to preserve a healthy Earth for future generations of people. Many Evangelical Protestants, particularly fundamentalist evangelicals, regard the Second Coming as being nearer at hand. Some, observing the formation of the United Nations, the establishment of the state of Israel, and certain other signs, believe humanity is already in the midst of the end times. If Jesus is returning soon—and if, as in certain evangelical doctrine, true Christians will be taken directly up to heaven in what is known as "the Rapture"—then there is no compelling reason to preserve Earth and protect its environment. As Glenn Scherer has written, "Many Christian fundamentalists feel that concern for our planet is irrelevant because it has no future."[80]

Perhaps the most widely recognized statement of the connection between fundamentalist eschatology and lack of concern for the environment was never actually uttered. According to Scherer, James Watt, the notoriously antienvironmentalist secretary of the interior under Ronald Reagan, told a Congressional committee in 1981 that he was unconcerned about the depletion of natural resources: "God gave us these things to use. After the last tree is felled, Christ will come back."[81] Alas, Watt, a member of the evangelical denomination, the Assemblies of God, said no such thing. What he actually said was, "I do not know how many future generations we can count on before the Lord returns, whatever it is we have to manage with a skill to have the resources needed for future generations."[82]

In their eagerness to discredit the religious right, observers such as Scherer may have exaggerated the importance of eschatology in shaping the environmental views of evangelicals. But this does not mean, as one author has concluded, that end-times theology plays no role in evangelical opposition to attempts to protect the global environment.[83] Environmental devastation and ecological crises are central to the plot of the *Left Behind* books and *The Late Great Planet Earth*.[84] In 2005, Hal Lindsey wrote that Hurricane Katrina signified that the Second Coming was "very near" and that Jesus would soon "snatch [believers] out of this world in the 'twinkling of an eye' " and "transform us from mortal to immortal and take us to be with Him." For this reason, he said, "There is no time to waste in frivolities that do not count for eternity."[85] A survey of religious activists has found that a lack of enthusiasm for protecting the environment is associated with fundamentalist evangelical beliefs, including dispensationalist eschatology and a belief in the proximity of the end times.[86] Authors of a second study have reported results that "strongly suggest that the complex of ideas in dispensational theology . . . may well condition fundamentalists, Pentecostals, and other evangelicals against active concerns with environmental policies."[87] Jim Wallis, editor of *Sojourners Magazine*, has chastised fellow evangelicals "who treat the imminent second coming of Jesus Christ as an excuse to ignore environmental issues and other concerns about this world."[88]

As noted in Chapter 4, Evangelical Protestants, Mainline Protestants, and Roman Catholics are all committed to the reduction of poverty around the world. Unlike their mainline and Catholic counterparts, however, many evangelicals regard this commitment as being incompatible with serious efforts to protect the global environment. The Cornwall Alliance has estimated that the Kyoto Protocol and other proposed actions to address climate change would cost a U.S. family of four between $1,000 and $4,000 per year and would "result in extensive unemployment." Beyond this, the Alliance contends, even if the Kyoto Protocol were fully implemented, it would barely affect Earth's temperature, but would cost the global economy at least $200 billion annually, with the heaviest burden falling on the "world's poorest families and countries. They would be prevented from developing the energy, jobs, and modern housing needed to eradicate poverty and disease, thus perpetuating the misery, despair, and death that pervade the developing world."[89]

While Mainline Protestants and Roman Catholics see addressing global climate change and other forms of environmental degradation as being crucial to sustainable economic growth—and hence the reduction of poverty—over the long run, some Evangelical Protestants demur. They believe that environmental protection will hinder economic growth and that certain environmental trends may not be undesirable. The Cornwall Alliance contends that warming of Earth and increased carbon dioxide levels in the atmosphere may actually be beneficial to crop growth and agricultural productivity.[90]

Other factors also help to explain differences among Evangelical Protestants, Mainline Protestants, and Catholics on protecting the global environment.[91] One of these concerns their attitudes regarding scientific claims. Mainline denominations and the Roman Catholic Church, having long ago abandoned a literal reading of the Bible, have no difficulty in accepting scientific accounts of creation. They are inclined to accept the view prevailing within the scientific community that climate change is real and that it is a consequence of human activities. On the other hand, many evangelicals, adhering to a literal interpretation of the book of Genesis, reject Darwinian evolution and are thus skeptical of science more generally. As the NAE's Richard Cizik noted shortly before his ouster, "Historically, evangelicals have reasoned like this: Scientists believe in evolution. Scientists are telling us climate change is real. Therefore, I won't believe what scientists are saying."[92] Many evangelicals continue to insist that there is little or no agreement among scientists on either the causes or the significance of global climate change. Calvin Beisner has written that the scientific "consensus" on global climate change is "fictional."[93] In June 2007, the Southern Baptist Convention adopted a resolution stating that "the scientific community is divided regarding the extent to which humans are responsible for recent global warming" and that "many scientists reject the idea of catastrophic human-induced global warming."[94]

Evangelicals are also more likely than either Mainline Protestants or Roman Catholics to regard environmentalism as idolatry—the worship of a false god. According to the Southern Baptist Convention, many Americans have "completely rejected God the Father in favor of deifying 'Mother Earth,' made environmentalism into a neo-pagan religion, and elevated animal and plant life to the place of equal—or greater—value with human life."[95] The Assemblies of God agree: "Today in our American culture, many people have turned their adoration from the Creator to the creation. They have gone to the extreme and are now worshiping the earth. We believe *worship* of the land, the sea, the oceans, and other attributes of the earth is an abomination to God—the Creator."[96]

The Assemblies of God fear that efforts to protect the environment will distract believers from the things that are truly important. "A major concern for Christians," they write, "is the overemphasis of the environment at the expense of spiritual issues effecting life and eternity."[97] Other evangelicals concur. Jerry Falwell told his listeners in 2007 that "alarmism over global warming" was "Satan's attempt to re-direct the church's primary focus."[98] The SBC has worried that "environmentalism is threatening to become a wedge issue to divide the evangelical community and further distract its members from the priority of the Great Commission" and the saving of souls.[99] This view is not, of course, shared by members of the Evangelical Climate Initiative and other evangelical environmentalists, but it is common within the evangelical community nonetheless.[100]

Some evangelicals, unlike most Mainline Protestants and Catholics, believe that environmental disaster is impossible, that human beings are incapable of doing serious damage to the creation of an omniscient and omnipotent God. Calvin Beisner has written that "just as good engineers build multiple layers of protection into complex buildings and systems, so also the wise Creator has built multiple self-protecting and self-correcting layers into His world. Positive and negative feedback mechanisms often minimize or quickly repair environmental damage." For this reason, "irreversible, catastrophic damage is rare to nonexistent in the world's history. What we see instead is a planet capable of recovering from many events we might shortsightedly see as permanent." Indeed, contends Beisner, God will not allow such damage to occur because to do so would violate the promise made to Noah after the flood that he would never again destroy the world. The "super-intending hand of God protecting the Earth," together with "the resiliency of the Earth because of God's wise design," he writes, "ought to make Christians inherently skeptical of claims that this or that human action threatens permanent and catastrophic damage to the Earth."[101]

Evangelicals, in contrast to many Mainline Protestants and Roman Catholics, tend to favor voluntary action and private, market-based solutions over regulation, national and international. The Cornwall Declaration states,

> We aspire to a world in which liberty as a condition of moral action is preferred over government-initiated management of the environment as a means to common goals. We aspire to a world in which the relationships between stewardship and private property are fully appreciated, allowing people's natural incentive to care for their own property to reduce the need for collective ownership and control of resources and enterprises, and in which collective action, when deemed necessary, takes place at the most local level possible.[102]

According to the ECI, "To protect freedom, unnecessary government regulations must be avoided. Government policies should be structured to allow the free market to solve the problem to the greatest extent possible. We should use the least amount of government power necessary to achieve the objective."[103]

To explain fully why Evangelical Protestants, more than either Mainline Protestants or Roman Catholics, favor free-market economics and oppose regulation is beyond the scope of this chapter. Part of the reason, however, concerns the origins of neoclassical economic theory and the important role played in its emergence in Britain by evangelical Christians. Adam Smith and David Ricardo argued that the so-called invisible hand would promote efficiency and lead to the unprecedented production of wealth, but they also believed that different economic classes had different interests that would inevitably set them one against another. As Gordon Bigelow has observed,

> The group that bridled most against these pessimistic elements of Smith and Ricardo was the evangelicals. . . . For them it was unthinkable that capitalism led to class conflict, for that would mean that God had created a world at war with itself. The evangelicals believed in a providential God, one who built a logical and orderly universe, and they saw the new industrial economy as a fulfillment of God's plan. The free market, they believed, was a perfectly designed instrument to reward good Christian behavior and to punish and humiliate the unrepentant.[104]

According to Bigelow, for evangelicals of Victorian England,

> The trials of economic life—the sweat of hard labor, the fear of poverty, the self-denial involved in saving—were earthly tests of sinfulness and virtue. . . . [T]hey regarded poverty as part of a divine program. Evangelicals interpreted the mental anguish of poverty and debt, and the physical agony of hunger or cold, as natural spurs to prick the conscience of sinners. They believed that the suffering of the poor would provoke remorse, reflection, and ultimately the conversion that would change their fate. In other words, poor people were poor for a reason, and helping them out of poverty would endanger their mortal souls. It was the evangelicals who began to see the business mogul as an heroic figure, his wealth a triumph of righteous will. The stockbroker, who to Adam Smith had been a suspicious and somewhat twisted character, was for nineteenth-century evangelicals a spiritual victor.[105]

Contemporary evangelical doctrine in the United States is of course considerably more compassionate in its attitudes toward the poor. But echoes of nineteenth-century evangelicalism are often heard in what is referred to as "prosperity theology" or the "prosperity gospel." Preached by televangelists such as Joel Osteen and the late Oral Roberts, the notion that material possessions are a sign of God's favor—that God wants Christians to be rich and will make them so—is highly controversial and has been rejected by many evangelical leaders.[106] There is greater consensus on the importance of private property and free markets, and the concomitant rejection of regulation. In 1978, the Southern Baptist Convention, in a Resolution On Economic Responsibility, stated that "the free enterprise system has been successful and should be kept."[107]

Opposition to regulation, together with a generally negative view toward international law and institutions (see Chapter 6), helps to explain why even those evangelicals who believe the global environment must be protected shun international solutions such as the Kyoto Protocol. In 2004, the editors of *Christianity Today*, while favoring action to combat global climate change, nevertheless agreed with a writer in the *Harvard International Review* who stated, "International coordination is likely to slow and divert truly effective action."[108] Indeed, as John Nagle notes, "In the end, the division among evangelicals regarding climate change largely disappears with respect to the dispute about the Kyoto Protocol and the use of international law to address climate change."[109]

Summary

Among U.S. Christians, Mainline Protestants are most likely to favor protection of the global environment and to view international treaties such as the Kyoto Protocol as an effective means of doing so. Evangelical Protestants, especially fundamentalists, are the least likely, with Roman Catholics in the middle, but closer to the mainline perspective.

The differences between the groups are grounded in a variety of factors: views regarding the relationship between humankind and nature, eschatology, attitudes toward science and the validity of scientific claims, the priority attached to goals besides environmental protection, and beliefs regarding free markets and governmental regulation of the economy. These factors are reflected in Table 7.1.

It is difficult to prove conclusively that the views of U.S. Christians have exerted a significant effect on U.S. environmental policy, and particularly on the U.S. commitment to international action to protect the environment. Some observers have contended that evangelical beliefs are responsible for the generally antienvironmental perspective of Republican lawmakers, beginning in the 1980s. Writing in 2004, Glenn Scherer took particular aim at House Majority Leader Tom DeLay and Sen. James Inhofe, chair of the Senate Environment and Public Works Committee, both evangelical Christians. According to Scherer,

> Neither DeLay nor Inhofe include environmental protection in "the Lord's work." Both have ranted against the [Environmental Protection Agency], calling it "the Gestapo." DeLay has fought to gut the Clean Air and Endangered Species acts. Last year, Inhofe invited a stacked-deck of fossil fuel-funded climate-change skeptics to testify at a Senate hearing that climaxed with him calling global warming "the greatest hoax ever perpetrated on the American people."[110]

The circumstantial evidence may seem compelling, but Scherer was unable to produce any direct evidence to link DeLay's and Inhofe's hostility toward environmental protection to their evangelical religious beliefs. Indeed, he noted that Inhofe never expressed his religious views in his capacity as committee chair.[111] It is certainly true that, given the lukewarm attitude among many evangelicals toward efforts at environmental protection, Republican leaders, including President George W. Bush, felt no pressure to act on environmental issues. Interestingly, in April 2008, Bush did for the first time acknowledge that human-induced global climate change was a fact, and he expressed a commitment to seeing the United States reduce its emissions of

Table 7.1: Views of U.S. Christians Regarding Protection of the International Environment

	Mainline Protestants	Evangelical Protestants	Roman Catholics
Protection of the Environment	Tend to regard it as a serious problem demanding prompt action, including national and international regulation	Divided; freestyle evangelicals are typically concerned with "creation care," but fundamentalists often are not. Oppose national and international regulation	Tend to regard it as a serious problem demanding prompt action, including national and international regulation
Relationship between Humans and Earth	Stewardship; humans are responsible for taking care of God's creation and not damaging it unduly	Divided; freestyle evangelicals tend toward a stewardship view; fundamentalists tend toward a subjectionist or dominion view—that God created Earth for humans to use as they see fit	Stewardship; humans are responsible for taking care of God's creation and not damaging it unduly
Proximity of the End Times	Unknowable, but quite possibly far in the future	Often believed to be near, based on a literal reading of the Bible and interpretation of world events	Unknowable, but quite possibly far in the future
View of Science	Respect science	Often distrust science because it is inconsistent with a literal reading of the Bible	Respect science
Relationship between Environment and Economy	Tend to see environmental protection as critical to long-term economic growth; emphasize sustainability	Tend to see environmental protection as hindering economic growth and thus contributing to poverty and human misery	Tend to see environmental protection as critical to long-term economic growth; emphasize sustainability
Believe that Environmental Protection is "Earth Worship" and Idolatry	No	Sometimes	No
Believe Environmental Protection Distracts People from More Important Spiritual Issues	No	Sometimes	No
Believe that Environmental Disaster is Impossible	No	Sometimes; either because God's promise to Noah after the flood precludes it, or because God created Earth with self-correcting mechanisms	No
Commitment to Laissez-Faire Economics	Low; do not believe capitalism was ordained by God; do believe that the system produces inequities that should be addressed through regulation and redistribution	High; tend to believe free markets were created by God as tests of human virtue; often believe that wealth is a sign of God's favor and that poverty is a sign of God's disfavor	Low; do not believe capitalism was ordained by God; do believe that the system produces inequities that should be addressed through regulation and redistribution

greenhouse gases by the year 2025. Many environmentalists were unimpressed, but others, including Philip Clapp of the Pew Environment Group, regarded the president's speech as marking "a significant political shift in the debate over U.S. climate policy."[112] To the extent that this is true, Bush's change in heart may have been at least partly the consequence of growing environmentalist sentiment among evangelicals, a large portion of his political base.

With Mainline Protestants and Roman Catholics solidly in the environmentalist camp, the evolution of attitudes among evangelicals is likely to be crucial in coming years. If, as Jim Wallis has suggested, the fundamentalist tide is ebbing and creation care has truly become a mainstream evangelical issue—one that evangelical voters regard as important—the political implications could be enormous. Candidates who espouse environmentally friendly policies are more likely to be elected. It will be increasingly easy for environmentally sensitive U.S. governments to enact policies aimed at curbing global climate change and other ecological problems, and it will be more difficult for presidents and Congressional leaders who oppose such policies to maintain their resistance.

Notes

1. Rachel Carson, *Silent Spring* (Boston, MA: Houghton Mifflin Co.; Cambridge: Riverside Press, 1962).
2. Information regarding CITES is at www.cites.org/.
3. Information regarding the Convention on Wetlands is at www.ramsar.org/.
4. Information regarding the UNCCD is at www.unccd.int/.
5. Robert Paarlberg, "The Eagle and the Global Environment: The Burden of Being Essential," in *Eagle Rules? Foreign Policy and American Primacy in the Twenty-First Century*, ed. Robert J. Lieber (Upper Saddle River, NJ: Pearson/Prentice-Hall, 2002), 325–27.
6. The National Oceanic and Atmospheric Administration (NOAA) provides a good basic overview of the issue at www.ozonelayer.noaa.gov/science/basics.htm.
7. Paarlberg, "Eagle and the Global Environment," 327–33.
8. A list of countries party to the Protocol is at http://maindb.unfccc.int/public/country.pl?group=kyoto.
9. Paarlberg, "Eagle and the Global Environment," 333–36.
10. The list of parties is available through the CBD's website at www.cbd.int/convention/parties/list/.
11. Barna Group, "Born Again Christians Remain Skeptical, Divided About Global Warming," September 17, 2007, www.barna.org/barna-update/article/20-donorscause/95-born-again-christians-remain-skeptical-divided-about-global-warming. It should be remembered that the Barna Group has a restrictive definition of evangelicals that understates their numbers compared to most other polling organizations. See Chapter 1.
12. Pew Forum, "U.S. Religious Landscape Survey," Report 2, 104.
13. Baylor ISR, "American Piety in the 21st Century," 24.
14. A good, brief account of Mainline Protestant advocacy on environmental issues is Michael Moody, "Caring for Creation: Environmental Advocacy by Mainline Protestant

Organizations," in *The Quiet Hand of God: Faith-Based Activism and the Public Role of Mainline Protestantism*, ed. Robert Wuthnow and John H. Evans (Berkeley, CA: University of California Press, 2002), 237–64.

15. The website for the NCC's Eco-Justice Program is at www.nccecojustice.org.
16. NCC, "NCC Spurs Four-Pronged, Interfaith Global Warming Strategy," August 18, 1998, www.ncccusa.org/news/news74.html.
17. NCC, "NCC Interfaith Climate Change Campaign Extends to 18 States," March 31, 2001, www.ncccusa.org/news/01news30.html.
18. NCC, "Open Letter to President Obama," October 8, 2008, www.nccecojustice.org/climate/presidentialletter.php.
19. NCC, "Carmichael Says New Emission Standards Will Protect Health, Reduce Global Warming," January 27, 2009, www.ncccusa.org/news/090127autostandards.html.
20. ELCA, *Caring For Creation: Vision, Hope, and Justice*, http://archive.elca.org/socialstatements/environment/.
21. UCC, "Resolution on Global Warming," www.uccecoaction.org/Warming99.html.
22. PCUSA, Washington Office, "Action Alert on Climate Change," January 4, 1999, www.pcusa.org/washington/issuenet/enviro-000900.htm.
23. PCUSA, "Kyoto Protocol, 1998" and "Kyoto Protocol, 1999," www.nccecojustice.org/downloads/anth/pres.pdf.
24. For links to the UMC's many denominational statements on the environment, see www.umc.org/interior.asp?mid=676.
25. UMC, "Environmental Justice for a Sustainable Future," *Book of Resolutions–2004*, http://archives.umc.org/interior.asp?ptid=4&mid=959.
26. Details of the bill (S. 2191) are at www.govtrack.us/congress/bill.xpd?bill=s110–2191.
27. Details of the bill (S. 3036) are at www.govtrack.us/congress/bill.xpd?bill=s110–3036.
28. ELCA, "Global Warming," http://archive.elca.org/advocacy/environment/lieberman-warner.html. For the letter itself, see www2.elca.org/advocacy/environment/WISC-L-W-bill-5.08-final.pdf.
29. Moody, "Caring for Creation," 248–49.
30. Moody, "Caring for Creation," 252.
31. John Paul II, "Peace with God the Creator, Peace with All of Creation," January 1, 1990, www.vatican.va/holy_father/john_paul_ii/messages/peace/documents/hf_jp-ii_mes_19891208_xxiii-world-day-for-peace_en.html.
32. USCC, *Renewing the Earth: An Invitation to Reflection and Action on Environment in Light of Catholic Social Teaching*, November 14, 1991, www.usccb.org./sdwp/ejp/bishopsstatement.shtml.
33. USCCB, *Global Climate Change: A Plea for Dialogue, Prudence, and the Common Good*, June 15, 2001, www.usccb.org./sdwp/international/globalclimate.shtml.
34. John H. Ricard, "U.S. Energy Policy Should Consider the Impact on the Poor," June 16, 2005, www.usccb.org/comm/archives/2005/05-149.shtml.
35. Ricard, "U.S. Energy Policy."
36. USCCB, "Letter to President Bush before the G-8 Summit," June 28, 2005, www.usccb.org./sdwp/international/g8bush.shtml.
37. Thomas G. Wenski, "Letter to Sen. Pete Domenici and Sen. Jeff Bingaman," March 13, 2006, www.usccb.org/sdwp/international/draft_2%20_consultation.pdf.
38. John L. Carr, "Written Testimony: Religious and Moral Dimensions of Global Climate Change," June 7, 2007, www.usccb.org/sdwp/ejp/climate/June07FinalTestimony.pdf.

39. USCCB, "Action Alert," May 30, 2008, www.usccb.org/sdwp/aa_climate_change.pdf. See also, USCCB, "Action Alert," June 5, 2008, www.usccb.org/sdwp/cloture_vote_climate.pdf.
40. USCCB, "Update: Climate Legislation," June 10, 2008, www.usccb.org/sdwp/alertsummaryjun1008.pdf.
41. NAE, "Environment and Ecology," www.nae.net/government-affairs/policy-resolutions/138-environment-and-ecology-1971-.
42. SBC, "Resolution on Environmental Stewardship," www.sbc.net/resolutions/amResolution.asp?ID=456.
43. A good account of the environmental movement among evangelicals, and opposition to it from other evangelicals, is John Copeland Nagle, "The Evangelical Debate over Climate Change," *University of St. Thomas Law Journal*, 5, no. 1 (Winter 2008): 52–86. Available for download at http://papers.ssrn.com/sol3/papers.cfm?abstract_id=1021712.
44. The homepage of the EEN is at www.creationcare.org.
45. Nagle, "Evangelical Debate over Climate Change," 61.
46. Nagle, "Evangelical Debate over Climate Change," 62.
47. Evangelical Environmental Network [hereinafter EEN], "On the Care of Creation: An Evangelical Declaration on the Care of Creation," www.creationcare.org/resources/declaration.php.
48. EEN, "Quick Facts and References," www.creationcare.org/resources/sunday/facts.php.
49. EEN, "Action Suggestions," www.creationcare.org/resources/sunday/actions.php.
50. NAE, *For the Health of the Nation*.
51. Laurie Goodstein, "Evangelical Leaders Swing Influence Behind Effort to Combat Global Warming," *New York Times*, March 10, 2005, www.nytimes.com/2005/03/10/national/10evangelical.html.
52. Quoted in Goodstein, "Evangelical Leaders Swing Influence."
53. Goodstein, "Evangelical Leaders Swing Influence."
54. The homepage of the Cornwall Alliance is at www.cornwallalliance.org/.
55. Cornwall Alliance, "Cornwall Declaration on Environmental Stewardship," www.cornwallalliance.org/articles/read/the-cornwall-declaration-on-environmental-stewardship/. Cornwall Alliance, "Cornwall Stewardship Agenda," www.cornwallalliance.org/articles/read/cornwall-stewardship-agenda/.
56. Cornwall Alliance, "Cornwall Stewardship Agenda."
57. Cornwall Alliance, "Cornwall Stewardship Agenda."
58. The homepage of the ECI is at http://christiansandclimate.org/.
59. Margot Roosevelt, "Evangelicals Go Green," *Time.com*, February 8, 2008, www.time.com/time/nation/article/0,8599,1157612,00.html.
60. ECI, "Climate Change: An Evangelical Call to Action."
61. Alan Cooperman, "Evangelicals Will Not Take Stand on Global Warming," *Washington Post*, February 2, 2006, A08, www.washingtonpost.com/wp-dyn/content/article/2006/02/01/AR2006020102132.html.
62. Ted Haggard, "Response to ISA Appeal Signers by NAE President Rev. Ted Haggard," January 25, 2006, www.pbs.org/moyers/moyersonamerica/green/nae_response.pdf.
63. Sheryl Henderson Blount, "Climate Change is Here to Stay," *Christianity Today*, March 30, 2007, www.christianitytoday.com/ct/2007/marchweb-only/113–52.0.html.

64. Sarah Pulliam, "Richard Cizik Resigns from the National Association of Evangelicals," *Christianity Today*, December 2008, www.christianitytoday.com/ct/2008/decemberweb-only/150-42.0.html.

65. Cornwall Alliance, "Evangelical Environmental Group Applauds National Association of Evangelicals, NAE Disavows Stance on Climate Change," www.cornwallalliance. org/press/read/evangelical-environmental-group-applauds-national-association-of-evangelicals/.

66. Quoted in Cornwall Alliance, "Evangelical Environmental Group Applauds National Association of Evangelicals."

67. Cornwall Alliance, "Evangelical Environmental Group Applauds National Association of Evangelicals."

68. The group's website is at www.we-get-it.org/.

69. Jim Wallis, "An Evangelical Climate Change," *Sojourners Magazine*, May 2006, www. sojo.net/index.cfm?action=magazine.article&issue=soj0605&article=060551.

70. Marsden, *For God's Sake*, 172.

71. Lynn White, Jr., "On the Historical Roots of Our Ecologic Crisis," *Science* (March 1967): 1203–07, www.jstor.org/stable/1720120.

72. "Larry King Live: America's Most Influential Evangelicals," February 1, 2005, http://transcripts.cnn.com/TRANSCRIPTS/0502/01/lkl.01.html.

73. *Hannity and Colmes*, Fox News Broadcast, June 20, 2001; quoted in Paul Maltby, "Fundamentalist Dominion, Postmodern Ecology," *Ethics & the Environment*, 13, no. 2 (Autumn 2008): 120, http://muse.jhu.edu/journals/ethics_and_the_environment/v013/13.2.maltby.html.

74. Raymond E. Grizzle, Paul E. Rothrock, and Christopher B. Barrett, "Evangelicals and Environmentalism: Past, Present, and Future," *Trinity Journal* (Spring 1998), http://findarticles.com/p/articles/mi_qa3803/is_199804/ai_n8791173/pg_14?tag=content;col1.

75. James L. Guth, Lyman A. Kellstedt, Corwin E. Smidt, and John C. Green, "Theological Perspectives and Environmentalism Among Religious Activists," *Journal for the Scientific Study of Religion*, 32, no. 4 (December 1993): 373–82, www.jstor.org/stable/1387177. By contrast, Woodrum and Hoban did not find a strong correlation between a belief in the literal accuracy of the Genesis creation account and subjectionist views. See Eric Woodrum and Thomas Hoban, "Theology and Religiosity Effects on Environmentalism," *Review of Religious Research*, 35, no. 3 (March 1994): 202, www.jstor.org/stable/3511888.

76. Douglas Lee Eckberg and T. Jean Blocker, "Christianity, Environmentalism, and the Theoretical Problem of Fundamentalism," *Journal for the Scientific Study of Religion*, 35, no. 4 (December 1996): 354, www.jstor.org/stable/i260038.

77. In early survey-based analyses, the dominion view—sometimes referred to as the "mastery-over-nature" view—was placed in conceptual opposition to a "unity-with-nature" view. The stewardship view was later proposed as an intermediate perspective (with humans above, but responsible for, the natural world). See Ronald G. Shaiko, "Religion, Politics, and Environmental Concern: A Powerful Mix of Passions," *Social Science Quarterly*, 8, no. 2 (June 1987): 243–62, http://pao.chadwyck.com.

78. UMC, "Environmental Justice for a Sustainable Future."

79. Maltby, "Fundamentalist Dominion, Postmodern Ecology," 121.

80. Glenn Scherer, "The Godly Must Be Crazy: Christian-Right Views are Swaying Politicians and Threatening the Environment," *Grist*, October 27, 2004, www.grist.org/news/maindish/2004/10/27/scherer-christian/.
81. Quoted in Scherer, "The Godly Must Be Crazy."
82. Quoted in Nagle, "Evangelical Debate over Climate Change."
83. Nagle, "Evangelical Debate over Climate Change."
84. Maltby, "Fundamentalist Dominion, Postmodern Ecology."
85. Hal Lindsey, "Signs from the Heavens," www.his-forever.com/a-printable_09_14_05.htm. See also Marsden, *For God's Sake*, 168.
86. Guth, Kellstedt, Smidt, and Green, "Theological Perspectives and Environmentalism."
87. James L. Guth, John C. Green, Lyman A. Kellstedt, and Corwin E. Smidt, "Faith and the Environment: Religious Beliefs and Attitudes on Environmental Policy," *American Journal of Political Science*, 39, no. 2 (May 1995): 377.
88. Jim Wallis, "Hearts and Minds: For the Health of the Nation," *Sojourners Magazine*, May 2005, www.sojo.net/index.cfm?action=magazine.article&issue=soj0505&article=050551.
89. Cornwall Alliance, "Cornwall Stewardship Agenda."
90. Cornwall Alliance, "Cornwall Stewardship Agenda."
91. Much of what follows draws on Nagle, "Evangelical Debate Over Climate Change."
92. *CNN Presents: God's Christian Warriors*, August 23, 2007; quoted in Nagle, "Evangelical Debate over Climate Change," 72.
93. E. Calvin Beisner, "Global Warming: Why Evangelicals Should Not Be Alarmed," www.ecalvinbeisner.com/freearticles/GW--Whynottobealarmed.pdf.
94. SBC, "On Global Warming," June 2007, www.sbc.net/resolutions/amResolution.asp?ID=1171.
95. SBC, "On Environmentalism and Evangelicals," June 2006, www.sbc.net/resolutions/amResolution.asp?ID=1159.
96. AOG, "Environmental Protection," www.ag.org/top/beliefs/contemporary_issues/issues_02_environment.cfm.
97. AOG, "Environmental Protection."
98. Falwell, "The Myth of Global Warming," http://trbc.org/new/sermons.php?url=20070225_11AM.html.
99. SBC, "On Environmentalism and Evangelicals."
100. Nagle, "Evangelical Debate over Climate Change," 78.
101. E. Calvin Beisner, "Biblical Principles for Environmental Stewardship," in *An Examination of the Scientific, Ethical and Theological Implications of Climate Change Policy*, ed. Roy W. Spencer, Paul K. Driessen, and E. Calvin Beisner (Interfaith Stewardship Alliance, 2005), available for download at www.cornwallalliance.org/articles/read/an-examination-of-the-scientific-ethical-and-theological-implications-of-climate-change-policy/.
102. Cornwall Alliance, "Cornwall Declaration."
103. ECI, "Principles for Federal Policy on Climate Change," available for download at http://christiansandclimate.org/policy-makers/.
104. Gordon Bigelow, "Let There Be Markets: The Evangelical Roots of Economics," *Harper's Magazine*, May 2005, www.harpers.org/archive/2005/05/0080538.
105. Bigelow, "Let There Be Markets."

106. David Van Biema and Jeff Chu, "Does God Want You to Be Rich?" *Time.com*, September 10, 2006, www.time.com/time/magazine/article/0,9171,1533448,00.html.

107. SBC, "Resolution on Economic Responsibility," June 1978, www.sbc.net/resolutions/amResolution.asp?ID=457.

108. "Heat Stroke: The Climate for Addressing Global Warming is Improving (Where We Stand: CT's View on Key Issues)," *Christianity Today*, 48, no. 10 (October 2004): 202. *Expanded Academic ASAP*. Web.

109. Nagle, "Evangelical Debate over Climate Change," 83.

110. Scherer, "The Godly Must Be Crazy."

111. Scherer, "The Godly Must Be Crazy."

112. J. R. Pegg, "Bush Climate Speech Covers Familiar Ground," *Environmental News Service*, April 1, 2008, www.ens-newswire.com/ens/apr2008/2008-04-16-10.asp.

CHAPTER 8

Conclusion

Religious Beliefs and Foreign Policy Preferences

This study has shown that there exist significant differences among Evangelical Protestants, Mainline Protestants, and Roman Catholics on a number of foreign policy issues. These differences are more pronounced at the organizational and "elite" levels than among the laity. This is, of course, because the doctrinal views of those who fill the pews on Sunday mornings are less likely to be consistent with denominational orthodoxy than the views of the denominational leadership. And in the end, it is theology and associated beliefs—not denominational affiliation—that most strongly affect foreign policy preferences.

It is partly for this reason that differences between fundamentalist evangelicals on the one hand and Mainline Protestants and Roman Catholics on the other tend to be greater than the differences between non-fundamentalist or freestyle evangelicals and other types of Christians. With respect to foreign policy preferences, it may make a certain amount of sense to distinguish, as Walter Russell Mead has done, between evangelicals and fundamentalists rather than lumping them together within the same category. At the least, it is important for observers of the contemporary U.S. religious scene to understand that fundamentalist views are not necessarily characteristic of evangelicals as a group and that the picture that one sometimes receives, particularly from journalistic and other popular accounts, of a monolithic evangelical movement is a gross oversimplification of reality.

Despite the complexity of the situation, one can still say that, in general, Evangelical Protestants are more favorably disposed toward the use of force than Mainline Protestants and Roman Catholics, less interested in protection of the international environment, more supportive of Israel, and less supportive of international institutions and international cooperation. The groups share a strong commitment to human rights, but Evangelical Protestants tend to focus on the rights of unborn children and religious freedom, while Mainline Protestants place more emphasis on a broader range of political, social, and economic rights, which they often conceive as matters of justice. Roman Catholics tend to align with Evangelical Protestants on aid for international family planning and religious freedom, but with Mainline Protestants on other human rights issues. The differences between the three groups in terms of foreign policy positions have their origins in underlying doctrinal differences regarding such matters as how the Bible should be interpreted, the view of God, eschatology, the view of Satan and of evil, and the view of the relationship between Christians and their churches on the one hand and civil government on the other. These conclusions are summarized in Tables 8.1 and 8.2.

Table 8.1: Summary of Foreign Policy Differences among U.S. Christians

	Mainline Protestants	Evangelical Protestants	Roman Catholics
Use of Force	Generally oppose use of force, favor negotiated settlements; favor arms control and disarmament efforts, oppose first use of nuclear weapons, oppose WMD, oppose land mines	Tend to support use of force and associated policies, few official positions on arms control and related issues	Presumption against use of force, favor arms control and disarmament efforts, oppose WMD, oppose land mines, oppose international arms trade
United Nations, International Law and Organizations	Support international law and institutions; see the United Nations as best hope for international peace	Generally not supportive of international law and institutions; tend to see the United Nations as ineffective or even evil	Church holds permanent observer status at the United Nations; generally very supportive of international law and institutions
Middle East	Emphasize rights of Palestinians as well as those of Israel; hope for negotiated settlement leading to formation of Palestinian state	More likely to offer unqualified support for government of Israel; generally oppose formation of a Palestinian state	Favor Roadmap to Peace and two-state solution; condemn both Palestinian terrorism and harsh Israeli responses to it; support assistance to Palestinian people
Human Rights	Emphasize broad range of rights, including political, social, economic, and cultural; often frame rights as matters of "justice"	Particularly concerned with freedom of religion and the rights of the unborn, but have recently broadened concerns to include human trafficking, poverty, hunger, and torture	High level of concern for rights of the unborn and with religious freedom; emphasize a broad range of rights, including economic, social, and political, framing them as matters of "justice"
International Environmental Protection	Highly concerned, support international agreements and regulation	Less concerned, but becoming more so; significant split between fundamentalists and others; generally oppose international agreements and regulation	Highly concerned, support international cooperation but Church usually does not take positions on specific agreements

Table 8.2: Explaining Foreign Policy Differences among U.S. Christians

	Mainline Protestants	Evangelical Protestants	Roman Catholics
View of War	Some pacifism, mostly just war theory, often with strong presumption against war	Some pacifism, mostly just war theory, with little or no presumption against war	Just war theory, with strong presumption against war
View of Government	Less likely to see government as deserving of deference, more likely to place "cross above flag"	More likely to see government as instituted by God to maintain order and punish wrong, deserving of deference	Vatican is a state; relatively low level of deference to governments of other states
Relationship between God and the United States	Less likely to see the United States as specially favored by God	More likely to see the United States as specially favored by God	Less likely to see the United States as specially favored by God
View of Evil and Satan	More likely to see Satan as metaphorical; evil exists, but it is the product of human society and human actions	More likely to see Satan as a supernatural being and to believe that some humans are his agents	More likely to see Satan as metaphorical and to see evil as the product of human society
View of God	More likely to see God as loving and nurturing; references to God may be feminine or gender-neutral; God often viewed as Distant or Benevolent	More likely to see God as judge or disciplinarian, references to God almost always masculine; God often viewed as Authoritarian	More likely to see God as loving and nurturing; references to God almost always masculine; God often viewed as Distant or Benevolent
View of Other Religions	More likely to believe other religions may contain some truth, should be respected	More likely to believe other religions are false	Officially hold other religions to be imperfect or even false, but participate actively in interfaith and ecumenical dialogue
Eschatology	Generally amillennialist	Often dispensationalist and premillennialist	Amillennialist
View of Discipleship and Mission	More emphasis on the "Second Great Commandment," to "love your neighbor as yourself"—social gospel orientation	More emphasis on the "Great Commission," to convert the world to Christ—salvation orientation	Relatively equal emphasis on the "Second Great Commandment" and the "Great Commission," on salvation and the social gospel
View of Human-Environment Relationship	Dominant metaphor: stewardship	Dominant metaphor: dominion; increasing emphasis on creation care and stewardship among non-fundamentalists	Dominant metaphor: stewardship

Religious beliefs are, of course, only one factor that helps to determine opinions concerning foreign policy. For this reason, it is important to consider whether or not the foreign policy preferences of certain types of U.S. Christians are more heavily affected by their religious views than the foreign policy preferences of other types of U.S. Christians. No data currently exist to demonstrate that this is (or is not) the case. The 2007 U.S. Religious Landscape Survey conducted by the Pew Forum on Religion & Public Life asked respondents what most influenced their thinking about government and public affairs. Among Evangelical Protestants, 28 percent reported that it was their religious beliefs. Among Mainline Protestants, only 8 percent stated that it was their religious beliefs, and among Roman Catholics, only 9 percent. These results are consistent with the fact that 79 percent of members of evangelical churches reported that their religion was very important to them, compared to 52 percent of members of mainline denominations and 56 percent of Roman Catholic believers.[1] The data suggest that among laypersons religious beliefs may be a more important determinant of foreign policy positions for Evangelical Protestants than for Mainline Protestants or Roman Catholics. At the same time, however, it is possible that religious beliefs influence the foreign policy preferences of members of the latter groups in subtle ways of which they are less consciously aware.[2]

Another issue that must be considered is whether the correlation (imperfect as it is) that exists between religious beliefs and foreign policy preferences is more apparent than real. Are the foreign policy preferences of various groups of U.S. Christians epiphenomenal, that is, a reflection not of religious beliefs or religious affiliation but of some other factor(s) that correlate strongly with these? It might, for example, be suggested that Evangelical Protestants have more hawkish views on the use of military force than Mainline Protestants and Roman Catholics not because of their evangelical beliefs but because they are more likely to be from the South and willingness to use force is more characteristic of Southern culture than culture in other parts of the United States.

It is difficult to dismiss this possibility entirely. Nevertheless, there are at least two arguments against it. First, at the institutional and leadership levels, there is frequently a clear logical connection between religious beliefs and foreign policy preferences, and policy positions are commonly supported by statements of doctrine and references to scripture. Can one exclude the possibility that such statements and references are justifications for positions adopted for other reasons, even unconscious ones? No, but this sort of uncertainty is inherent in any study that seeks to identify, via the consultation of documents, interviews, and other similar sources, to discern the motives of individuals and the institutions they represent. Second, in the analysis of public opinion survey data, it is often possible via statistical means to control for the influence of other factors or variables. At least one study explicitly examined the possibility that demographic factors commonly associated with political orientation (e.g., the region of the United States in which an individual was born and raised) were responsible for differences among Christians on social issues. It found that demographic factors did not account for such differences. Rather, the author concluded, regarding different groups of Christians, that "their religious convictions lead them in different ideological directions due in part to their differences on how they read the Bible, the nature of salvation, the role of the Church, and differences in their denominational background."[3] If this is true concerning social issues, it seems reasonable to assume that it is true with regard to foreign policy issues as well.

The Impact of Religion on Foreign Policy

Chapter 2 of this volume was devoted to articulating the various ways in which religion influences U.S. foreign policy. Examples of this influence were provided in both that chapter and in succeeding ones. Broadly speaking, there are at least five mechanisms through which religious institutions and religious beliefs affect U.S. behavior abroad: (1) the incorporation of religious beliefs into underlying cultural norms, (2) outreach and education efforts by religious organizations that influence the foreign policy discourse, (3) lobbying and other forms of political action by religious institutions, (4) voting by people of faith, and (5) the religious beliefs of policymakers themselves.

With respect to voting and electoral politics, the effect on foreign policy of religious beliefs may be more indirect than direct. For example, since at least the 1980s conservative evangelicals have tended to vote Republican in national elections in part because of their religiously grounded opposition to abortion and gay rights. While certain foreign policy issues—the Middle East, in particular—may have helped to determine their votes, the most salient issues have been largely domestic. Nevertheless, the impact on foreign policy has been profound. Republican policymakers may have been supported by conservative evangelicals primarily on the basis of their stances on social issues, but once elected they have of course pursued foreign policies, and these policies have in many cases been quite different from those that would likely have been pursued by Democratic policymakers. It is difficult, for example, to imagine Al Gore, as president, invading Iraq or opposing the Kyoto Protocol as the administration of George W. Bush did.

For members of the executive branch and Congress, the religious beliefs and foreign policy preferences of religious constituencies may in some cases *propel* foreign policy in a particular direction; in others, they may *constrain* foreign policy from being taken in a certain direction. Pressure from religious groups, especially conservative evangelicals, played a major role in the passing of the International Religious Freedom Act of 1998 and in a variety of human rights initiatives under the administration of George W. Bush. At the same time, conservative evangelical support for the government of Israel helped to prevent the Bush administration from taking that government to task for actions regarding Jewish settlements on the West Bank that were contrary to the administration's own declared policy.

How does the influence of religion on U.S. foreign policy compare to that of other factors, individual, societal, and international? To answer this question would require the articulation of a comprehensive theory of U.S. foreign policy and is thus beyond the scope of this volume; it may well be impossible. Certainly, the impact of religion varies from time to time and issue to issue. Over the past few decades, religious influence seems to have been strongest in the realm of human rights policy and, perhaps, Middle East policy. It seems to have been strongest during the administration of George W. Bush and generally stronger under Republican administrations than Democratic ones.

The analysis contained in the preceding chapters of this volume suggests a number of conclusions regarding *when*—as opposed to *how*—religion is likely to affect U.S. behavior abroad:

1. Religion is likely to influence U.S. foreign policy when religious values and beliefs are so deeply embedded that they become a part of the cultural fabric of society, even to the point that their religious origins are not widely recognized.

In part because of the emphasis on the separation of church and state in this country, a significant portion of the population—including many Christians—views with suspicion efforts by religious institutions to influence policy decisions for overtly religious reasons. When policymakers offer explicitly religious justifications for policy, they may be supported by those segments of the population that share their religious views, but opposed by those that do not. Thus, when the religious foundation of certain deeply embedded cultural beliefs is not widely recognized, and is, partly for that reason, relatively immune to challenge, religion can significantly affect policy. The obvious example here is exceptionalism. Although exceptionalist beliefs are stronger among Evangelical Protestants than other Christian groups, they are nevertheless prevalent within the latter groups and throughout American society.

2. Religion is likely to influence U.S. foreign policy when the religious views of policymakers influence their approach to foreign policy issues.

By definition, policymakers have a significant influence on policy. Whether or not their religious beliefs affect policy depends partly on the holding of such beliefs by policymakers and the importance of those beliefs in the formation of their policy positions. As noted in Chapter 2 and elsewhere, the foreign policy of George W. Bush seems to have been heavily influenced by his religious beliefs and the beliefs of some of his advisors. Religious beliefs have influenced the foreign policies of other presidents, including Jimmy Carter, for whom their beliefs were critical to shaping their view of the world.

3. Religious institutions are most likely to influence U.S. foreign policy when they speak with a single voice on foreign policy issues.

Religious organizations had little influence on Bush administration policy concerning Iraq because they were divided. While Mainline Protestant denominations and the Roman Catholic bishops were strongly and unanimously opposed to the invasion of Iraq in 2003, the Southern Baptist Convention and other Evangelical Protestant denominations were either in favor of it or remained neutral. Thus, the Bush administration was not strongly pushed in either direction. By contrast, emerging consensus among Roman Catholics, Mainline Protestants, and, increasingly, Evangelical Protestants on global climate change helped cause the administration to shift its position and acknowledge the reality of the phenomenon. Should this coalition hold together, it is likely to continue to influence U.S. policy on protection of the international environment in the years ahead.

4. Religion is most likely to influence U.S. foreign policy when the members of religious organizations strongly and overwhelmingly support the positions articulated by the organizational leadership.

One of the reasons that Mainline Protestant denominations have had relatively little success in influencing foreign policy decisions in recent years is that the institutional leadership tends to be more liberal, both theologically and politically, than the laity. Hence, these organizations do not wield the leverage, especially in the electoral realm, that they might otherwise wield. The Roman Catholic Church has found itself in somewhat the same position, although on certain issues—abortion being the most important—the Church is more unified than most Mainline Protestant denominations. Evangelical Protestant organizations, on the other hand, tend to reflect much more accurately the views of their membership, a fact that gives them increased influence in discussions with policymakers.

5. Religion is most likely to influence U.S. foreign policy when religiously inspired views on foreign policy issues held by policymakers or articulated by religious organizations and leaders are reinforced by, or at least are not contrary to, important economic, political, and/or strategic imperatives.

Sometimes, as in the case of Jimmy Carter's human rights policies, the impact of religion on policy is trumped by other considerations. The most important of these is typically national security. It is possible that in the post–Cold War world, such factors might assume lesser importance than they once did, but this remains to be seen.

Private Foreign Policies of Religious Organizations

This book has focused on the implications of religion—beliefs, believers, and institutions—for the foreign policy of the U.S. government. It is important to note, however, that religious organizations, from denominations down to individual congregations—often pursue their own private foreign policies, interacting directly with foreign citizens and occasionally foreign governments. Robert Wuthnow wrote in 2009 that

> American Christianity is more engaged in the wider world than ever before. There are more American missionaries, more faith-based humanitarian and relief workers, and more short-term volunteers serving abroad now than in the past. . . . Nearly all U.S. congregations are involved in some kind of international ministry, whether it be collecting money for global hunger programs, sponsoring missionaries, or working directly with international nongovernmental agencies.[4]

The longest-running private foreign policy conducted by U.S. religious groups is missionary work. Exactly how many missionaries are currently operating in countries outside the United States is difficult to determine, in part because they are sponsored by so many different types of organizations: denominational boards, individual congregations, and nondenominational organizations. Moreover, some "mission" organizations focus almost entirely on traditional missionary work—preaching, leading Bible studies, evangelizing, and establishing new congregations—while others divide their energies among a broader range of activities, including humanitarian relief and advocacy.[5]

In any event, the scope of the missionary work conducted by religious organizations is enormous. According to the United States Catholic Mission Association, more than 3,000 U.S. Catholics—clergy, members of religious orders, and laypersons—serve as missionaries outside of North America, with the largest numbers in Africa, the Far East, and Central and South America.[6] Missionary efforts of the Roman Catholic Church are overseen by the Congregation for the Evangelization of Peoples in Rome, but are administered primarily by religious orders (e.g., Maryknoll, the Benedictines, Franciscans, Dominicans, Carmelites, and Jesuits) and by dioceses and archdioceses. Since the Second Vatican Council, the Church has emphasized humanitarian work as much as proselytizing and conversion.

Not surprisingly, among Protestant churches, the evangelical denominations are the most active missioners. The International Mission Board of the Southern Baptist Convention has an annual budget of nearly $300 million and manages 5,000 full-time professional missionaries as well as 30,000 short-term volunteers. The Assemblies of God World Missions has 2,500 full-time missionaries in the field. By contrast, the Worldwide Ministries division of the Presbyterian Church (USA), which also provides food, medical, disaster, and development assistance, supports only 400 long-term and 75 short-term missionaries. The number of denominational mission boards has more than doubled over the past century, rising from 46 in 1900 to 115 in 2001.[7]

This increase, dramatic as it is, has been overshadowed by the growth of nonde-nominational mission groups, which increased from a mere 28 in 1900 to 575 in 2001. The largest of these organizations are New Tribes Mission and Campus Crusade for Christ, which together have about 2,600 employees working abroad. According to Wuthnow, "faith missions" take in nearly three-quarters of mission-oriented revenue and account for 60 percent of U.S. missionaries in the field. Overall, estimates suggest that there are roughly 120,000 American missionaries, professional and volunteer, working overseas. What is the effect of their efforts? Again, it is difficult to determine with a great deal of accuracy, but the International Mission Board of the SBC, to take just one example, claims to be responsible for 600,000 baptisms around the world every year.[8]

Missionary work by religious organizations has been generally compatible with the foreign policy of the U.S. government, which is typically not opposed to efforts to spread Christianity around the globe. In the realm of humanitarian relief, the private foreign policies of religious organizations are actually supported by the government. Or, perhaps it would be more accurate to say that the religious organizations serve as part of the U.S. foreign policy apparatus. Since the 1950s, faith-based organizations have been "trusted allies for distributing food and administering other government-sponsored relief and development programs."[9] In 2003, for example, Catholic Relief Services received nearly three-quarters of its funding from the U.S. government, while Church World Services received 64 percent. The scope of some of these programs, like the scope of the missionary work conducted by U.S. religious groups, is extremely large. During the first decade of the twenty-first century, the foreign expenditures of major faith-based relief agencies totaled well over $2 billion per year. As Wuthnow notes, "The Adventist Development and Relief Agency was present in 120 countries, World Vision International in 100, Catholic Relief Services in 90, Feed the Children in 51, [and] Lutheran World Relief in 30."[10] The organizations were active in nearly every part of the globe.

Although the private foreign policies of religious organizations have often been compatible with, or supportive of, official U.S. foreign policy, they have sometimes been conducted in direct opposition to it. During the 1980s, Mainline Protestant organizations, as well as some Roman Catholic groups, were at the forefront of the so-called Sanctuary Movement. This movement was part of a more general opposition to the Reagan Administration's Central American policy, especially its support of the Contra rebels in Nicaragua and of right-wing dictatorships in Guatemala and El Salvador.[11]

Toward the end of the Carter administration, the U.S. Congress had passed, and Carter had signed into law, the 1980 Refugee Act. The Act expanded the range of persons entitled to enter the United States as refugees from those fleeing communism to those who had "a well-founded fear of persecution" regardless of the political orientation of the government of the country from which they were fleeing.[12] The adoption of the Refugee Act coincided with a large-scale migration of persons from certain Central American countries. Guatemala was enmeshed in a civil war; during the 1980s, 50,000 Guatemalans lost their lives and another 100,000 disappeared. The Guatemalan military was later found to be responsible for more than 90 percent of the over 600 massacres that took place in Guatemalan villages during the war. In El Salvador, also in the throes of civil war, the Salvadoran military, in 1980 alone, killed more than 10,000 people.[13] Human rights abuses, including torture, were rampant. According to one estimate, between 1981 and 1990, more than one million Salvadorans and Guatemalans entered the United States, mainly through Mexico.[14]

As part of its Cold War policy, the Reagan administration was actively aiding the right-wing, anti-Communist governments of both El Salvador and Guatemala. For this reason, and because U.S. law forbad the provision of foreign assistance to governments engaged in large-scale violations of human rights, the administration refused to acknowledge that persons fleeing Guatemala and El Salvador might have a well-founded fear of persecution. Instead, it argued consistently that they were economic migrants seeking a higher standard of living and therefore ineligible to remain in the United States.[15] Between 1980 and 1986, the U.S. Immigration and Naturalization Service (INS) denied more than 97 percent of the applications for political asylum filed on behalf of Central American refugees. By 1985, 32,000

Salvadorans had been deported from the United States to their home country, where more than 100 disappeared, were tortured, or were killed.[16]

Frustrated by their inability to assist Central American refugees in securing asylum, a Quaker meeting and a Presbyterian congregation in Tucson, Arizona, decided in 1982 to provide sanctuary for these individuals, helping to smuggle them into the United States and moving them well north of the border with Mexico (sometimes as far as Canada), away from the watchful eyes of U.S. immigration authorities. Led initially by Quaker activist Jim Corbett and Presbyterian minister John Fife, and subsequently by the Chicago Religious Task Force on Central America, a kind of modern underground railroad spread rapidly across the country. Refugees were provided not only protection from U.S. authorities, but in many cases food, clothing, education, medical care, and employment.[17]

At its zenith in the mid-1980s, more than 150 faith congregations—Christian and Jewish—participated directly in the Sanctuary Movement, while another thousand or more offered moral and sometimes financial backing.[18] At the denominational level, as well as the local level, Mainline Protestant denominations were at the forefront of the movement. The American Lutheran Church, the United Methodist Church, the Presbyterian Church (USA), the United Church of Christ, and the American Baptist Church openly declared their support. In 1984, the National Council of Churches "urged a moratorium on the deportation of aliens to Central America and asked the government to cease harassing and prosecuting the Sanctuary Movement." The NCC subsequently "recommended serious consideration of the Sanctuary Movement as an expression of Christian duty to the suffering stranger."[19]

It is impossible to know exactly how many Central American refugees were aided by religious organizations—and others—in direct defiance of U.S. policy. One estimate suggests that the Sanctuary Movement protected "tens of thousands of individuals and families, enabling them to start a new life in the U.S."[20] Echoes of the movement, and evidence of the continuing relevance of the idea of sanctuary in Christian thought, can be seen today in the New Sanctuary Movement that is committed to blocking the enforcement of current U.S. immigration policy and particularly to preventing the deportation of undocumented aliens. As of this writing, chapters of the New Sanctuary Coalition, which was founded in 2007, have been formed in 13 states and the District of Columbia. The New York City chapter, the largest, has more than 20 member faith communities, including several Catholic parishes and a number of Mainline Protestant congregations.[21]

Religion and Foreign Policy in the Obama Administration

What will be the influence of religion on U.S. foreign policy under Barack Obama? Although it is too early, at this writing, to know exactly how Obama's beliefs might influence his policies, it is interesting to note that within a month of assuming the presidency, Obama, expanding his predecessor's faith-based initiatives, created the

Office of Faith-Based and Neighborhood Partnerships and placed it under the White House Domestic Policy Council, a move "widely seen as an effort to involve a religious perspective in the administration's policy decisions."[22]

For a U.S. Christian, Barack Hussein Obama's formative years were unusual. In *The Audacity of Hope*, he recounts his upbringing in a kind of interfaith family whose members, while acquainted with religion, were largely skeptical of it. His father, who was divorced from his mother when Obama was two, had been raised Muslim, but became an atheist. His stepfather was Muslim, but had "grown up in a country (Indonesia) that easily blended its Islamic faith with remnants of Hinduism, Buddhism, and ancient animist traditions." Obama's mother, the strongest influence on him, was a declared secularist who believed that "a working knowledge of the world's great religions was a necessary part of any well-rounded education." Obama describes growing up in a home in which "the Bible, the Koran, and the Bhagavad Gita sat on the shelf alongside books of Greek and Norse and African mythology. On Easter or Christmas Day," he writes, "my mother might drag me to church, just as she dragged me to the Buddhist temple, the Chinese New Year celebration, the Shinto shrine, and ancient Hawaiian burial sites. In sum, my mother viewed religion through the eyes of the anthropologist; it was a phenomenon to be treated with a suitable respect, but with a suitable detachment as well." Obama's exposure to multiple religious traditions was also a result of his schooling; as a child in Jakarta, Indonesia, he attended both a Catholic school and a public school in which he studied the precepts of Islam.[23]

As an adult, Obama became a committed Christian and was baptized at Trinity United Church of Christ in Chicago, where he remained for 20 years, resigning his membership following controversial remarks by the pastor, the Reverend Jeremiah Wright, during the 2008 presidential campaign. Affiliated with the predominantly white United Church of Christ, one of Mainline Protestantism's most liberal denominations, Trinity's congregation is largely African American. Given his somewhat unconventional, eclectic religious upbringing and his longtime membership in a black UCC congregation, it is not surprising that Obama's religious views and the policy preferences that might flow from them are generally liberal. Stephen Mansfield, a conservative evangelical and author of *The Faith of George Bush* and *The Faith of Barack Obama*, has described Obama's views in the following terms:

I think Barack Obama believes about Jesus and about conversion what your average evangelical does. He believes that Jesus is the son of God and that he died for the sins of the world and God raised him from the dead again. Where he begins to depart from orthodox evangelical Christianity probably begins with his view of scripture. He believes some of it might be of human origin, and some scriptures may be of more weight than others. So in a sense, [his is a] traditional theological liberalism that tends to treat scripture as being at least partially of human origin. But then you add that sort of young postmodern twist. Postmodernists don't really reconcile systems of thought. In fact, they're not sure systems of thought are possible. Theologically speaking, they might pick one from column A and two from column B, whether it all fits together or not. So he's a theological liberal with a postmodern emphasis.[24]

Beyond the impact of Obama's beliefs, the political environment in the United States and the new president's relationship to particular religious groups favors some shifts in foreign policy on the part of his administration. Being lightly supported by conservative Christians, Obama need not worry about alienating his political base by pursuing foreign policies that many evangelicals regard as anathema. This should free him to move in new directions, particularly in the Middle East. Already, Obama has attempted to repair the U.S. image in the Arab and Muslim world. Unlike his predecessor, he has taken a stern approach to the government of Israel, insisting that the construction of Jewish settlements on the West Bank must cease and that Israel must accept a two-state solution.[25] Previous U.S. administrations said much the same thing publicly, but privately were more flexible. According to Israeli officials, the Bush administration agreed to allow the expansion of Jewish settlements on the West Bank despite its declared opposition to them.[26]

The Obama administration has been much firmer in its rhetoric, seeking to close certain "loopholes" that the Israeli government has exploited, particularly the "natural growth" of existing settlements, which Israeli leaders have maintained is consistent with a settlement freeze. In some of the administration's sharpest remarks, Secretary of State Hillary Clinton, said of Obama, "He wants to see a stop to settlements—not some settlements, not outposts, not 'natural growth' exceptions."[27]

Although neither Obama nor members of his administration have publicly threatened to withdraw U.S. economic and/or diplomatic support from Israel if Israel does not comply with U.S. demands, they seem more determined than their predecessors. Prior to meeting with conservative Israeli prime minister Benjamin Netanyahu in May 2009, administration officials traveled to Capitol Hill to brief members of Congress on the shift in U.S. policy and to secure their backing. According to one account, Netanyahu, expecting to be supported by his traditional allies in Congress, was "stunned" to discover that many had fallen in line with the administration.[28] Aaron David Miller, of the Woodrow Wilson International Center for Scholars, has stated of the administration, "They've concluded, 'We're going to force a change in behavior.'"[29] Whether or not they will succeed remains to be seen, but early signs suggest that they might. Under pressure from Washington, Netanyahu has for the first time publicly accepted the notion of a Palestinian state, although he has attached conditions—that it be demilitarized and that it allow Israel to control the airspace over its territory, among others—that are likely to be unacceptable to Palestinian negotiators.[30]

The Obama administration also has begun to shift policy on protection of the international environment. During his campaign for the presidency, Obama pledged to reduce U.S. emissions of carbon dioxide by 80 percent, a promise he repeated following his election.[31] In March 2009, the administration's climate envoy, Todd Stern, said that the United States would involve itself in negotiating a successor treaty to the Kyoto Protocol in "a robust way."[32] As of this writing, a successor treaty has not been negotiated, but the United States, together with China, Brazil, India, and South Africa, concluded an agreement in December 2009 aimed at limiting the rise in global temperatures by 2050 to 2° Celsius above preindustrial levels. The so-called Copenhagen Accord, to which most of the other 188 nations of the world assented, did not establish binding goals for reducing emissions of greenhouse gases, but it did provide for the articulation of individual national goals, as well as for monitoring and reporting programs that would enable the tracking of progress toward their attainment. It also provided a potential springboard for additional climate talks to be held under U.N. auspices in Mexico City in 2010.[33]

Toward the Future

What does the future hold for the influence of religion on U.S. foreign policy? The election of Obama in November 2008 caused some observers to proclaim the dawn of "a post-evangelical America." Lisa Miller wrote for *Newsweek*, "For at least four decades, white evangelicals have been the religion-and-politics story in this country." She continued,

> If this week's exit polls tell us anything about religion, they remind us that there are tens of millions of voters in this country who believe in God, read their Scripture, pray, regularly attend a house of worship—and do not consider themselves born-again Christians. In 2008, 44 percent of Americans who go to religious services more than once a week voted for Obama; in 2004, just 35 percent of those people voted for Kerry.[34]

Although in certain states, such as Colorado, Indiana, and Florida, Obama's share of the vote among white evangelicals was much higher than Kerry's, overall it was only slightly higher, about 3 percent. Concluded Miller, "the religious vote for Obama did not reflect a massive shift in ideologies and priorities among evangelicals but rather muscle-flexing by a coalition of others of faith," including African Americans, Latinos (who are largely Roman Catholic), and Mainline Protestants.[35]

Some analysts saw in the formation of this coalition the beginnings of a potential realignment of the American electorate. According to Stephen Schneck, director of the Life Cycle Institute of the Catholic University of America, "In the long term, this could be huge. There are swing Catholics and swing Protestants even within the evangelicals. To the extent Obama can mobilize those people as part of a new Democratic coalition, that marginalizes the Republicans even further."[36]

This exaggerated rhetoric is surely premature. The "new Democratic coalition"—to the extent that it exists—is not necessarily a religious coalition; it was not formed entirely, or perhaps even largely on the basis of religion. African Americans, including those who are not religious, presumably supported Obama in overwhelming numbers for reasons having less to do with faith and more to do with race and his positions on a variety of issues of concern to them. The emergence of this coalition does not necessarily signal the end, despite the sensationalist headlines, of evangelical influence in U.S. politics. Neither does it portend the revival of liberal Christianity in the United States. Black Protestants and Latinos tend to be fairly conservative on social issues, although less so on others. The Mainline Protestant denominations that have been the most theologically and politically progressive—for example, the United Methodist Church and the Episcopal Church—have suffered the most significant declines in membership over the past several decades. Some observers, noting Obama's frequent invocations of Jesus and his quoting of scripture, believe that this is part of a political strategy designed to revive the Christian left and to reinvigorate those politically moderate-to-liberal Christians who felt powerless for much of the last 30 to 40 years.[37] This may be both the strategy and the effect, but that it signals anything remotely approaching a fundamental shift in U.S. electoral politics—and a consequent shift in the foreign policies pursued by this country over the longer term—is highly debatable.

Clues to the future impact of religion on the foreign policy of the United States are more likely to be found in three other trends. The first of these is *the declining percentage of Americans who describe themselves as Christian*. According to the most recent American Religious Identification Survey (ARIS), the number of Americans who identified themselves as Christian fell from 86 percent of the U.S. population in 1990 to 76 percent in 2008. Although there was a slight increase in the percentage of Americans adhering to other faiths during this period, the greatest growth occurred in the category of those who identified themselves as having no theistic beliefs or no religion. This group, which ARIS referred to as "Nones," represented 8.2 percent of the population in 1990, but 15.0 percent of the population in 2008. The data suggest that as a nation, Americans are becoming both less Christian and less religious.[38] Should this trend continue, all other things being equal, one can probably expect a lessening of the influence of religion on U.S. foreign policy over time.

A second development worth watching is *declining denominational loyalty among U.S. Christians and especially Protestants*. The Pew Religious Landscape Survey found that roughly a third of those raised in the Roman Catholic Church had subsequently changed their religious affiliation, while nearly half of those raised in Protestant churches had done so. More than a quarter of Protestants had moved from one Protestant "family" (e.g., Lutheranism, Methodism) to another. Most Evangelical Protestants who left one Protestant family for another remained within the evangelical tradition; Mainline Protestants who switched denominations were about as likely to join a largely evangelical church family as to remain within the mainline tradition.[39] Declining denominational loyalty and a diminishing sense of denominational identity among U.S. Protestants—trends that are also reflected in the relatively recent explosion of nondenominational churches, including many mega-churches—do not necessarily suggest a waning of religious influence on foreign policy. They do suggest, however, a further loss of influence over the views of church members on the part of church leaders and institutions, particularly within Mainline Protestant denominations. This could result in a deterioration of the political power of such organizations and their impact on foreign policy decisions.

A third trend to bear in mind is *the growing division within the Evangelical Protestant ranks between fundamentalists and other evangelicals,* especially the so-called freestyle evangelicals. As earlier chapters have made clear, fundamentalists tend to be more theologically and politically conservative than other evangelicals. On certain issues—protection of the international environment being the most obvious—the split within the evangelical community has widened during the last decade. If freestyle evangelicals emerge as the dominant faction, or even as a substantial counterweight to the fundamentalists, the implications for U.S. foreign policy could be significant. Because the positions of freestyle evangelicals on political, social, and economic issues tend to be closer to those of Mainline Protestants and Roman Catholics, there is greater potential for cooperation with those groups and the institutions that represent them. On issues such as the environment and Middle East policy, the impact of this development, should it occur, could be dramatic.

Notes

1. Pew Forum, "U.S. Religious Landscape Survey," Part 2, 77, 24.
2. On this last point, I am indebted to James L. Guth.
3. Charles F. Hall, "The Christian Left: Who are They and How are They Different from the Christian Right?" *Review of Religious Research,* 39, no. 1 (September 1997): 41, www.jstor.org/stable/3512477.
4. Robert Wuthnow, *Boundless Faith: The Global Outreach of American Churches* (Berkeley, CA: University of California Press, 2009), 235.
5. Wuthnow, *Boundless Faith,* 125.
6. United States Catholic Mission Association, "U.S. Catholic Mission Handbook," 2004–2005 Survey Findings, available for download at www.uscatholicmission.org/Mission%20Handbook.htm.
7. Wuthnow, *Boundless Faith,* 125–28.
8. Wuthnow, *Boundless Faith,* 129–30, 126.
9. Wuthnow, *Boundless Faith,* 125.
10. Wuthnow, *Boundless Faith,* 132–33.
11. Two of the best books on this movement are Ann Crittenden, *Sanctuary: A Story of American Conscience and the Law in Collision* (New York: Weidenfeld & Nicolson, 1988); and Renny Golden and Michael McConnell, *Sanctuary: The New Underground Railroad* (Maryknoll, NY: Orbis Books, 1986).
12. Susan Gzesh, "Central Americans and Asylum Policy in the Reagan Era," *Migration Information Source,* April 2006, www.migrationinformation.org/Feature/display.cfm?ID=384.
13. "Sanctuary Movement: Immigration and Naturalization Service, Chicago Religious Task Force on Central America," www.jrank.org/cultures/pages/4415/Sanctuary-Movement.html.

14. Gzesh, "Central Americans and Asylum Policy."
15. Gzesh, "Central Americans and Asylum Policy."
16. "Sanctuary Movement."
17. Crittenden, *Sanctuary.*
18. Gzesh, "Central Americans and Asylum Policy."
19. Kurtz and Fulton, "Love Your Enemies?" 368.
20. The New Sanctuary Movement, "Building on a Powerful Tradition," www.newsanctuary-movement.org/build-tradition.htm.
21. The New Sanctuary Coalition of New York City, members list, www.newsanctuarynyc.org/memberslist.php.
22. Eamon Javers, "Obama invokes Jesus more than George W. Bush," *Politico*, June 9, 2009, www.politico.com/news/stories/0609/23510_Page3.html.
23. Barack Obama, *The Audacity of Hope: Thoughts on Reclaiming the American Dream* (New York: Three Rivers Press, 2006), 203–205.
24. Quoted in Jessica Ramirez, "Barack's Beliefs," *Newsweek* web exclusive, August 7, 2008, www.newsweek.com/id/151233.
25. Mark Landler and Isabel Kershner, "Israeli Settlement Growth Must Stop, Clinton Says," *New York Times*, May 29, 2009, www.nytimes.com/2009/05/28/world/middleeast/28mideast.html?_r=1&fta=y.
26. Ethan Bronner, "Israelis Say Bush Agreed to West Bank Growth," *New York Times*, June 3, 2009, www.nytimes.com/2009/06/04/world/middleeast/04israel.html?scp=15&sq=Obama%20settlements%20Israel%20two-state&st=cse.
27. Landler and Kershner, "Israeli Settlement Growth Must Stop."
28. Nadia Hijab, "The Obama Difference," *New York Times*, June 8, 2009, www.nytimes.com/2009/06/09/opinion/09iht-edhajib.html?scp=10&sq=Obama%20Netanyahu%20Congress&st=cse.
29. Quoted in Landler and Kershner, "Israeli Settlement Growth Must Stop."
30. Howard Schneider, "Netanyahu Backs 2-State Goal," *Washington Post*, June 15, 2009, www.washingtonpost.com/wp-dyn/content/article/2009/06/14/AR2009061400741.html.
31. John M. Broder, "Obama Affirms Climate Change Goals," *New York Times*, November 10, 2008, www.nytimes.com/2008/11/19/us/politics/19climate.html.
32. Elisabeth Rosenthal, "Obama's Backing Raises Hope for Climate Pact," *New York Times*, March 1, 2009, www.nytimes.com/2009/03/01/science/earth/01treaty.html.
33. Andrew C. Revkin and John M. Broder, "A Grudging Accord in Climate Talks," *New York Times*, December 19, 2009, www.nytimes.com/2009/12/20/science/earth/20accord.html?scp=1&sq=Broder%20John&st=cse.
34. Lisa Miller, "A Post-Evangelical America: The Religious Building Blocks of Obama's Victory," *Newsweek* web exclusive, November 6, 2008, www.newsweek.com/id/167917.
35. Miller, "A Post-Evangelical America."
36. Quoted in Javers, "Obama invokes Jesus more than George W. Bush."
37. Javers, "Obama invokes Jesus more than George W. Bush."
38. Barry A. Kosmin and Ariela Keysar, "American Religious Identification Survey (ARIS 2008): Summary Report," March 2009, www.americanreligionsurvey-aris.org/reports/ARIS_Report_2008.pdf.
39. Pew Forum, "U.S. Religious Landscape Survey," Report 1, 30–32.

Selected Bibliography

This bibliography consists of two sections. The first lists the websites of major churches, denominations, and other religious organizations, research centers specializing in the study of religion and/or religion and politics, and religion-based nondenominational or ecumenical/interfaith advocacy organizations that seek to exert influence on foreign policy and related issues. Entries for individual documents located on these websites are, with a few important exceptions, omitted from the bibliography. Full citations for these documents are in the notes. The second section lists all other sources cited in this book, except that entries for newspaper articles and web-based sources that are largely factual (as opposed to analytic) have been omitted. Full citations for these sources are also in the notes.

I. Websites

A. Churches, Denominations, and Other Religious Organizations

American Baptist Churches USA. www.abc-usa.org.
Assemblies of God (USA). www.ag.org.
Christian Church (Disciples of Christ). www.disciples.org.
Christian Reformed Church in North America. www.crcna.org.
Church of the Brethren. www.brethren.org.
Church of the Nazarene. www.nazarene.org.
Churches of Christ. www.church-of-christ.org.
Episcopal Church. www.episcopalchurch.org.
Evangelical Lutheran Church in America. www.elca.org.
Holy See Mission to the United Nations. www.holyseemission.org.
Lutheran Church—Missouri Synod. www.lcms.org.
Mennonite Church USA. www.mennoniteusa.org.
National Association of Congregational Christian Churches. www.naccc.org.
National Association of Evangelicals. www.nae.net.
National Conference of Catholic Bishops. See United States Conference of Catholic Bishops.
National Council of Churches. www.ncccusa.org.
Presbyterian Church (USA). www.pcusa.org.
Reformed Church in America. www.rca.org.
Religious Society of Friends (Quaker). www.quaker.org.
Salvation Army. www.salvationarmy.org.
Southern Baptist Convention. www.sbc.net.
United Church of Christ. www.ucc.org.
United Methodist Church. www.umc.org.
United States Catholic Conference. See United States Conference of Catholic Bishops.
United States Conference of Catholic Bishops. www.usccb.org.
Vatican: The Holy See. www.vatican.va.
World Council of Churches. www.oikoumene.org.

B. Research Centers

Association of Religion Data Archives. www.thearda.com.
Barna Group. www.barna.org.
Hartford Institute for Religion Research. www.hirr.hartsem.edu.
Institute for Studies of Religion, Baylor University. www.isreligion.org.
Pew Forum on Religion & Public Life. www.pewforum.org.

C. Religion-Based Non-Denominational or Ecumenical/Interfaith Advocacy Organizations

American Israel Public Affairs Committee. www.aipac.org.
Christian Coalition of America. www.cc.org.
Cornwall Alliance for the Stewardship of Creation. www.cornwallalliance.org.
Evangelical Climate Initiative. www.christiansandclimate.org.
Evangelical Environmental Network. www.creationcare.org.
Focus on the Family. www.focusonthefamily.com.
Interfaith Stewardship Alliance. www.interfaithstewardship.org.
National Religious Partnership for the Environment. www.nrpe.org.
Religious Coalition for Reproductive Choice. www.rcrc.org.

II. Other Sources

Abrams, Elliott, ed. *The Influence of Faith: Religious Groups and U.S. Foreign Policy.* Lanham, MD: Rowman & Littlefield, with the Ethics and Public Policy Center, 2001.
—. "Introduction." In *The Influence of Faith: Religious Groups and U.S. Foreign Policy,* edited by Elliot Abrams, vii–x. Lanham, MD: Rowman & Littlefield, Ethics and Public Policy Center, 2001.
Amstutz, Mark R. "Faith-Based NGOs and U.S. Foreign Policy." In *The Influence of Faith: Religious Groups and U.S. Foreign Policy,* edited by Elliott Abrams, 175–87. Lanham, MD: Rowman & Littlefield, with the Ethics and Public Policy Center, 2001.
Angell, Norman. *The Great Illusion: A Study of the Relation of Military Power in Nations to Their Economic and Social Advantage.* New York: Putnam, 1910.
Axelrod, Robert, and Robert O. Keohane. "Achieving Cooperation under Anarchy: Strategies and Institutions." *World Politics,* 38, no. 1 (October 1985): 226–54, www.jstor.org/stable/2010357.
Bandow, Doug. "Crackpot Theology Makes Bad Foreign Policy." June 4, 2002, www.cato.org/dailys/06-04-02.html.
Bates, Stephen. "'Godless Communism' and its Legacies." *Society,* 41, no. 3 (March/April 2004): 29–33, www.springerlink.com/content/641a3blyhj5qma5l/.
Baumgartner, Jody C., Peter L. Francia, and Jonathan S. Morris. "A Clash of Civilizations? The Influence of Religion on Public Opinion of U.S. Foreign Policy in the Middle East." *Political Research Quarterly,* 61, no. 2 (June 2008): 171–79, www.jstor.org/stable/20299723.
Baylor Institute for Studies of Religion. "American Piety in the 21st Century: New Insights to the Depth and Complexity of Religion in the US." Selected Findings from the Baylor Religion Survey, September 2006, www.baylor.edu/content/services/document.php/33304.pdf.
Beisner, E. Calvin. "Biblical Principles for Environmental Stewardship." In *An Examination of the Scientific, Ethical and Theological Implications of Climate Change Policy,* edited by Roy W. Spencer, Paul K. Driessen, and E. Calvin Beisner. Interfaith Stewardship Alliance, 2005. Available for download at www.cornwallalliance.org/articles/read/an-examination-of-the-scientific-ethical-and-theological-implications-of-climate-change-policy/.

—. "Global Warming: Why Evangelicals Should Not Be Alarmed." *Reformed Perspective,* September 2007, 21–23, http://reformedperspective.ca/images/stories/PDFs/global907.pdf.

Bell, Daniel. "The End of American Exceptionalism." *The Public Interest,* 41 (Fall 1975): 193–224. Available for download at http://pao.chadwyck.com/journals/displayItemFromId.do?QueryType= journals&ItemID=g035#listItem81.

Bellah, Robert N. "Civil Religion in America." *Daedalus,* 96, no. 1 (Winter 1967): 1–21, www.jstor.org/stable/20027022.

Bigelow, Gordon. "Let There Be Markets: The Evangelical Roots of Economics." *Harper's Magazine,* May 2005, www.harpers.org/archive/2005/05/0080538.

"Blessed Be *the Name* of the Lord." *Christianity Today,* May 8, 2008, www.christianitytoday.com/ct/2008/may/17.21.html.

Blount, Sheryl Henderson. "Climate Change Is Here to Stay." *Christianity Today,* March 30, 2007, www.christianitytoday.com/ct/2007/marchweb-only/113–52.0.html.

Blumenthal, Max. "Onward Christian Soldiers." *Salon.com,* April 15, 2003, http://dir.salon.com/story/news/feature/2003/04/15/in_touch/.

Boyer, Paul S. *When Time Shall Be No More: Prophecy Belief in Modern American Culture.* Cambridge, MA: Belknap/Harvard University Press, 1992.

—. "When U.S. Foreign Policy Meets Biblical Prophecy." *Alternet,* February 20, 2003, www.alternet.org/story/15221.

Brands, H. W. "The Idea of the National Interest." In *The Ambiguous Legacy: U.S. Foreign Relations in the "American Century,"* edited by Michael J. Hogan, 120–51. New York: Cambridge University Press, 1999.

Brinkley, Douglas. "Jimmy Carter's Modest Quest for Global Peace." *Foreign Affairs,* 74, no. 6 (November–December 1995): 90–100, www.jstor.org/stable/20047382.

Broadway, Bill. "Evangelicals' Voices Speak Softly about Iraq." *Washington Post,* January 25, 2003, www.washingtonpost.com/ac2/wp-dyn/A40893-2003Jan24?language=printer.

—. "Religious Leaders' Voices Rise on Iraq." *Washington Post,* September 28, 2002, www.proquest.com.

Brown, Michael E., Sean M. Lynn-Jones, and Steven E. Miller, eds. *Debating the Democratic Peace, an International Security Reader.* Cambridge, MA: MIT Press, 1996.

Brzezinski, Zbigniew. *Power and Principle.* New York: Farrar, Straus, Giroux, 1983.

Bumiller, Elizabeth. "Evangelicals Sway White House on Human Rights Issues Abroad." *New York Times,* October 26, 2003, www.nytimes.com/2003/10/26/world/evangelicals-sway-white-house-on-human-rights-issues-abroad.html?pagewanted=1.

Caldwell, Deborah. "Despite Controversy, Iraq Beckons as Evangelical Mission Field." *Religion News Service,* April 24, 2003, http://pewforum.org/news/display.php?NewsID=2186.

—. "Poised and Ready." *Beliefnet,* April 2003, www.beliefnet.com/story/123/story_12365.html.

—. "Why Iraq Beckons." *Beliefnet,* April 2003, www.beliefnet.com/story/124/story_12448.html.

Calo, Zachary R. "Catholic Thought, Political Liberalism, and the Idea of Human Rights." www4.samford.edu/lillyhumanrights/papers/Calo_Catholic.pdf.

Campolo, Tony. "The Ideological Roots of Christian Zionism." *Tikkun,* 20, no. 1 (January–February 2005): 19–20, www.tikkun.org/article.php/Campolo-roots-of-christian-zionism.

Carr, E. H. *The Twenty Years' Crisis, 1919–1939: An Introduction to the Study of International Relations.* London: Macmillan & Co., 1941.

Carroll, James. "The Bush Crusade." *The Nation,* September 20, 2004, www.commondreams.org/views04/0902-06.htm.

Carson, Rachel. *Silent Spring.* Boston, MA: Houghton Mifflin Co.; Cambridge: Riverside Press, 1962.

Christopher, Paul. *The Ethics of War and Peace: An Introduction to Moral and Legal Issues.* Englewood Cliffs, NJ: Prentice-Hall, 1994.

Claude, Inis L., Jr. *Swords into Plowshares: The Problems and Progress of International Organization,* 4th ed. New York: Random House, 1984.

"CNN Live Saturday: Interview with Albert Mohler, Charles Kimball." *CNN.com,* May 10, 2003, http://edition.cnn.com/TRANSCRIPTS/0305/10/cst.11.html.

Cooperman, Alan. "Bush's Remark about God Assailed." *Washington Post*, November 22, 2003, www.washingtonpost.com/ac2/wp-dyn/A4697- 2003Nov21?language=printer.

—. "Evangelicals Will Not Take Stand on Global Warming." *Washington Post*, February 2, 2006, www.washingtonpost.com/wp- %09dyn/content/article/2006/02/01/AR2006020102132.html.

—. "Openly Religious, to a Point." *Washington Post*, September 1, 2004, www.washingtonpost.com/wp-dyn/articles/A24634-2004Sep15.html.

Copeland, Dale C. "Economic Interdependence and War: A Theory of Trade Expectations." *International Security*, 20, no. 3 (Winter 1995–1996): 5–41, www.jstor.org/stable/i323313.

Crittenden, Ann. *Sanctuary: A Story of American Conscience and the Law in Collision.* New York: Weidenfeld & Nicolson, 1988.

CUNY Graduate Center. "American Religious Identification Survey (2001)," www.gc.cuny.edu/faculty/research_briefs/aris/key_findings.htm.

Davis, Tami R. and Sean M. Lynn-Jones. "Citty upon a Hill." *Foreign Policy*, no. 66 (Spring 1987): 20–38, www.jstor.org/stable/1148662.

Domke, David. *God Willing? Political Fundamentalism in the White House, the "War on Terror," and the Echoing Press.* London: Pluto Press, 2004.

Donnelly, Jack. *Universal Human Rights in Theory and Practice*, 2nd ed. Ithaca, NY: Cornell University Press, 2003.

Doyle, Michael. "Kant, Liberal Legacies, and Foreign Affairs." Part I, *Philosophy & Public Affairs*, 12, no. 3 (Spring 1983): 205–35, www.jstor.org/stable/2265298.

—. "Liberalism and World Politics." *American Political Science Review*, 80, no. 4 (December 1986): 1151–61, www.jstor.org/stable/1960861.

Duhigg, Charles. "Evangelicals Flock into Iraq on a Mission of Faith." *Los Angeles Times*, March 18, 2004, www.pipeline.com/~rougeforum/evangelicalsinvade.html.

Easton, Nina J. "With Antipoverty Call, Evangelicals Seek New Tone." *Boston Globe*, July 5, 2005, www.boston.com/news/nation/washington/articles/2005/07/05/with_antipoverty_call_evangelicals_seek_new_tone/.

Eckberg, Douglas Lee and T. Jean Blocker. "Christianity, Environmentalism, and the Theoretical Problem of Fundamentalism." *Journal for the Scientific Study of Religion*, 35, no. 4 (December 1996): 343–55, www.jstor.org/stable/i260038.

Ellsworth, Tim. "Baptists Adrift in Doctrinal Confusion." *SBC Life*, October/November 2001, www.sbclife.org/articles/2001/10/sla6.asp.

Elman, Colin. "Horses for Courses: Why *Not* Neorealist Theories of Foreign Policy?" *Security Studies*, 6, no. 1 (Autumn 1996): 7–53.

Erlanger, Steven. "Netanyahu, In U.S., Woos Conservatives." *New York Times*, January 20, 1998, www.nytimes.com/1998/01/20/world/netanyahu-in-us-woos-conservatives.html.

Evangelicals against Torture. "An Evangelical Declaration against Torture: Protecting Human Rights in an Age of Terror," www.evangelicalsforhumanrights.org/storage/mhead/fullstatement.pdf.

"Evangelicals Ask Bush for Even Mideast Tack." *The Christian Century*, July 31, 2002, www.proquest.com.

Falwell, Jerry. "God is Pro-War," *World Net Daily*, January 31, 2004, http://worldnetdaily.com/news/article.asp?ARTICLE_ID=36859.

Farlee, Robert Buckley, ed. *Honoring Our Neighbor's Faith.* Minneapolis, MN: Augsburg Fortress, 1999.

Farr, Thomas F. *World of Faith and Freedom: Why International Religious Liberty is Vital to American National Security.* Oxford: Oxford University Press, 2008.

Fukuyama, Francis. "The End of History." *National Interest* (Summer 1989), www.unc.edu/home/rlstev/Text/Fukuyama%20End%20of%20History.pdf.

—. *The End of History and the Last Man.* New York: Free Press, 1992.

Garrity, Patrick. "Warnings of a Parting Friend (US Foreign Policy Envisioned by George Washington in his Farewell Address)." *National Interest*, no. 45 (Fall 1996): 14–26, www.mtholyoke.edu/acad/intrel/garrity.htm.

Gerson, Michael J. *Heroic Conservatism: Why Republicans Need to Embrace America's Ideals (And Why They Deserve to Fail If They Don't)*. New York: HarperOne, 2007.

Glad, Betty. *Jimmy Carter: In Search of the Great White House*. New York: W. W. Norton & Co., 1980.

—. *An Outsider in the White House: Jimmy Carter, His Advisors, and the Making of American Foreign Policy*. Ithaca, NY and London: Cornell University Press, 2009.

"God's Christian Warriors." *CNN.com*, August 23, 2007, http://transcripts.cnn.com/TRANSCRIPTS/0708/23/cp.01.html

Golden, Renny, and Michael McConnell. *Sanctuary: The New Underground Railroad*. Maryknoll, NY: Orbis Books, 1986.

Goodstein, Laurie. "Evangelical Leaders Swing Influence Behind Effort to Combat Global Warming." *New York Times*, March 10, 2005, www.nytimes.com/2005/03/10/national/10evangelical.html.

—. "Falwell to Mobilize Support for Israel." *New York Times*, January 21, 1998, www.nytimes.com/1998/01/21/world/falwell-to-mobilize-support-for-israel.html.

—. "Seeing Islam as 'Evil' Faith, Evangelicals Seek Converts." *New York Times*, May 27, 2003, www.nytimes.com/2003/05/27/national/27ISLA.html?ex=1215144000&en=1fc28e95510c4a7b&ei=5070.

Green, John C. "The American Public and Sympathy for Israel: Present and Future." *Journal of Ecumenical Studies*, 44, no. 1 (Winter 2009): 1–15.

—. "The American Religious Landscape and Political Attitudes: A Baseline for 2004." Pew Forum for Religion & Public Life, September 9, 2004, http://pewforum.org/docs/index.php?DocID=55.

—. "Evangelicals and Civic Engagement: A View from (near) the Top." *Ethics and Public Policy*, May 22, 2002, www.eppc.org/programs/ecl/conferences/eventID.29,programID.31/conf_detail.asp.

—. "Evangelicals v. Mainline Protestants." *Frontline*, April 29, 2004, www.pbs.org/wgbh/pages/frontline/shows/jesus/evangelicals/evmain.html.

Grizzle, Raymond E., Paul E. Rothrock, and Christopher B. Barrett. "Evangelicals and Environmentalism: Past, Present, and Future." *Trinity Journal* (Spring 1998), http://findarticles.com/p/articles/mi_qa3803/is_199804/ai_n8791173/pg_14?tag=content;col1.

Guth, James L. "Bush and Religious Politics." In *Ambition and Division: Legacies of the George W. Bush Presidency*, edited by Steven E. Schier, 87–109. Pittsburgh, PA: University of Pittsburgh Press, 2009.

—. "Militant and Cooperative Internationalism Among American Religious Publics, 2008." Prepared for the Annual Meeting of the International Studies Association, February 16–20, 2010.

—. "Religion and Roll Calls: Religious Influences on the U.S. House of Representatives, 1997–2002." Presented at the annual meeting of the American Political Science Association, August 30–September 2, 2007.

—. "Religious Leadership and Support for Israel: A Study of Clergy in Nineteen Denominations." Presented at the annual meeting of the Southern Political Science Association, January 3–7, 2007.

Guth, James L., Cleveland R. Fraser, John C. Green, Lyman A. Kellstedt, and Corwin E. Smidt. "Religion and Foreign Policy Attitudes: The Case of Christian Zionism." In *Religion and the Culture Wars: Dispatches from the Front*, edited by Green, Guth, Smidt, and Kellstedt, 330–60. Lanham, MD: Rowman & Littlefield, 1996.

Guth, James L., John C. Green, Lyman A. Kellstedt, and Corwin E. Smidt. "Faith and Foreign Policy: A View from the Pews." *Review of Faith and International Affairs* (Fall 2005), 3–10.

—. "Faith and the Environment: Religious Beliefs and Attitudes on Environmental Policy." *American Journal of Political Science*, 39, no. 2 (May 1995): 364–82, www.jstor.org/stable/2111617.

Guth, James L., John C. Green, Corwin E. Smidt, Lyman A. Kellstedt, and Margaret M. Poloma. *The Bully Pulpit: The Politics of Protestant Clergy*. Lawrence: University of Kansas Press, 1997.

Guth, James L., Lyman A. Kellstedt, Corwin E. Smidt, and John C. Green. "Theological Perspectives and Environmentalism Among Religious Activists." *Journal for the Scientific Study of Religion*, 32, no. 4 (December 1993): 373–82, www.jstor.org/stable/1387177.

Gzesh, Susan. "Central Americans and Asylum Policy in the Reagan Era." *Migration Information Source*, April 2006, www.migrationinformation.org/Feature/display.cfm?ID=384.

Hall, Charles F. "The Christian Left: Who are They and How are They Different from the Christian Right?" *Review of Religious Research,* 39, no. 1 (September 1997): 27–45, www.jstor.org/stable/3512477.

Hartsock, Nancy C. M. "Prologue to a Feminist Critique of War and Politics." In *Women's Views of the Political World of Men,* edited by Judith Stiehm, 123–50. Dobbs Ferry, NY: Transnational Publishers, 1984.

Hartz, Louis. *The Liberal Tradition in America.* New York: Harcourt, Brace, 1955.

"Heat Stroke: The Climate for Addressing Global Warming is Improving (Where We Stand: CT's View on Key Issues)." *Christianity Today,* 48, no. 10 (October 2004), www.christianitytoday.com/ct/2004/october/10.26.html.

Hertzberg, Hendrick. "Jimmy Carter." From an essay written for *Character Above All,* www.pbs.org/newshour/character/essays/carter.html.

Hersh, Seymour M. "Annals of National Security: Up in the Air. Where is the Iraq War Headed Next?" *New Yorker,* December 5, 2005, www.newyorker.com/archive/2005/12/05/051205fa_fact.

Hertzke, Allen D. *Freeing God's Children.* New York: Rowman & Littlefield, 2004.

—. *Representing God in Washington: The Role of Religious Lobbies in the American Polity.* Knoxville, TN: University of Tennessee Press, 1988.

—. "The Role of Evangelicals in the New Human Rights Movement." Address at the USC Annenberg School for Communication Conference on Religion, Politics, and Public Policy, Los Angeles, CA, September 22, 2004, http://faculty-staff.ou.edu/H/Allen.D.Hertzke-1/speeches.html.

—. "Roman Catholicism and the Faith-Based Movement for Global Human Rights." *Review of Faith and International Affairs,* 3, no. 3 (Winter 2005), www.rfiaonline.org/archives/issues/3–3/93-faith-based-movement.

Hijab, Nadia. "The Obama Difference." *New York Times,* June 8, 2009, www.nytimes.com/2009/06/09/opinion/09iht-edhajib.html?scp=10&sq=Obama%20Netanyahu%20Congress&st=cse.

Hoge, Dean R. "A Test of Theories of Denominational Growth and Decline." In *Understanding Church Growth and Decline, 1950–1978,* edited by Dean R. Hoge and David A. Roozen, 179–97. New York: Pilgrim Press, 1979.

Hudson, Valerie M., ed. *Culture and Foreign Policy.* Boulder, CO: Lynne Rienner & Co., 1997.

Huntington, Samuel P. "Clash of Civilizations?" *Foreign Affairs,* 72, no. 2 (Spring 1993): 22–49, www.jstor.org/stable/20045621.

—. *The Clash of Civilizations and the Remaking of World Order.* New York: Simon & Schuster, 1996.

Ikenberry, G. John. "America's Liberal Grand Strategy: Democracy and National Security in the Post-War Era." In *American Foreign Policy: Theoretical Essays,* 4th ed., edited by G. John Ikenberry, 274–96. New York: Longman/Addison-Wesley, 2002.

Inboden, William III. *Religion and American Foreign Policy, 1945–1960: The Soul of Containment.* New York: Cambridge University Press, 2008.

Iriye, Akira. *Cultural Internationalism and World Order.* Baltimore, MD: Johns Hopkins University Press, 1997.

James, Robison B., Barbara Jackson, Robert E. Shepherd, Jr., and Cornelia Showalter. *The Fundamentalist Takeover in the Southern Baptist Convention: A Brief History,* 4th ed. Macon, GA: Cooperative Baptist Fellowship of Georgia, 2006, www.sbctakeover.com/index.htm.

Javers, Eamon. "Obama invokes Jesus more than George W. Bush." *Politico,* June 9, 2009, www.politico.com/news/stories/0609/23510_Page3.html.

Jelen, Ted G. "Religion and Foreign Policy Attitudes: Exploring the Effects of Denomination and Doctrine." *American Politics Quarterly,* 22, no. 3 (July 1994): 382–400.

—. "Research in Religion and Mass Political Behavior in the United States: Looking Both Ways After Two Decades of Scholarship." *American Politics Quarterly,* 26, no. 1 (January 1998): 110–34. *Expanded Academic ASAP.* Web.

"Jerry-miad / Falwell blames liberals, gays, judges for terror." *Pittsburgh Post-Gazette,* September 17, 2001, www.post-gazette.com/forum/20010917edfal17p3.asp.

Johnson, James Turner. "Just Cause Revisited." In *Close Calls: Intervention, Terrorism, Missile Defense, and "Just War" Today,* edited by Elliott Abrams, 3–38. Washington, DC: Rowman & Littlefield, with the Ethics and Public Policy Center, 1998.

Judis, John. "The Chosen Nation: The Influence of Religion on U.S. Foreign Policy." Policy Brief 37, Carnegie Endowment for International Peace, March 2005, www.carnegieendowment.org/files/PB37.judis.FINAL.pdf.

Kang, K. Connie. "Presbyterians and the Trinity: Let Us Phrase." *Los Angeles Times*, June 30, 2006, http://articles.latimes.com/2006/jun/30/local/me-trinity30.

Katzenstein, Peter J., ed. *The Culture of National Security: Norms and Identity in World Politics*. New York: Columbia University Press, 1996.

Keeter, Scott. "Election '06: Big Changes in Some Key Groups." Pew Research Center for the People & the Press, November 16, 2006, http://pewresearch.org/pubs/93/election-06-big-changes-in-some-key-groups.

Keeter, Scott, and David Masci. "Science in America: Religious Belief and Public Attitudes." Pew Research Center, December 18, 2007, http://pewresearch.org/pubs/667/science-in-america-religious-belief-and-public-attitudes.

Kellstedt, Lyman A. "The Meaning and Measurement of Evangelicalism: Problems and Prospects." In *Religion and Political Behavior in the United States*, edited by Ted G. Jelen, 3–21. New York: Praeger, 1989.

Kelly, Mark. "God Challenging Southern Baptists to Reach Muslims." SBC International Mission Board, June 20, 2003, www.imb.org/main/news/details.asp?LanguageID=1709&StoryID=942.

Keohane, Robert O. "International Institutions: Two Approaches." *International Studies Quarterly*, 32, no. 4 (December 1988): 379–96, www.jstor.org/stable/2600589.

—. *International Institutions and State Power: Essays in International Relations Theory*. Boulder, CO: Westview Press, 1989.

Kirby, Dianne. "Harry Truman's Religious Legacy: The Holy Alliance, Containment and the Cold War." In *Religion and the Cold War*, edited by Dianne Kirby, 77–101. New York: Palgrave/Macmillan, 2003.

Klaus, Byron D. "Compassion Rooted in the Gospel that Transforms." *Enrichment Journal*, http://enrichmentjournal.ag.org/200402/200402_016_compassion.cfm.

Kohut, Andrew, and Bruce Stokes. *America against the World: How We are Different and Why We are Disliked*. New York: Henry Holt, 2006.

Kosmin, Barry A., and Ariela Keysar. "American Religious Identification Survey (ARIS 2008): Summary Report." March 2009, www.americanreligionsurvey-aris.org/reports/ARIS_Report_2008.pdf.

Kristof, Nicholas D. "Evangelicals a Liberal Could Love." *New York Times*, February 3, 2008, www.nytimes.com/2008/02/03/opinion/03kristof.html?

—. "Giving God a Break." *New York Times*, June 10, 2003, www.nytimes.com/2003/06/10/opinion/10KRIS.html?

Kurtz, Lester, and Kelly Goran Fulton, "Love Your Enemies? Protestants and United States Foreign Policy." In *The Quiet Hand of God: Faith-Based Activism and the Public Role of Mainline Protestantism*, edited by Robert Wuthnow and John H. Evans, 364–80. Berkeley, CA: University of California Press, 2002.

Lang, Anthony F., Jr. "The Catholic Church and American Foreign Policy." Carnegie Council, October 11, 2002, www.cceia.org/resources/articles_papers_reports/79.html.

"Larry King Live: America's Most Influential Evangelicals." February 1, 2005, http://transcripts.cnn.com/TRANSCRIPTS/0502/01/lkl.01.html.

Lugo, Luis, Allen Hertzke, Richard Cizik, and Joel H. Rosenthal. "Evangelical Reflections on the U.S. Role in the World." Carnegie Council on Ethics and International Affairs, September 15, 2005, www.cceia.org/resources/transcripts/5230.html.

Maltby, Paul. "Fundamentalist Dominion, Postmodern Ecology." *Ethics & the Environment*, 13, no. 2 (Autumn 2008): 119–41, http://muse.jhu.edu/journals/ethics_and_the_environment/v013/13.2.maltby.html.

Marsden, Lee. *For God's Sake: The Christian Right and US Foreign Policy*. London and New York: Zed Books, 2009.

Marsh, Charles. "Wayward Christian Soldiers." *New York Times*, January 20, 2006, www.nytimes. com/2006/01/20/opinion/20marsh.html?ex=1295413200&en=9611bfdb755d0d6d&ei=5090& partner=rssuserland&emc=rss.

Martin, Lisa L. "Institutions and Cooperation: Sanctions During the Falkland Islands Conflict." *International Security*, 16, no. 4 (Spring 1992): 143–78, www.jstor.org/stable/i323297.

Martin, William. "The Christian Right and American Foreign Policy." *Foreign Policy*, 114 (Spring 1999): 66–80, www.jstor.org/stable/1149591.

Mayer, Jeremy D. "Christian Fundamentalists and Public Opinion Toward the Middle East: Israel's New Best Friends?" *Social Science Quarterly*, 85, no. 3 (September 2004): 695–712, www3.interscience. wiley.com/cgi-bin/fulltext/118763830/HTMLSTART.

Mazlish, Bruce, and Edwin Diamond. *Jimmy Carter: A Character Portrait*. New York: Simon and Schuster, 1979.

McCleary, Rachel M. *Global Compassion: Private Voluntary Organizations and U.S. Foreign Policy since 1939*. Oxford: Oxford University Press, 2009.

McLennan, Scotty. "What Would Jesus Do? The Three Christian Positions on War." *Stanford Daily*, October 2, 2001. Reprinted in PrayerinAmerica.org, "Prayer in America," www.prayerinamerica. org/wp-content/downloads/get-involved/themes/Armed-Conflict.pdf.

McManus, Mike. "Evangelicals Embrace Global Millennial Goals." *VirtueOnline*, October 18, 2007, www.virtueonline.org/portal/modules/news/article.php?storyid=6915.

Mead, Walter Russell. "God's Country?" *Foreign Affairs*, 85, no. 5 (September–October 2006): 24–43, www.jstor.org/stable/20032068.

—. *Special Providence: American Foreign Policy and How it Changed the World*. New York: Routledge, 2002.

Mearsheimer, John J. "The False Promise of International Institutions." *International Security*, 19, no. 3 (Winter 1994–95): 5–49, www.jstor.org/stable/2539078.

—. *Tragedy of Great Power Politics*. New York: W. W. Norton & Co., 2001.

Mearsheimer, John J., and Stephen M. Walt. *The Israel Lobby and U.S. Foreign Policy*. New York: Farrar, Straus and Giroux, 2007.

—. "The Israel Lobby." *London Review of Books*, March 23, 2006, www.lrb.co.uk/v28/n06/print/mear01_. html.

—. "The Israel Lobby and U.S. Foreign Policy." A working paper for the John F. Kennedy School of Government, Harvard University; available at http://ksgnotes1.harvard.edu/Research/wpaper.nsf/ rwp/RWP06–011.

Millbank, Dana. "Guess Who Came to the Evangelicals' Dinner." *Washington Post*, October 12, 2007, www.washingtonpost.com/wp-dyn/content/article/2007/10/11/AR2007101102537.html.

Miller, Lisa. "A Post-Evangelical America: The Religious Building Blocks of Obama's Victory." *Newsweek* (web exclusive), November 6, 2008, www.newsweek.com/id/167917.

Mitrany, David. *A Working Peace System*. Pittsburgh, PA: Quadrangle Books, 1966.

Moody, Michael. "Caring for Creation: Environmental Advocacy by Mainline Protestant Organizations." In *The Quiet Hand of God: Faith-Based Activism and the Public Role of Mainline Protestantism*, edited by Robert Wuthnow and John H. Evans, 237–64. Berkeley, CA: University of California Press, 2002.

Morgenthau, Hans J. *Politics among Nations: The Struggle for Power and Peace*, 4th ed. New York: Alfred A. Knopf, 1967.

Muravchik, Joshua. *The Uncertain Crusade: Jimmy Carter and the Dilemmas of Human Rights Policy*. Lanham, MD: Hamilton Press, 1986.

Myers, Kenneth A. "CT Classic: Do Jews Really Need Jesus?" *Christianity Today*, August 2002 (web only), www.christianitytoday.com/ct/2002/augustweb-only/8-12-52.0.html.

Nagle, John Copeland. "The Evangelical Debate over Climate Change." *University of St. Thomas Law Journal*, 5, no. 1 (Winter 2008): 52–86. Available for download at http://papers.ssrn.com/sol3/ papers.cfm?abstract_id=1021712.

Nardin, Terry, ed. *The Ethics of War and Peace: Religious and Secular Perspectives*. Princeton, NJ: Princeton University Press, 1996.

National Public Radio. "Profile: Silent Evangelical Support of Bush's Proposed War against Iraq." *Morning Edition*, February 26, 2003, www.npr.org/programs/morning/transcripts/2003/feb/030226.hagerty.html.

Nelson, Keith L. and Spencer C. Olin, Jr. *Why War? Ideology, Theory, and History*. Berkeley, CA: University of California Press, 1979.

Nurser, John S. [Canon John Nurser]. "The 'Ecumenical Movement' Churches, 'Global Order,' and Human Rights: 1938–1948." *Human Rights Quarterly*, 25, no. 4 (November 2003): 841–81, www.jstor.org/stable/20069697.

——. *For All Peoples and All Nations: The Ecumenical Church and Human Rights*. Washington, DC: Georgetown University Press, 2005.

Obama, Barack. *The Audacity of Hope: Thoughts on Reclaiming the American Dream*. New York: Three Rivers Press, 2006.

Owen, John M. "How Liberalism Produces Democratic Peace." *International Security*, 19, no. 2 (Autumn 1994): 87–125, www.jstor.org/stable/2539197.

Paarlberg, Robert. "The Eagle and the Global Environment: The Burden of Being Essential." In *Eagle Rules? Foreign Policy and American Primacy in the Twenty-First Century*, edited by Robert J. Lieber, 325–41. Upper Saddle River, NJ: Pearson/Prentice-Hall, 2002.

Payne, Richard J. *The Clash with Distant Cultures: Values, Interests, and Force in American Foreign Policy*. Albany, NY: State University of New York Press, 1995.

Pegg, J. R. "Bush Climate Speech Covers Familiar Ground." *Environmental News Service*, April 1, 2008, www.ens-newswire.com/ens/apr2008/2008-04-16-10.asp.

Perlez, Jane. "The World: Suddenly in Sudan, A Moment to Care." *New York Times*, June 17, 2001, www.nytimes.com/2001/06/17/weekinreview/the-world-suddenly-in-sudan-a-moment-to care.html?scp=1&sq=Suddenly%20in%20Sudan&st=cse.

Pew Forum on Religion & Public Life. "Americans Struggle with Religion's Role at Home and Abroad." March 20, 2002, http://pewforum.org/surveys.

——. "Different Faiths, Different Messages: Americans Hearing about Iraq from the Pulpit, but Religious Faith Not Defining Options." March 19, 2003, http://pewforum.org/publications/surveys/iraq-war.pdf.

——. "Religion and Politics: Contention and Consensus (Part II)." July 24, 2003, http://pewforum.org/docs/?DocID=28#1.

——. "U.S. Religious Landscape Survey: Religious Affiliation: Diverse and Dynamic." February 2008. The full report is available for download at http://religions.pewforum.org/reports.

——. "U.S. Religious Landscape Survey: Religious Beliefs and Practices: Diverse and Politically Relevant." June 2008. The full report is available for download at http://religions.pewforum.org/reports.

Pew Research Center for the People & the Press. "Religion and the Presidential Vote: Bush's Gains Broad-Based." December 6, 2004, http://people-press.org/commentary/?analysisid=103.

Podles, Leon J. "God Has No Daughters: Masculine Imagery in the Liturgy." *Catholic Culture*. Previously published in *Homiletic & Pastoral Review* (November 1995): 20–27, www.catholicculture.org/library/view.cfm?recnum=613.

Posner, Sarah. "Pastor Strangelove." *The American Prospect*, May 21, 2006, www.prospect.org/cs/articles?articleId=11541.

Pulliam, Sarah. "Richard Cizik Resigns from the National Association of Evangelicals." *Christianity Today*, December 2008, www.christianitytoday.com/ct/2008/decemberweb-only/150-42.0.html.

Quandt, William B. *Peace Process: American Diplomacy and the Arab-Israeli Conflict Since 1967*, 3rd ed. Washington, DC: Brookings Institution, 2005.

Ramirez, Jessica. "Barack's Beliefs." *Newsweek*, August 7, 2008, www.newsweek.com/id/151233.

Ray, James Lee. *Democracy and International Conflict: An Evaluation of the Democratic Peace Proposition*. Columbia, SC: University of South Carolina Press, 1995.

"Religion and Ethics Newsweekly/UN Foundation Survey Explores Religion and America's Role in the World." *Religion and Ethics Newsweekly,* October 22, 2008, www.pbs.org/wnet/religionandethics/ episodes/by-topic/civil-society/religion-ethics-newsweeklyun-foundation-survey-explores-religion-and-americas-role-in-the-world/1190/.

Religious Coalition for Reproductive Choice. "Words of Choice: Countering Anti-Choice Rhetoric," www.rcrc.org/pdf/Words_of_Choice.pdf.

"Religious Right Backs Special Role At UN for Catholic Church." *Church and State,* May 1, 2000, www. thefreelibrary.com/Religious+Right+Backs+Special+Role+At+UN+For+Catholic+Church-a062402432.

Ribuffo, Leo P. "Religion in the History of U.S. Foreign Policy." In *The Influence of Faith: Religious Groups and U.S. Foreign Policy,* edited by Elliott Abrams, 1–27. Lanham, MD: Rowman & Littlefield, with the Ethics and Public Policy Center, 2001.

Roberts, Carl W. "Imagining God: Who is Created in Whose Image?" *Review of Religious Research,* 30, no. 4 (June 1989): 375–86, www.jstor.org/stable/3511298.

Roosevelt, Margot. "Evangelicals Go Green." *Time,* February 8, 2008, www.time.com/time/nation/ article/0,8599,1157612,00.html.

Rosecrance, Richard. *The Rise of the Trading State: Commerce and Conquest in the Modern World.* New York: Basic Books, 1986.

Rossi, Joseph S., S. J. *American Catholics and the Formation of the United Nations.* Melville Studies in Church History, vol. IV. Lanham, MD: University Press of America, 1993.

—. *Uncharted Territory: The American Catholic Church at the United Nations, 1946–1972.* Washington, DC: Catholic University Press of America, 2006.

Rummel, Rudolph J. "Democracies *Are* Less Warlike than Other Regimes." *European Journal of International Relations,* 1, no. 4 (December 1995): 457–79. Available for download at http://ejt. sagepub.com/content/vol1/issue4/.

Ruotsila, Markku. *The Origins of Christian Anti-Internationalism: Conservative Evangelicals and the League of Nations.* Washington, DC: Georgetown University Press, 2008.

Russett, Bruce. *Grasping the Democratic Peace: Principles for a Post-Cold War World.* Princeton, NJ: Princeton University Press, 1993.

Russett, Bruce, and Jon R. Oneal. *Triangulating Peace: Democracy, Interdependence, and International Organizations.* New York: W. W. Norton & Co., 2001.

Savranskaya, Svetlana, and Thomas Blanton, eds. "The Reykjavik File: Previously Secret Documents from U.S. and Soviet Archives on the 1986 Reagan-Gorbachev Summit." From the collections of The National Security Archive, George Washington University, Washington DC. National Security Archive Electronic Briefing Book No. 203, www.gwu.edu/~nsarchiv/NSAEBB/NSAEBB203/index. htm.

Scherer, Glenn. "The Godly Must Be Crazy: Christian-Right Views are Swaying Politicians and Threatening the Environment." *Grist,* October 27, 2004, www.grist.org/news/maindish/2004/10/27/ scherer-christian/.

Schneider, Howard. "Netanyahu Backs 2-State Goal." *Washington Post,* June 15, 2009, www.washington-post.com/wp-dyn/content/article/2009/06/14/AR2009061400741.html.

Schweller, Randall L. "Fantasy Theory." *Review of International Studies,* 25, no. 1 (January 1999): 147–50, www.jstor.org/stable/20097582.

Shaiko, Ronald G. "Religion, Politics, and Environmental Concern: A Powerful Mix of Passions." *Social Science Quarterly,* 68, no. 2 (June 1987): 243–62, http://pao.chadwyck.com.

Shriver, Peggy L. "Evangelicals and World Affairs." *World Policy Journal,* 23, no. 3 (Fall 2006): 52–58. *Expanded Academic ASAP.* Web.

Simon, Bob. "Zion's Christian Soldiers: The '60 Minutes' Transcript." *Washington Report on Middle East Affairs,* December 2002, www.wrmea.com/archives/december02/0212068.html.

Sirgiovanni, George. *An Undercurrent of Suspicion: Anti-communism in America During the Cold War.* New Brunswick, NJ: Transaction Publishers, 1990.

Smith, Gaddis. *Morality, Reason, and Power: American Diplomacy in the Carter Years.* New York: Hill and Wang, 1986.

Smith, Robert O. "Between Restoration and Liberation: Theopolitical Contributions and Responses to U.S. Foreign Policy in Israel/Palestine." *Journal of Church and State,* 36, no. 4 (Autumn 2004): 833–60. *Expanded Academic ASAP.* Web.

Smith, Tom W. "Classifying Protestant Denominations." *Review of Religious Research,* 31, no. 3 (March 1990): 225–45, www.jstor.org/stable/3511614.

Smith, Tony. "National Security Liberalism and American Foreign Policy." In *American Foreign Policy: Theoretical Essays,* 4th ed., edited by G. John Ikenberry, 258–74. New York: Longman/Addison-Wesley, 2002.

Spanier, John. *Games Nations Play,* 7th ed. Washington, DC: Congressional Quarterly Press, 1990.

Steensland, Brian, Jerry Z. Park, Mark D. Regnerus, Lynn D. Robinson, W. Bradford Wilcox, and Robert D. Woodbury. "The Measure of American Religion: Improving the State of the Art." *Social Forces,* 79, no. 1 (September 2000): 291–318, www.jstor.org/stable/2675572.

Steinfels, Peter. "An Evangelical Call on Torture and the U.S." *New York Times,* July 21, 2007, www.nytimes.com/2007/07/21/us/21beliefs.html.

Stockman, Farah. "Christian Lobbying Finds Success: Evangelicals Help to Steer Bush Efforts." *Boston Globe,* October 14, 2004, www.boston.com/news/nation/articles/2004/10/14/christian_lobbying_finds_success/.

Stoddard, Ed. "Slavery Campaign Closes Gap among Evangelicals." *Boston Globe,* April 1, 2007, www.boston.com/news/nation/articles/2007/04/02/slavery_campaign_closes_gaps_among_evangelicals/.

Tocqueville, Alexis de. *Democracy in America,* Vol. 1. New York: Doubleday & Co., 1969.

Toolin, Cynthia. "American Civil Religion from 1789 to 1981: A Content Analysis of Presidential Inaugural Addresses." *Review of Religious Research,* 25, no. 1 (September 1983): 39–49, www.jstor.org/stable/3511310.

Unger, Craig. "How George Bush Really Found Jesus." *Salon.com,* November 8, 2007, www.salon.com/books/feature/2007/11/08/house_of_bush/print.html.

Utley, Jon Basil. "America's Armageddonites." *Antiwar.com,* October 11, 2007, www.antiwar.com/utley/?articleid=11735.

Van Biema, David, and Jeff Chu. "Does God Want You to Be Rich?" *Time.com,* September 10, 2006, www.time.com/time/magazine/article/0,9171,1533448,00.html.

Wagner, Donald. "Evangelicals and Israel: Theological Roots of a Political Alliance." *Christian Century,* November 4, 1998, 1020–26, www.religion-online.org/showarticle.asp?title=216.

Wald, Kenneth D. "Religious Elites and Public Opinion: The Impact of the Bishops' Peace Pastoral." *Review of Politics,* 54, no. 1 (Winter 1992): 112–43, www.jstor.org/stable/1407929.

Waldman, Steven. "Why Evangelicals are Abandoning Bush." *Huffington Post,* November 2, 2006, www.huffingtonpost.com/steven-waldman/why-evangelicals-are-aban_b_33137.html.

Waldman, Steven, and John Green. "Evangelicals v. Fundamentalists." *Frontline,* April 29, 2004, www.pbs.org/wgbh/pages/frontline/shows/jesus/evangelicals/vs.html.

—. "Freestyle Evangelicals: The Surprise Swing Vote." *Beliefnet,* www.beliefnet.com/story/129/story_12995_1.html.

Wallis, Jim. "An Evangelical Climate Change." *Sojourners Magazine,* May 2006, www.sojo.net/index.cfm?action=magazine.article&issue=soj0605&article=060551.

—. "Hearts and Minds: For the Health of the Nation." *Sojourners Magazine,* May 2005, www.sojo.net/index.cfm?action=magazine.article&issue=soj0505&article=050551.

Waltz, Kenneth N. *Theory of International Politics.* Reading, MA: Addison-Wesley Publishing Co., 1979.

Walzer, Michael. *Just and Unjust Wars: A Moral Argument with Historical Illustrations,* 4th ed. New York: Basic Books, 2006.

Warren, Heather A. *Theologians of a New World Order: Reinhold Niebuhr and the Christian Realists, 1920–1948.* New York: Oxford University Press, 1997.

Weber, Timothy P. "How Evangelicals Became Israel's Best Friend." *Christianity Today*, October 5, 1998, www.christianitytoday.com/ct/8tb/8tb038.html.

—. *Living in the Shadow of the Second Coming: American Premillennialism, 1875–1982*. Chicago, IL: University of Chicago Press, 1987.

Weigel, George. "The Catholic Human Rights Revolution." *Crisis*, July/August 1996, www.ewtn.com/library/CHISTORY/HRREVOLU.TXT.

—. Tranquillitas Ordinis: *The Present Failure and Future Promise of American Catholic Thought on War and Peace*. Oxford: Oxford University Press, 1987.

White, Lynn, Jr. "On the Historical Roots of Our Ecologic Crisis." *Science*, March 1967, 1203–07, www.jstor.org/stable/1720120.

Williams, Robert E., Jr., and Dan Caldwell. "*Jus Post Bellum*: Just War Theory and the Principles of Just Peace." *International Studies Perspectives*, 7, no. 4 (November 2006): 309–20, www3.interscience.wiley.com/cgi-bin/fulltext/118607018/HTMLSTART.

Wilson, James Q. "American Exceptionalism." *The American Spectator*, September 2006, http://spectator.org/archives/2006/10/02/american-exceptionalism.

Winthrop, John. "A Model of Christian Charity," http://religiousfreedom.lib.virginia.edu/sacred/charity.html.

Woodrum, Eric, and Thomas Hoban. "Theology and Religiosity Effects on Environmentalism." *Review of Religious Research*, 35, no. 3 (March 1994): 193–206, www.jstor.org/stable/3511888.

Wuthnow, Robert. *Boundless Faith: The Global Outreach of American Churches*. Berkeley, CA: University of California Press, 2009.

Wuthnow, Robert, and John H. Evans, eds. *The Quiet Hand of God: Faith-Based Activism and the Public Role of Mainline Protestantism*. Berkeley, CA: University of California Press, 2002.

Zinn, Howard. "The Power and the Glory: Myths of American Exceptionalism." *Boston Review* (Summer 2005), http://bostonreview.net/BR30.3/zinn.html.

Zunes, Stephen. "Is the Israel Lobby Really that Powerful?" *Tikkun*, 21, no. 4 (July/August, 2006): 49, www.tikkun.org/article.php/Zunes-IstheIsraelLobbyThatPowerful.

Index